HEADS AND TALES

A HISTORY OF BADSEY SCHOOLS

HEADS AND TALES

A HISTORY OF BADSEY SCHOOLS

BY
MAUREEN SPINKS

THE BADSEY SOCIETY

HEADS AND TALES: A HISTORY OF BADSEY SCHOOLS

This first edition published in 2004 by
The Badsey Society, 4 High Street, Badsey, Evesham WR11 7EW, England.
Text copyright © Maureen Spinks 2004.
Photographs and illustrations copyright © as indicated.

Graphic design by Richard Phillips.

Printed by Russell Press Limited, Nottingham.

ISBN 0 9547 4690 2

THE BADSEY SOCIETY

The Badsey Society was formed at a meeting in the village in February 2002.
The Society exists to promote the understanding and study of the parish and village of Badsey, including Aldington, and the surrounding area. For further information see the website – WWW. BADSEY.ORG.UK/SOCIETY

Another Badsey Society Publication –
A Brief History of Badsey and Aldington, 2nd edition, T C Sparrow, 2002. 0 9547 4691 0.

COVERS

Front and back cover: Badsey First School, 2003, illustrated by Ian Gibson.
Back cover: From the old to the new – photos of Badsey schoolchildren 1903 and 2003.
Bottom picture back row: Jonathan Spinks, son of the author; Gina Phillips, daughter of the Chairman of Governors; William Pask, whose mother works at the school. Front row: David Waters, great-grandson of Beryl Hall whose botanical illustrations feature in the book; Eleanor Hardwick, great-great niece of Cecilia Barnard, Lena Crisp and Harry Crisp who feature in the 1903 photo; Connor Trotman, third generation Badsey pupil.

The illustrator, Ian Gibson, trained at Portsmouth College of Art. He works as a self-employed artist and has a wide repertoire, mainly in watercolour. He moved to Badsey in 1997 and specialises in local views and artist's impressions of buildings.

CONTENTS

ACKNOWLEDGEMENTS

I would like to begin by offering my heartfelt thanks to Richard Phillips who has designed the layout and put in long hours preparing the book for print. The project has benefited enormously from Richard's invaluable work. I would also like to thank Ian Gibson for his lovely cover design and other illustrations; committee members of The Badsey Society for their support, in particular local author and historian Terry Sparrow, who always responded promptly to my many queries, and Will Dallimore and Tony Jerram for assistance in the title of the book.

I am indebted to the current Headteacher of Badsey First School, Elizabeth Spencer, and the previous Head, Gerry Hughes, for allowing me access to school Log Books and Admissions Registers, and for lending their support to the project. I have been privileged to make contact with former Headteachers or their descendants: Trevor Clark, who contacted me from Spain; Mary Chaplin, widow of Hugh Chaplin; Richard Harvey, son of Maurice Harvey; Margaret Amos, daughter of Frank and Jean Amos and granddaughter of John McDonald. As for early Headteachers, Audrey New (née Harrison) has provided information about Ruth Silvester and Barry Moss has put some flesh on the bones of John Sheppard, the first known teacher.

As far as former pupils and staff are concerned, Pat Goldstraw (née Barnard) who knows the school from so many aspects as pupil, teacher, parent, Governor and Trustee, has been of enormous help. Other people who were at school during the years of Mr Amos' headship and provided information are: Michael Barnard, Joan Bearman (née Martin), John Bird, Peggy Bird (née Keen), Jim Brailsford, Bob Butler, Molly Corbett (née Evans), Evelyn Day (née Crane), Esmé Dennick (née Jelfs), Don Hartwell, Lorna Howarth (née Bayliss), Lionel Knight, Evelyn McKanan-Jones (née Barnard), Doreen Moore (née Ballard), Fred Roberts. In response to a newspaper article, two evacuees, Stanley Hayes and Bill Coton, contacted me. From the post-war period, I would like to thank: Wendy Beasley (née Tomkins), Robert Bennett, John Dallimore, Will Dallimore, Karen Evans (née Woodcock), Pat Gorin, John Hall, Jean James, David Miller, Zena Rogers (née Bennett). Also a big thank you to the many people in the village who did their best to put names to the faces in the class photos, and former pupils who contacted me via the Friends Reunited website.

The following people have loaned photographs or memorabilia for inclusion in the book: Pete Addis (p 118), Marion Allen (pp 148-149), Margaret Amos (pp 43, 74-76, 90, 95, 169), Badsey First School (pp 31, 34, 38, 44, 53-54, 56, 63, 69, 127, 131-132, 137, 140-141, 149, 154-155, 157-159, 160, 170-171), Joan Bearman (p 104), Robert Bennett (p 120), John Bird (pp 98, 105), Robert Butler (pp 91, 96), David Caswell (p 99), Hazel Dance (p 109), Sue Daniels (p 59), Esmé Dennick (pp 93, 114), Susan Dix (p 170), Gladys Dodd (p 78), Pat Goldstraw (pp 35, 39, 46, 50, 55, 59, 65, 71, 74, 115, 146), Pat Gorin (pp 113, 135), Molly Haines (p 79), John Hall (p 114), Peggy Hancock (p 33), Don Hartwell (168), Jack Hartwell (p 89), Stanley Hayes (p 100), Steve Hiatt (p 107), Adrian Hough (pp 144, 180), Kathryn Hough (p 180), Emmeline Hughes (p 89), Jean James (pp 129, 135, 138, 148, 150), Lionel Knight (p 72), Joyce Major (p 123), Ivor Martin (pp 61, 67, 125, 168), Roger Martin (pp 61, 67, 125, 168), Fred Mason (pp 51, 79, 91), David Miller (pp 111, 118, 121, 126), Muriel Morcombe (p 123), Audrey New (p 26), Louise Phillips (p 160), Richard Phillips (pp 22, 25, 55, 99, 153, 163, 192), Terry Sparrow (p 68), Peter Stewart (p 57), Jane Thompson (p 96), Allan Warmington (p 39), Brian Wells (p 112), Pat Westmacott (pp 78, 121), Shirley Wilce (p 109), Kate Wilson (p 113), Tracey Wright (p 146); The Evesham Journal (pp 4, 143). Where possible, I have attempted to establish copyright and permission to reproduce, but I apologise for any omissions.

My thanks go to Hilary Jobson (née Crane) and Dulcie Cleaver (née Jelfs) and to the Lawes Agricultural Trust for permission to publish the letters about market gardening (p 86); to Joan Bayliss for permission to publish her husband's drawings (pp 84-85); to Angela Waters for permission to publish her grandmother's drawings (p 87); to Diane Sims (née Burford) and Cathy McMeikan for permission to publish their poems (pp 128, 164); to the Church of England Record Centre for permission to publish documents relating to The National Society (pp 20, 21, 28, 30); to the Governing Body of Christ Church, Oxford, for permission to print documents (pp 15, 41); to Worcestershire Record Office for permission to print documents (pp 10, 12, 14, 19, 73, 178); to Michael Barnard for his sketches (pp 80, 98, 103, 191).

Thanks are due to my sister, Beth, for accommodation in London, whilst conducting searches at the Public Record Office and Lambeth Palace Library (and for looking after her nephew!); also to the proof-readers Sarah Pask and Louise Phillips. Finally to my husband, Tony, for his support throughout the project, valuable comments on the text, and forbearance when the book seemed to dominate the household in the final stages of production!

The Badsey Society is grateful for the support of an Awards for All grant from the Lottery Commission in publishing this book.

AWARDS FOR ALL

FOREWORD

BY ELIZABETH SPENCER

I took up my post as Headteacher of Badsey First School on 11th April 2002. A former pupil at the school from 1958-1964, I deemed it a great privilege to be returning as Headteacher. Moreover, I experienced a feeling of "coming home", as my connections with the school reach back to the beginning of the 20th century when my grandmother was a pupil here.

I began my education at Badsey in the care of Mrs Churchill, in what is now Mrs Bevington's classroom. My overwhelming memories are of a zoo set out in a tray of sand and the smell of warm wax crayons and milk. Miss Smith came next. I remember sitting on the floor, just a few metres from where my desk is now, listening enthralled as she recounted the adventures of a little girl in a striped dress, Milly-Molly-Mandy. In Mrs Gorin's class, we chanted our tables and in Mr Hunt's class, the girls sewed cotton dresses, which were sent as nighties to children in Africa. Miss Saunders' classroom was the kitchen. To this day I still dread the thought of semolina and the tapioca puddings! I emerged, aged 11, with the school prize for reliability and friends with whom I often reminisce.

As one to whom education in Badsey matters enormously, it gives me great pleasure to commend this book to you.

For Jonathan
and for all past and present Badsey pupils and staff

Maureen Spinks has lived in Badsey since 1993. She studied History at The University of Sheffield and now works at The University of Gloucestershire. She is Secretary of The Badsey Society, Clerk to the Governors at Badsey First School, a Parent Governor at Blackminster Middle School and a regular contributor to the Badsey website. *Picture courtesy the Journal Series, Evesham. A Newsquest publication.*

INTRODUCTION

This book has been a labour of love over the last seven years. When my son started at Badsey First School as a four-year-old in 1997, I began to take an interest in the history of this Victorian village school. What was fascinating for me was the fact that many of the children at the school had parents, grandparents and earlier forebears who had attended the school. Since then, my researches have taken me far and wide. I have spent many a happy hour talking to former pupils. I have spent yet more hours perusing school Log Books and Minute Books. I have undertaken research at the Public Record Office at Kew and entered the lofty portals of Christ Church Library, Oxford, and Lambeth Palace Library, London, home of the Archbishop of Canterbury. I thus had a wealth of information, but there came a time when I had to start putting it into book shape.

The year 2004 seemed to be an appropriate date and deadline to work towards as it marks the 150th anniversary of the founding of the school that we know today as Badsey First School. It was in 1854 that the young Reverend Thomas Hunt, newly arrived in the village, established the National School of Badsey, Aldington and Wickhamford, under the auspices of the Church of England. Since then, the school has undergone four name changes: Badsey Board School in 1893, Badsey Council School in 1903, Badsey County Primary School in 1948 and Badsey First School in 1975. As well as a name change, there was a location change. In 1895, the school moved from the High Street (in the building now occupied by the British Legion) to its current site on School Lane.

It is interesting to see how Badsey School has developed over the last 150 years, and why we have such a diversity of education within the state sector. I hope that this book, by attempting to set the history of the school within an historical framework, will provide some answers. It is also fascinating how, in time, the wheel comes full circle. For a long period in the 19th century the curriculum was very narrow, concentrating almost exclusively on the "three Rs" (Reading, Writing and Arithmetic), but the dawning of the 20th century saw a more enlightened approach to education with teachers being given freedom to show initiative in syllabus and method. In the 1990s there was once again government intervention in the curriculum, but today the emphasis is beginning to switch again to a more creative approach. Who knows what the future holds?

I have enjoyed writing this book and I hope that you will enjoy reading it.

Maureen Spinks
The Willows, High Street, Badsey, Worcestershire

Stephen Field Evesham Worces...
December 18 1841

SEWARD's

CHARITY.

M DCC LIV.

SEWARD's CHARITY

IN FAVOR OF THE

PARTICULAR BAPTISTS.

I *Elizabeth Seward,* of the Parish of *Bengworth,* **in the County of** *Worcester,* Widow, do make this my last Will and **Testament** in manner following; (that is to say) I give and bequeath

---

And upon further Trust that my said Trustees shall from time to time, and at all times hereafter, pay the *Interest,* Dividends, or yearly Produce of the Sum of *Four hundred Pounds South Sea Annuities,* other Part of my said Two thousand Pounds South Sea Annuities, as the same shall be from time to time received, *to the said* Jacob More *during his Life, and after his Death to each and every succeeding Minister or* Teacher *of the said Congregation at* Bengworth *aforesaid; to the Intent and Purpose that he and they shall therewith or thereout pay for* Teaching poor Children to Read, *whose Parents are not able to pay for the same, of the Place and Schools after mentioned,* (*that is to say*) Badsey near Evesham, *and at* Two Schools in Evesham, *and One in* Bengworth *aforesaid; viz. to pay* Six Shillings a Month *to* Badsey *aforesaid, and to the said* Three other Schools Four Shillings per Month *each;* which are the same Sums which were allowed or paid to them by my late dear Husband.

£ 400 New South Sea Annuities, Badsey, Evesham, and Bengworth Schools.

Extracts from the will of Elizabeth Seward, dated 1753, bequeathing money for an educational charity which still exists to this day.

10

Woodcut by Thomas Bewick.

1

EARLY EDUCATION IN BADSEY

Before the 19th century, the majority of children in England had little opportunity for education. Rigid class distinctions divided the country. The upper and middle classes, anxious to maintain the established order, had two theories about the education of the poor. The first theory was that schooling would be dangerous; the second held that simple schooling was a benefit, allowing the poor to read the scriptures and to earn a useful if humble living while learning gratitude to their social betters. Badsey was more fortunate than most in that there does seem to have been some kind of educational establishment in the village from at least the 17th century. Meanwhile, the upper classes were educated at one of the great public schools in the land. For example, in the first half of the 18th century, the Seward boys of Seward House were educated at Westminster School.

17th Century – John Sheppard's School

The earliest mention of a school in Badsey is 1658. Walter Savage of Broadway wrote of his seven-year-old son in his journal on 6th July 1658: "Watt went to school at Badsey being Tewsday". The Savages lived at Broadway Court (long since demolished), some five miles distant from Badsey. The school was probably for younger children, as by a year or two later, Watt (who went on to become Town Clerk of Worcester) was attending school at Todenham and then Burford.

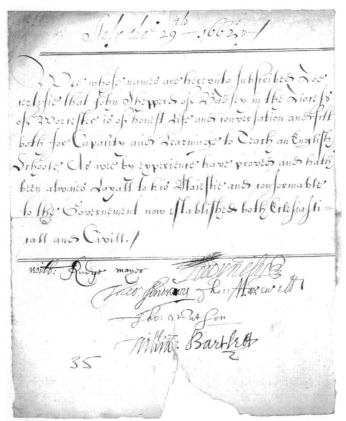

Teacher's licence for John Sheppard, 1662, the first known school teacher in Badsey. © The Diocese of Worcestershire.

The school that young Walter Savage attended may well have been one run by John Sheppard. A teacher's licence for John Sheppard of Badsey exists in the diocesan records at Worcestershire Record Office. The licence, dated 29th July 1662, states:

> We whose names are hereunto subscribed do certify that John Sheppard of Badsey in the diocese of Worcester is of honest life and conversation and is fit both for capacity and learning to teach in English schools as now by experience have proved and hath been always loyal to his Majesty and conformable to the government now established both ecclesiastical and civil.

From the beginning of the 17th century, teachers were appointed by the diocesan bishop, and licences were issued through the ecclesiastical courts. The bishops' licences were required before legally teaching in any school, though generally it applied to grammar or endowed schools rather than smaller village institutions. Many unlicensed schoolmasters taught quite illegally. It is interesting that Badsey should have had a licensed schoolmaster, presumably indicating a school of some standing. After the restoration of the monarchy in 1660, the 1662 Act of Uniformity required all schoolmasters to be loyal to the Church of England.

It is not known where the school was situated or for how long it lasted. Possibly it may have been located in the church, a common practice in village schools in those days. From the Badsey parish registers, it can be gleaned that John Sheppard lived in Badsey from at least the 1630s until his death in 1672. His sons, Thomas and John, were baptised in 1634 and 1639 respectively. It is possible, though, that the John Sheppard referred to could have been John, the son, who, at the time of the licence in 1662, was a young married man about to start a family. It was obviously a family where education was important because John Sheppard's descendants then moved to Bretforton where, for the next 200 years, they provided an unbroken line of Parish Clerks.

18th and 19th Centuries – Baptist School

From the mid-18th century, a Baptist school existed at Seward House. Money for the school was provided as part of an endowment made by Elizabeth Seward. Elizabeth was the widow of Benjamin Seward, the sixth of seven sons of John and Mary Seward, who had moved to Badsey in the early 1690s, living in the house which still bears their name. All their sons were baptised in St James' Church, Badsey, but with the growth in non-conformity, a number of the brothers embraced new ways of worship. Benjamin and Elizabeth were members of the Particular Baptists at Bengeworth and lived at the Mansion House, Bengeworth (now The Evesham Hotel). Benjamin died in March 1753 and Elizabeth died the following year.

Elizabeth Seward's will, dated 2nd June 1753, settled the interest on £4,550 (most of which was invested in the South Sea Company) to various charitable purposes. This included the interest or dividends of £400 South Sea annuities "for teaching poor children to read, whose parents are not able to pay for the same, of the place and schools after mentioned, that is to say, Badsey near Evesham, and at two schools in Evesham and one in Bengeworth". Elizabeth, in making her bequest, was ensuring that the work started by her husband, Benjamin, would continue: "to pay six shillings a month to Badsey aforesaid, and to the said three other schools four shillings per month each; which are the same sums which were allowed or paid to them by my late dear husband". Jacob More, the Minister at Bengeworth, was the man responsible for ensuring that this particular bequest was complied with.

Seward House at that time was occupied by the eldest surviving son, Henry Seward, and later his son, Henry. Although a clergyman of the established church, young Henry seems to have been happy to allow the schoolmistress appointed by the Baptist Minister to teach the children in his house. A report on the *State of the Bishopric of Worcester* in 1782 states under Badsey, "a few children taught to read at Mr Seward's expense". Henry died in 1790, aged 33, his wife having predeceased him. There was no heir and Seward House then passed into other hands, so it is likely that the school moved to another location.

The schoolmistress during this early period was most probably Mary Mellen (or Malin, Melyn, Meling or Miland, as the name sometimes appeared). In the burial register for 1788, the burial is recorded of Mary Mellen, whose occupation was described as "School Dame". Mary's husband, Richard, had died in 1766, leaving her with five daughters and two sons, the youngest being only six, so one assumes she would have been grateful for the six shillings payment.

Eighty years after Elizabeth Seward's death, we have evidence that the bequest was still being administered according to the terms of the will. According to a report of the Charity Commissioners in 1836, the money had been regularly received and employed for the purposes expressed in the will. Samuel Lewis, in his *Topographical Directory of England*, 1840, refers to a small endowed school in Badsey for the instruction of nine poor children, under a mistress who received £3 12s 0d, the bequest of Elizabeth Seward. In the same year, Bentley tells us that Mrs Sarah Sheaf kept a preparatory school. The school continued in a small way until 1880, after which time, after several years of wrangling over the distribution of the bequest, an educational charity was established (see Appendix G).

18th and 19th Centuries – Sunday School

It is likely that a Sunday School was in existence around the end of the 18th century. From about 1780, Sunday Schools began to be attached to parish churches in England. Sunday Schools were cheap and ran outside working hours and were the beginning of real popular education; the movement grew at a phenomenal rate. The scholars were taught spelling as a preparation for reading the Bible. A perusal of the marriage registers for this period indicates a level of literacy as a large number of people were able to sign their

Seward House where the Baptist School was first located.

Document showing the appointment of William Barnard, Schoolmaster, as Parish Clerk and Sexton in 1842. William Barnard was in charge of the Sunday School which, at that time in Badsey, was the only real opportunity for children to have the chance of an education.

name, so it is assumed they received a basic education from attendance at a Sunday School.

Another reason for assuming that Badsey was part of this vanguard is because a Vestry Meeting of 1839 met "to consider the re-establishment of the Sunday School". At the meeting on 25th June, it was resolved that the Sunday School project should go ahead and a committee was formed of five principal inhabitants. The "principal inhabitants" were deemed to be: from Badsey, Reverend William Byrd, Edward Appelbee and William Collett and from Aldington, Richard Ashwin and Thomas Byrd. Subscriptions were raised from 20 people, the highest amount being received from the Byrd family of The Poplars who donated £2. The school was under the supervision of the Assistant Curate, Reverend Thomas Griffith, son-in-law of the absentee vicar Charles Phillott.

It may have taken a year or two for the Sunday School to be established, as no children were listed as scholars in the 1841 census. But from 1842, William Barnard was in charge and, for the next 12 years, the Sunday School was the principal educator of children in the parish teaching basic reading and writing in addition to the scriptures. 39-year-old William Barnard, originally from Cirencester, moved to Badsey from Evesham in 1842, in which year he was formally appointed Parish Clerk and Sexton of Badsey and Wickhamford. He was described

Two extracts from the Badsey census return of 1851. The first shows the family of William Barnard, Parish Clerk and Schoolmaster. He was also the enumerator who conducted the census. The second shows Elizabeth Wheatley, Schoolmistress. What a coincidence that, 150 years later, Elizabeth Spencer (née Wheatley) should become Headmistress of Badsey School!

as a schoolmaster, but other records refer to him as a tailor, so it is assumed that he was a tailor by profession, who also taught in the Sunday School.

The Sunday School was still in existence in the early 1850s when the newly-appointed Reverend Hunt, writing in March 1853, mentioned the Sunday School which was held in his barn. The 1851 census records a number of children listed as scholars. William Barnard was Schoolmaster and Mrs Elizabeth Wheatley and Mrs Kitty Hartwell were Schoolmistresses. Out of 81 children aged five to ten living in Badsey and Aldington, these were the numbers relating to school attendance:

Scholar	50
Nothing listed	24
Working on land	5
At home	1
Farmer's daughter	1

The child at home was eight-year-old Henry Byrd of Ivy House, Aldington, who presumably had a home tutor before being sent away to school. The farmer's daughter was six-year-old Frances Sheaf of Seward House, who probably had a governess.

The National Debate

The success of Sunday Schools aroused interest in a national system of day schools. The government in the early part of the 19th century was reluctant to take on the role of educating the masses, so it was left to the church to take on this role. In 1811, the Anglicans established *The National Society for Promoting the Education of the Poor in the Principles of the Established Church throughout England and Wales,* whilst the non-conformists formed *The British & Foreign School Society.* These two organisations arose out of the work of Andrew Bell, a Scottish clergyman (1753-1832), and Joseph Lancaster, a Quaker (1778-1838). Thus began a debate that split national opinion and was to hinder educational progress until 1870 when education for all became compulsory. Both Bell and Lancaster started schools, but the

Above: Letter of 1853 from the Reverend Thomas Hunt to Dr John Bull of Christ Church, Oxford, appealing for help in establishing a school. Reproduced by kind permission of the Governing Body of Christ Church, Oxford.

Below: The Reverend Thomas Hunt.

establishment of these schools was haphazard and depended on local circumstances.

The idea that the state should help provide education was only accepted gradually in 19th century England. Other European countries had begun state systems, for example Holland in 1808. The church clung to its traditional monopoly, and church leaders considered voluntary effort enough to provide the schooling that was required. There were many failed attempts during the first half of the 19th century. In 1807, the philanthropist, Samuel Whitbread, proposed a Poor Law Bill in which a key place was given to education. He hoped that a system of parochial elementary schools, like that adopted in Scotland, would reduce crime and pauperism (in 1803, one-ninth of the population of England was receiving poor relief). But the bill was defeated, mostly by the Bishops who disliked the proposal that democratic committees should run the schools. It was important, however, in being the first of a series of attempts to secure state intervention in popular education.

The Reform Act of 1832 gave the franchise to the middle classes and the question of educational reform was again reconsidered. J A Roebuck suggested compulsory schooling for all, the country divided into school districts, each under a committee, all overseen by a Minister of Public Instruction. His plan was too ambitious, yet government interest was sufficient to allow a grant of £20,000 to be made to help school-building by the National and British Societies. This modest act of 1833 was a historic turning point, the first practical act involving the state in England's schooling. Detailed surveys showed that many children were untouched by education. At last, in 1839, a Committee of the Privy Council was appointed to consider "all matters affecting the education of the people". Its first Secretary was Dr James Kay-Shuttleworth (1804-1877). In the decades that followed, there was an increase in schools throughout the land. The National Society's desire was to found a church school in every parish in the land. To this end, they were prepared to offer financial assistance in the form of a grant of money towards the cost of building a school.

The Pressure for More Formal Education

In Badsey by the 1840s, there was recognition that a school was required and a site was given by Richard Ashwin of Aldington Manor, but no further progress was made. It was not until 25-year-old Reverend Thomas Henry Hunt arrived as Vicar in 1852 that things began to happen. With reforming zeal, he soon set about amending the years of neglect caused by absentee vicars. One of his main areas of concern was the poor educational facilities and he felt strongly that a National School should be established.

But the main obstacle in Badsey was that many of the larger landowners were non-resident and did not feel inclined to contribute towards the cost of providing a school from which their own children would gain no benefit. Hunt, despite all the fervour and enthusiasm of youth, found it difficult to change their minds in order to procure funds for the erection and support of the proposed school, and his own private resources were insufficient to accomplish the project.

Reverend Hunt thus set out his concerns in a letter to Dr John Bull, Canon of Christ Church. (The Dean and Chapter of Christ Church, Oxford, had, since 1546, been the patrons of the parishes of Badsey, Aldington and Wickhamford.) He found "a crying necessity" for a National School in parishes with a population of 650, and no educational facility except a Sunday School. (He did not feel that the Baptist School was worthy of mention, or it probably did not suit his case.) The reply from Reverend Bull is not available, but it was obviously a positive response as, less than two months later, Hunt was forwarding the plans for the school. In neighbouring Offenham, a National School was being erected, and at Bretforton a school had opened in 1847. It was now time for Badsey to have the educational establishment that it deserved.

The National School.

2

THE NATIONAL SCHOOL 1854-1893

School-building was proceeding at a fast pace all over the country, taking advantage of the School Sites Act of 1841 in order to acquire land for such purposes. Having received confirmation of support from his patrons, Reverend Hunt was able to proceed with his plans for the establishment of a school in Badsey, and quickly set about commissioning some plans.

Building the School

The land which Richard Ashwin had donated was 80 feet by 42 feet in a location now occupied by the British Legion in the High Street. Reverend Hunt immediately commissioned a local Evesham builder, George Hunt (not a relative), to draw up plans. "He begs me to send you up a side elevation, and thinks that you will not deem this too ornate," wrote Reverend Hunt to his patron in May 1853. "And he would wish to know what alterations you would require; a great many new schools have risen up about here, and they are all somewhat similar to the one sent for your inspection." These plans did not come to fruition, however, as the state was beginning to take more control of education.

The Government's Committee of the Privy Council had in 1840, as one of its first tasks in improving standards, begun the control of school sites and buildings. By 1847, an album of designs by the architect, H E Kendall, established the model Victorian church school. "The styles of the Middle

Ages are best suited for school houses … because the buildings themselves partake … of a semi-religious character." Playgrounds and "galleries" (rows of seats) on the Scottish model became popular. Single school-rooms were common, although Kay-Shuttleworth, the Committee's first Secretary, favoured the curtain to divide groups.

A E Perkins of Worcester was appointed architect and William Shelswell the builder. In accordance with the specifications of the time, Perkins' design had just one room, 37 feet long by 17 feet wide, to house 78 children, with a separate entrance for boys and girls and separate playgrounds; the toilets and coal store were at the rear. The walls were to be of brick, with stone dressing, and the roof of timber and slate. A teacher's residence was not part of the plan.

Funding the Project

The money for building the school came from two main sources: public subscription and the government. In addition, smaller grants were received from the Diocesan Board and The National Society. As soon as Reverend Hunt had received the go-ahead for the project, an appeal was made to parishioners for subscriptions. A Vestry meeting in July 1853 agreed that £29 9s 7d (accruing from the sale in 1837 of six cottages belonging to the parish of Badsey) should be granted in aid of the erection of a National Day School. When completing The National Society's "Application for Aid" form, to further his claim, Reverend Hunt wrote in an accompanying letter: "The children of the poor in both parishes are growing up in gross ignorance, the nearest school being distant over two miles. The population is rapidly increasing and the want of a school is severely felt by the parish, who see a painful contrast between their own children and those of the neighbouring parishes, in most of which schools exist."

The final costs for building the school were as follows:

School site	Donation
Building	£225 19s 6d
Rejected plans	£10
Fittings	£88 5s 6d
Legal expenses	£16 9s 10d
Architect's commission	£20
TOTAL	**£360 14s 10d**

Local funds	£194 18s 10d
Committee of Council	£125 16s 0d
Diocesan Board	£20
National Society	£20
TOTAL	**£360 14s 10d**

Union with The National Society

To obtain a grant from The National Society, a school had to be "in union" with the Society, and must comply with the building specifications laid down by the Committee of Council. On 18th March 1854, Thomas Hunt, on behalf of himself and the other Managers, signed the formal document uniting the Badsey school with *The National Society for Promoting the Education of the Poor in the Principles of the Established Church throughout England and Wales*. In doing so, he promised that the children would receive religious instruction of the Church of England and attend church regularly, that the Master or Mistress would be a member of the Church of England, that a report on progress would be made every year and that periodic inspections would be allowed.

One month later, a Trust Deed was signed in which it specified that the Trustees were to be the Minister and Churchwardens of Wickhamford and their successors and that the principal officiating Minister was for the time being to have the control of the religious teaching and Sunday School. The reason why the Churchwardens of Wickhamford were specifically mentioned and not Badsey is not known. Perhaps it was deemed important to mention Wickhamford specifically because the Vicar held the two benefices in plurality but was resident at Badsey. Certainly, the terms of the Trust Deed were to cause much confusion nearly 100 years later when the old school building was being sold, as it was initially assumed that it referred to a school at Wickhamford, long since discontinued.

The School Managers were to be the

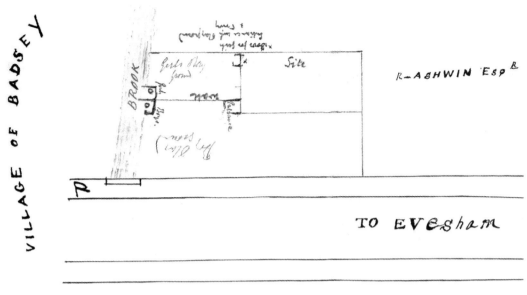

VILLAGE OF BADSEY

BROOK

Site

R-ASHWIN Esp^B

TO EVESHAM

Scale. 10 20 30 40 feet

Above: Original sketch plan showing the location of the proposed school. The site was bounded on its southern perimeter by the brook, which now goes underground at Manorside, but can be seen on the opposite side of the High Street on the south side of Green Leys. The original plan had the playgrounds on the south side of the school with toilets emptying into the brook! This plan was rejected in favour of the plan below.

Below: The approved plan of 1854 no longer exists, but this plan of 1926 shows the improved design of the school, with the original building placed more centrally on the plot, playgrounds to north and south, and the toilets placed at the rear (EC stands for earth closet). An extension was added in 1873.

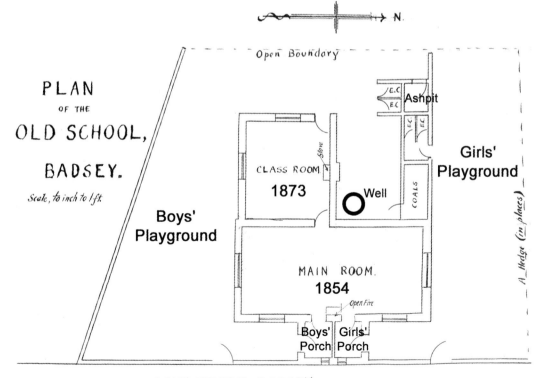

N.

PLAN OF THE OLD SCHOOL, BADSEY.

Scale, to inch to 1ft.

Open Boundary

E.C
E.C   Ashpit

E.C
E.C

CLASS ROOM
1873

Stove

Well

COALS

Girls' Playground

A Hedge (in places)

Boys' Playground

MAIN ROOM.
1854

Open Fire

Boys' Porch   Girls' Porch

HIGH STREET, BADSEY. → To Evesham, Littleton,

The formal agreement of 1854 uniting Badsey School with The National Society.

Minister and three other persons (though from the beginning it seems there were five in total), who must be members of the Church of England and subscribers of at least 20 shillings a year, to be elected by subscribers of at least 10 shillings a year. The first Managers were the Reverend Thomas Hunt, Samuel Taylor of Wickhamford Manor, Richard Ashwin of Aldington Manor, Thomas Appelbee of Harrington House, Badsey, and Thomas Sheaf of Seward House, Badsey. There was also to be a ladies' committee of not more than four.

The Opening of the School

The foundation stone was laid on 1st August 1854, and The United Badsey, Aldington and Wickhamford National School opened its doors to pupils on 1st November 1854. The first Mistress of the school was Miss Sarah Bradley. In 1855, *Billings' Directory* described the school as "a neat building of recent creation … Sarah Bradley mistress, average number of

scholars 45 …". Miss Bradley was well thought of as Mistress and in 1862 she was presented with a Bible by a few friends, as a token of esteem and high approval of the manner in which she had conducted the school.

The school's income was received in three ways: school fees, annual local subscription and a government grant. The fees set in 1854 were 3d (if possible) for the first child of a family, 2d for the next and 1d for the next in the family. An annual local subscription of £20 was promised, but the Managers hoped it would be made up to £35. The principal funding came from a yearly grant. Payment of this grant depended directly on the inspector's report. From 1862 nationwide, a ruthless system of "payment by results" was introduced.

The Curriculum

In 1862, the Revised Code was introduced, which influenced the curriculum of the elementary school. Every year there was an examination in Reading, Writing and Arithmetic. For more than one generation of teachers and scholars, the daily routine became an unremitting grind in the "three Rs" (Reading, Writing and Arithmetic), with constant repetition and rote learning being the normal method of instruction. Individual initiative was crushed as teachers endeavoured to meet the conditions of the Code and discipline was severe. The teachers' desire to obtain a good result arose partly from the fact that, in the early days especially, their salaries often depended upon the amount of grant the school obtained. Unfortunately the Log Books for this period at Badsey do not survive, but the books which survive for other schools give an indication of the teachers' chronic anxieties at the time of inspection.

Religious instruction also had to be given, though it did not earn any financial reward, and the girls were required to learn needlework. From 1867, additional "specific" subject grants were offered for English grammar, geography and history, and in 1875 these were converted into "class" subjects, with the grant earned by the proficiency of the whole group rather than of the individual pupils.

Self-Improvement Association

The arrival of a school in the village awakened people's enthusiasm for knowledge and gave them a desire to continue improving themselves after leaving school at ten. The Badsey Self-Improvement Association was formed in the 1860s and funds were used to buy books such as *Chambers' Dictionary*. We may like to consider it as an early example of "life-long learning" which today's government in 2004 is keen to promote! At its annual feast in January 1869, the speaker emphasised the absolute necessity for young men to perfect themselves in reading in order to be able to understand what they read. Thomas Hall (1817-1907) spoke of the difference between the present time and when he was a boy, he having left school at five years old. In his young days, when men and boys met together it was generally to teach one another what they ought

not to know. Mr Joseph Jones apologised for the opinion he had first formed of the group, having believed them to be a branch of the Reform Association and had called their place of meeting a sedition shop!

Attendance Before Compulsory Education

No attendance register exists for the early history of the National School but, judging from the number of children listed as "scholar" in the census returns, it would seem that a majority of Badsey, Aldington and Wickhamford children attended school, even though there was no legal compulsion until 1870 to do so (except for pauper children and those working in factories and workshops covered by special attendance legislation). Around 61% of children living in Badsey, Aldington and Wickhamford, in the age-range 5-10 were listed as "scholar" in the 1861 census.

RULES

To be observed by the Parents of Children attending the National

School at _____

Parents who wish to get their children admitted into the above-named school, may do so by applying to the Master on any Monday morning, at a quarter before 9 o'clock.

Parents are requested to pay particular attention to the following rules :—

1. The children are to assemble at the school on every week-day morning at a quarter before 9, and every afternoon at a quarter before 2 o'clock, except Saturday, which is a holiday.

2. On the Sunday the children meet in the morning at   , and in the afternoon at   o'clock.

3. The school hours are from 9 to 12, and 2 to 5, in the summer ; and from 9 to 12, and 2 to 4, in the winter.

4. The children must be sent to school clean and neat in person and dress.

5. No child may stay from school without leave from the Master.

6. Leave of absence will be readily granted, either by application personally or by note: this application must be made before, and not after, the child absents itself.

7. If any child come late or be absent, a ticket of suspension will be sent, requiring a reason from the parent.

8. If the ticket be disregarded, the child will not be allowed to attend the school until a satisfactory answer has been given by the parent.

9. Every child must bring   a week, to be paid in advance every Monday morning: if there should be three children in one family desirous of attending the school, the third will be admitted free.

10. No child will be admitted under the age of six years.

N.B. No child will be admitted until it has been vaccinated.

Sold at the *National Society's Depository*, Sanctuary, Westminster.

The National Society rules, which had to be displayed in every school.

In a return to Christ Church of 1872, Hunt indicated that the average attendance was 58, which was probably a good indicator of numbers before the school was enlarged under the Act of 1870; but for special events, the attendance numbers rose. A report in *The Evesham Journal* in May 1869 about the Badsey Wake indicates that 119 schoolchildren partook of tea. The Wake began with a service at the church, followed by a procession to the field next to the Vicarage where the festivities took place.

The Baptist School

At the time the National School opened in 1854, the Baptist School was still in existence. Reverend Thomas Hunt described it as "a very small charity for Infant School at which about five or six children under six are taught their alphabet, but little else".

The Jones family who for several generations had been prominent landowners in the village were responsible for its continued existence. In 1861, Ann Jones was the Mistress, operating from Malvern House, where she lived with her widowed mother. Ann married a Wesleyan Minister and moved away from the village. By 1872, her 15-year-old niece, Edith, was in charge. The school was probably being conducted at Badsey Manor House, where Edith's father was tenant farmer as

Below: Badsey Hall today, once the home of a young ladies' boarding school for about 20 years in the 19th century. Badsey Hall has also been called the Stone House and Montpelier.

Malvern House had been let. Edith was still in charge in 1880. The last recorded Mistress of the school was Edith's younger sister, Mary Eliza, who had charge in 1881 when the family was living at Oakleigh, Old Post Office Lane. These were the final years of the Baptist School. The school was not recognised by the Education Committee as none of the Jones' girls was a qualified teacher, and thus the teaching was not judged "efficient".

Other Educational Establishments

During the 1860s, when the state educational debate was very much to the fore, two private schools for young ladies opened in Badsey. It is possible that a few of the wealthier families in the village may have sent their daughters to one of these establishments.

The first to open was a school run by the Misses Crossley, at Montpelier House (now known as Badsey Hall, 42 High Street). At the time of the 1871 census, 24-year-old Harriet Crossley was the Head, assisted by her elder sister, Anne, and a Music Teacher and a teenage assistant. The school had 25 boarding pupils who came from all over the country, ranging in age from seven to 15. By 1881, another sister, Emma Crossley, was in charge. The school had less boarding pupils, but may well have had a number of day pupils. Certainly, Emma Bell and her sisters, the daughters of Edwin Bell, a Market Gardener who lived at The Poplars, attended the school during the 1880s when the National School was experiencing financial difficulties. The school had closed by 1888 but, to this day, the names of three of the girls, Helena, Camilla and Roma, remain etched on one of the panes of glass in the sitting-room.

In July 1869, another school opened at Malvern House, the former home of the Baptist School. The proprietor was Mrs Mary Mallet, assisted by her daughter and other assistants. The advertisement which appeared in *The Evesham Journal* indicated that the school would take both boarding and day pupils. However, with the Misses Crossley's boarding school just a short distance away, Mrs Mallet appears to have been unsuccessful in breaking into the boarding market. The 1871 census records just one scholar (and that was the Mallet's youngest daughter, Edith!), whereas the Crossley establishment had 25 boarders. Whilst the advertisement indicated that children over the age of ten could also be taken, obviously Mrs Mallet felt unable to provide an adequate education, as another daughter, 13-year-old Jane, was a pupil at the Crossleys' school. The school had closed by 1891.

Compulsory Education for All

Until the latter part of the 19th century, the church had a monopoly on education but, by the late 1860s, the climate was favourable for wide state intervention in elementary schooling. England's survival as an industrial power and parliamentary democracy depended on the provision of education for the whole population. Disraeli's Reform Act of 1867 gave the vote to virtually all male householders and doubled the franchise overnight. Men who were neither literate nor propertied could now exercise a vote and education reform came to the fore.

The widened electorate of 1868 returned a liberal Government "ardent for reform". W E Forster set about preparing an education bill, his aims being "to cover the country with good schools" and "to get the parents to send their children to these schools". His remit was not easy as his task was to forge a compromise between two extremes: those which demanded free, compulsory, state schooling for all, free from religious colouring, and supported by extremist non-conformists, Liberals and Trades Unionists, and those supported by Church of England and Conservative interests, which fought to protect church schools. His compromise plan, aimed to "fill the gaps", was devised with considerable political skill. Where schooling was "sufficient, efficient and suitable", no action would be taken; where it was not, a School Board would be set up to create and run state elementary schools, financed by a local rate, government grant and "school pence" from pupils. The churches were placated and voluntary agencies

Malvern House today. In the 19th century it was for a time the Baptist School and then a private school. The advertisement below appeared in "The Evesham Journal" of 3rd July 1869.

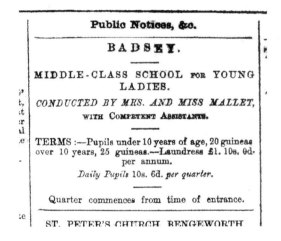

were given six months to build church schools in ill-provided areas before any School Board was established. Thus the chief stumbling block for previous Bills was surmounted and Forster's Act became law on 9th August 1870, bringing some schooling within the reach of every English child.

But not everyone was happy with this "dual system" of Board and church elementary schools, a debate which carries on to the present day. There was some bitterness at this "compromise upon a compromise" which caused a serious split in the Liberal party. Churchmen, by contrast, spoke against the "godless" Board schools.

The Impact of the 1870 Education Act

As a result of Forster's Education Act, the country was divided into school districts, based on civil parishes and the boroughs. Each district was surveyed to see if its "educational condition" was adequate. On 22nd December 1871, H F Pooley, Inspector of Returns, issued a report on the parishes of Badsey, Wickhamford and Aldington, in which he stated that out of a total of 769 inhabitants for the three parishes, 625 (81%) were of the class whose children might be expected to attend elementary school. An analysis of the 1871 census (on whose figures the report was written) gives us a clue as to which children would not be expected to attend the village school. It would have included the Reverend Hunt's children, the children of local farmers and landowners, and the children at the two young ladies' boarding establishments that existed in the village.

Based on a rate of one in five of this class, school accommodation was required for 125 children (81 children from Badsey, 24 from Aldington and 20 from Wickhamford). The school had been built to accommodate 78 children, so provision for an extra 47 was required. The Managers had taken advantage of the six-month period when voluntary agencies were given the chance to put right any deficiency because the report indicates that plans were already in hand for an extension, which the Inspector felt was adequate. A grant was awarded in January 1873 and work commenced shortly after. An extra room was added at the rear to accommodate the Infant children. The building work cost £193, of which £25 was given by Christ Church. By 26th October 1873, the new classroom was complete and ready for use.

Attendance After Compulsory Education

School Attendance Committees were set up in 1876, even in voluntary districts, declaring it was a parent's duty to see his child educated. School Attendance Officers were appointed to check on truants. Mundella's Act of 1880 forced all Committees to make by-laws, making attendance compulsory for every child at least to the age of ten, and thereafter to 13 unless he or she could pass a special leaving examination or gain exemption by making a certain number of school attendances.

But not all parents welcomed these initiatives since, not only was there a loss of income from the children's labour, but school fees had to be paid as well. Whilst the "school pence" was not a big sum of money, where there were several children in the family, this could represent a considerable outlay. Often parents reacted by simply keeping the youngsters away if they had no money for fees. Not until 1891 did an extra government grant at last make free schooling possible for virtually all elementary scholars.

The Teaching Staff

During the latter part of the 19th century, women dominated the teaching profession. Most teachers were extremely young; in 1870, about half were mere teenage apprentices. Miss Bradley was in charge of the school from 1854 until the 1860s, with one Assistant to help. By 1871, Miss Ann Meredith and her sister, Jemima, were the Mistress and the Assistant Mistress at the school. According to a return made by Reverend Hunt to Christ Church in 1872, Ann Meredith, a Certificated teacher, received a salary of £30 a year, a furnished residence worth £8, one ton of coal worth £1 and half the government grant in 1872 worth £21 15s 0d. Jemima received a salary of £10 a year. The sisters' accommodation, according to the 1871 census, was in the cottage which is now No 20 Brewers Lane.

The school then went through a succession of Heads: young women in their twenties, who had charge of a large number of children with little assistance and few resources. Miss Colbourn was the head in 1876 and by 1880 Ruth Silvester was in charge of the school. She is believed to have had family connections with the village, as she lodged with Robert and Elizabeth Silvester at what is now the Spar shop. From then until 1888, the Mistress of the time lodged at the Silvesters' house. Other Mistresses included Antoinette Marsden and Letitia Stone. Miss Stone was born at West

Above: Artist's reconstruction from architect's plans of the National School building in the 1870s after the extension was built in 1873.

Right: The old school building as it appears today. Mr George Henry Stewart, on behalf of the Boy Scouts, bought the property in October 1951 from the Diocesan Board for £350. Both the Boy Scouts and The British Legion were interested in buying the property but the Scouts were allowed to buy it as they had leased the building and made a number of improvements. In June 1962, as the Scouts had built a new hut on the Recreation Ground, Mr Stewart sold the building to the present owners, The British Legion (now The Royal British Legion) for £500.

Bromwich, Staffordshire, which was also the home-town of Ruth Silvester. It is possible that Miss Stone was recommended to take on the Badsey headship by Ruth, who had just married and settled in the village.

Under Miss Stone's headship, an excellent examination in 1885 at that year's school inspection resulted in an improved grant. Miss Stone, however, was experiencing a number of difficulties because of under-resourcing and left in 1885. She was replaced by Elizabeth Wagstaff, whose tenure lasted three years but who, some years later, returned as Mrs Mason to take on the post of Head of the Infant Department at the new Board School, a post which she held until 1922. During Miss Wagstaff's headship, good teaching also resulted in an increased grant but she, too, was concerned about the lack of qualified assistance. Accordingly, Miss Elizabeth Smith was duly appointed Assistant Mistress; she had been a Pupil Teacher at Blockley National School, Elizabeth Wagstaff's home village.

The Ladies' Committee

The terms of the original Trust Deed mentioned a "ladies' committee of not more than four". During the 1880s, the wives of School Managers Arthur Savory and Julius Sladden helped at the school. The first indication of Mrs Eugenie Sladden visiting the school is 8th October 1881, when she writes in her diary: "I went to the school to help Mrs Savory sell the work, but we were cold as nobody came to buy." Mrs Sladden was referring to the needlework done by the girls, which was sold to cover the cost of materials. From then on, until Reverend Hunt retired and in between giving birth to a succession of children, Mrs Sladden frequently went to help out at school, often going to visit her friend, Mrs Frances Savory at Aldington Manor, afterwards. She was at school on 13th November 1882, just a week before giving birth to her daughter, Ethel.

In February 1883, we learn from her diary that there was an inspection at the school. Mrs Sladden was unable to go, as she had to look after her own children, but she was able to meet the Inspectors the next day with Mrs

Ruth Silvester, Mistress in 1880. After a short spell teaching in Coventry, she returned to Badsey to marry John Cull the baker. Her children, and many of her grandchildren and great-grandchildren attended Badsey School.

Savory. At the beginning of February 1884, Mrs Sladden did not feel well enough to go in to school (Arthur was born just a week or two later), so asked Miss Corbett to go instead. Georgina Corbett, a single woman in her forties, lived at Harrington House with her widowed father. Later in the year, she became the first female Manager of the school, an uncommon position for women in those days. Hamilla Hunt, the eldest daughter of the Vicar, also visited from time to time; on one occasion in June 1884, she distributed prizes.

The diary also records the illnesses that affected attendance such as this entry for July 1885: "I went to the school, several children there had whooping cough and a great many were away with it." The Sladdens' children did not attend the local school but instead were educated at home in their early years. "May began lessons with Jack," wrote Mrs Sladden in her diary on 29th September 1884, speaking of her eldest two children, aged nearly four and nearly six at the time.

Queen Victoria's Jubilee

The school participated in the village's celebrations for Queen Victoria's Golden Jubilee in 1887. The schoolchildren, each with a ticket attached to their satchel or back, together with the choir and parishioners, marched with banners from the Vicarage along the High Street as far as The Manor, led by the Toddington Brass Band. After a church service, a cold dinner was served in Mr John Byrd's field at the rear of the church, everyone having been asked to bring his own plate, knife, fork, cup and saucer. A programme of sports was then conducted, followed by dancing. The proceedings were concluded with a display of fireworks (home-made by the Reverend Sealy Poole of Evesham!) from the church tower.

Growing Financial Difficulties

For some years the school had been experiencing financial difficulties. In the six months after the 1870 Education Act became law, there was a frenzy of church activity throughout the land. But after that, voluntary effort gradually faded, dependent as it was upon the uncertainties of private subscription.

This was certainly true in Badsey where, by 1872, according to a form completed for Christ Church by the Reverend Hunt, the school's finances were beginning to run into trouble. Subscriptions amounted to £29 19s 9d, school fees £18 8s 2d, government grant £43 10s 0d, leaving a deficit of £91 17s 11d to be made good by himself. From time to time, Hunt wrote to his patrons at Christ Church for financial assistance, the following concluding sentence of a letter dated June 1879 being typical: "If you would consider my petition, I should feel deeply obliged as with three boys at school and Sandhurst and two girls to educate, and all to feed, £20 a year extra would be something for the poor bairns." (Hunt's children, of course, did not attend the local school.)

By the 1880s, the financing of the school was proving to be a real problem and it also seems that the Managing Committee, as required by the terms of the original trust deed,

had lapsed, possibly because two of its long-standing members had recently died or moved away. In 1881, a new Managing Committee was formed at a first School Meeting. In addition to the Vicar, the Churchwardens of Badsey (Julius Sladden), Aldington (Arthur Savory) and Wickhamford (George Pethard) became ex-officio members, and four other members were elected annually at the General Meeting of subscribers. Julius Sladden, who had moved to Seward House just a couple of years earlier, proposed the resolution: "That it is desirable to continue the Badsey, Aldington & Wickhamford CE School on the voluntary system." It was seconded by Arthur Savory, who had moved to Aldington Manor as a tenant farmer in 1873, and carried unanimously.

The Annual School Meeting in 1883 confirmed the desire to continue under the voluntary system and subscribers thanked Reverend Hunt for clearing the existing debt of £26. There was discussion about a £50 legacy left by Miss Sarah Byrd of The Poplars. It was hoped to raise enough money by subscription to equal the amount, and thus be able to afford a School Teacher's residence. The project was felt desirable, not only because it would enable the Mistress the convenience of being close to her school, but she would also be in a position to protect the school from damage and destruction. The members at the meeting were surprised and alarmed to hear that the parish was unable to deter its children from breaking the school windows and doing continual and wilful damage.

Despite mounting financial pressures, Reverend Hunt managed to fend off a School Board during his tenure, but it was just a matter of time. He retired in 1887 and from then on, the situation became more serious.

The Crisis Deepens

The Reverend Charles Granville Gepp succeeded Reverend Hunt in December 1887. He found the school in a poor state financially, and immediately provided bibles and prayer books for school use, as well as a subscription of £5 but, unlike Hunt, he was unprepared to continue bailing out the school financially.

At the subscribers' meeting in May 1888, it was agreed that it would be necessary to call a public meeting of parishioners to discuss the parlous state of the school finances. A letter was also read from Reverend Hunt who, although retired to Shropshire, still took a keen interest in the school. He reminded them of the £50 bequest made by the late Miss Sarah Byrd for the good of the school, to be apportioned as he felt fit.

A meeting of ratepayers was called for August and the Vicar laid before the meeting four alternatives: to levy a voluntary rate, to increase the voluntary subscription, to raise the school fees, or to have a School Board. The School Board option had no supporters, and raising of the school fees was felt undesirable. The meeting was split between the first two options, but eventually decided in favour of subscriptions. Despite canvassing from house to house, the subscriptions from the three parishes amounted to just over £8.

The School Managers met on 18th January 1889, at which meeting they decided they had no alternative but to resign. A Parish Meeting was called for 29th January, with a notice convening the meeting posted on the church

August. 1888

Badsey, Aldington and Wickhamford Schools.

At an adjourned meeting of the ratepayers, held in the Schoolroom, Badsey, on Thursday evening, August 16, 1888, it was unanimously resolved, on the motion of Mr. Sladden, seconded by Mr. Steward, "That a circular setting forth the present unsatisfactory condition of the School finances be forthwith printed and distributed amongst the ratepayers, and that an appeal be made to them, and to the inhabitants of the three parishes generally, to raise by voluntary subscription the amount necessary for carrying on the School.

The estimated expenses amount to an average of £125 per annum. The yearly receipts (without the voluntary subscriptions) amount to an average of £80, leaving a sum of not less than £40 to be made up by voluntary subscriptions from the three parishes. For the last two years the voluntary subscriptions have averaged only £26.

Last year the sum of £20 2s. was subscribed by the Dean and Chapter of Christ Church, Oxford, and five individuals, leaving £6.3s. 6d. as the total amount contributed by the three parishes. ////

Unless the required amount is made up, the Managing Committee will have no alternative but to resign; the School will be closed, and a School Board will be forced upon the Parish.

[TURN OVER.]

Above and below: Subscription form sent to all parishioners of Badsey, Aldington and Wickhamford in August 1888. This form was returned by Wingfield John Smith of Wickhamford Mill, who agreed to pay 5s annually. Note the underlining and addition of exclamation marks to certain parts of the form! Edward Wilson, Frederick Bullock, Elijah Crisp and John Mason conducted the canvas (John Mason was shortly to marry Elizabeth Wagstaff, the Mistress of Badsey School).

If you are in favour of carrying on the School on the Voluntary System please fill up the annexed form.

I am willing to subscribe £ : 5 s. : d. annually to the Badsey, Aldington and Wickhamford Schools, the subscriptions to be collected in the month of September.

Signed, Wingfield John Smith

Date, Sept 15th. 1888.

First page of bank book for Badsey National School. Arthur Savory was the Treasurer. The entries for Wagstaff relate to Miss Elizabeth Wagstaff, Mistress 1885-1888. The entries for Smith relate to Miss Elizabeth Smith, Assistant Mistress 1888-1889.

doors, and other prominent places. Reverend Gepp explained the impossibility of carrying on the school at all with the funds at their disposal. The Managers stated their intention to resign: "We, the undersigned Managers of the Badsey, Aldington and Wickhamford Schools, hereby declare our intention of resigning office and decline to incur any responsibilities of the said schools after the close of the financial year ending 31st January 1889." The Managers also passed a resolution that "we are unable and unwilling any longer to maintain the above school on the voluntary system".

Gepp wrote to the Department saying that the present Managers had resigned owing to their inability to maintain the school for lack of funds, but indicated that they were willing to carry on the school until a Board was formed, especially as an inspection was due shortly. The inspection took place on 5th February and the Education Department was duly notified two days later that, as it had become impossible to fund such necessaries as coal and firewood, the school must be closed without delay. The school limped on throughout February, and then a notice was publicly read and posted in the schoolroom on 28th February stating that the school would close on 8th March.

Closure

And so the school closed in March 1889. There was opposition to a School Board but not enough support for a voluntary school. Numerous meetings were held but matters drifted with no real conclusion. Reverend Gepp wrote to the Reverend J Duncan, Secretary of The National Society, informing him of the situation. Duncan, desperate to try and retrieve the situation, enclosed some information about The National Society for distribution. Gepp did not mince his words in his reply:

"The contents of the leaflets are quite familiar to my parishioners. They know perfectly well what the change means; but, for all that, they will not subscribe. Meeting after meeting has been held for at least eight years past (as the Minutes of the Vestry Book testify), committees of management have been formed, subscriptions have been promised (and never paid). Every expedient has been tried, and failed, with a sad monotony which has wearied on to the five or six persons who have hitherto borne the burden.

"The fact is, the school has been in a hopeless condition for some years past. My predecessor, the Reverend T H Hunt, adopted the simple but (as I consider it) suicidal, policy of paying off the deficit, from time to time, out of his own pocket; thereby, it is true, staving off the evil day temporarily, but really adding to the difficulties and complications of the question."

The Evesham Journal reported the state of affairs in its issue of 22nd June 1889: "The village children have now for several months experienced the pleasures of perfect freedom from educational control. This is, of course, a state of things which cannot be tolerated for long."

At the request of the Secretary of The National Society, the Reverend Edward Houghton of Blockley, Secretary of the Worcester Diocesan Education Society, was asked to act as The National Society's representative to try and save the school. Houghton was dismayed to find that it was almost a fait accompli that the Trustees had decided to transfer the school to a School Board, and that he had only been invited to confer with the Trustees about the most favourable terms in which the transfer could be made. He suggested additional and augmented subscriptions and augmentation of school fees. Having obtained permission from Reverend Gepp, who felt that "there is no hope", he spent some hours in canvassing the parishioners, who he claimed were unanimously in favour of maintaining a voluntary school. In the meantime, the Education Department issued a Final Notice expiring on 29th September as a deadline for making voluntary provision.

At a meeting of parishioners on 30th July 1889, at which the Vicar was not present, the proposal to maintain the school under the voluntary system was passed unanimously. So, for the time being, Reverend Houghton had gained a reprieve for Badsey National School, and had obtained promises of subscriptions sufficient to enable the school to be continued. New Managers were elected who made an immediate inspection of the premises. New heating apparatus was required, repairs to furniture, gallery, hat pegs needed, and the whole building needed painting. An advertisement for new staff was placed in *The Schoolmaster* and *Schoolmistress* newspapers.

Temporary Reprieve

The school reopened on Monday 30th September 1889 under the headship of Miss Alice Kelland. The advertisement had specified a Mistress "not under 25". Miss Kelland was aged only 20 at the time of her appointment, but she proved to be a capable Head. No Log Books survive from this period, but an Admissions Register was begun in January 1890, which indicates a school roll of 115.

Demise of the National School

At the Annual School Meeting in both April 1891 and 1892, Reverend Gepp impressed upon the parishioners the necessity of increased support if the Managers were to maintain the standard of efficiency. The Inspector's report was "exceedingly satisfactory" but he had made certain "recommendations", which had to be

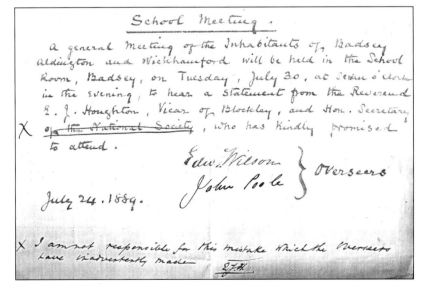

Announcement of a meeting (one of many) held in 1889 to discuss the future of the National School. Note the correction made by Reverend Houghton, who was Secretary of the local Diocesan Board rather than of the National Society.

In 1890, it became compulsory for all schools to keep an Admissions Register and a special printed book was provided for this purpose. Miss Kelland entered 115 children into the register on 30th January 1890. From the order in which the children appear in the register, it seems they were entered in order of Standard as the Head has written down the eldest boys followed by the eldest girls, then another group of younger boys followed by girls. The first person on the list was 11-year-old William Sparrow, great-uncle of village historian, Terry Sparrow. In later years, Mr McDonald wrote in the margin to indicate what happened to the pupils in adulthood; for example, George Enstone emigrated to Canada.

implemented as soon as possible. Reverend Gepp emphasised that the Managers had not been extravagant; instead the problem was with the ever-increasing demands made by the Education Department. The education in elementary schools was becoming more costly every year. The cost of education per head at Badsey was 35s 0d, while the average cost per head of all the Church Schools in England and Wales was 36s 11½d; and if they took Board Schools throughout the country, the average was 45s 11½d per head. Free education for any child aged 4-14 was to become compulsory from September 1892, so money could not be raised from fees. The population of the three parishes was increasing rapidly. The school buildings could accommodate only 120 and there were already

130 on the register, with a certainty that this number would increase. Reverend Gepp concluded by saying that, if parishioners wanted the school to be maintained as a voluntary school, there were just two courses open: either to increase the subscriptions or to consent to a voluntary rate. As subscriptions had not worked in the past it was agreed to

Advertisement in The Schoolmaster magazine, 1889. Miss Alice Kelland was offered the job.

Badsey National School narrowly escaped becoming a Board School in 1889, when a Final Notice was issued by the Board of Education. The terms of the conditions were satisfied on that occasion, but less than four years later, a Final Notice was issued on 7th February 1893 which was acted upon.

levy a voluntary rate on the parish and a committee of volunteers for collecting the rates was formed.

Arthur Savory, writing many years later in his book, *Grain and Chaff from an English Manor,* said: "The large farmers were being gradually ruined by foreign competition, and the small market gardeners, in occupation of the land as it fell vacant, could not be induced to subscribe, although their own children were the sole beneficiaries." He went on to say that, on the suggestion of a voluntary rate, one old parishioner announced the feeling of many that she did not intend "to pay no voluntary rate until I'm obliged".

But the end of the National School was in sight. Following a further inspection in September 1892, the newly-appointed Inspector, Mr M J Barrington Ward, made certain recommendations with which the Managers felt unable to comply. Reverend Gepp wrote to the Education Department stating that there was no funding available and regretting that, as far as the Managers could see, they would be unable to carry on the school as a voluntary school after April. In an Education Department Minute paper, Barrington Ward made it clear that what was desirable at Badsey in 1889 (ie the creation of a school Board) was desirable now. "The school has been moribund for some time, and the Correspondent finds it impossible to stir up local interest in school affairs (so he tells me). The proposed Union may therefore be announced."

In the meantime, Reverend Gepp received a letter from the Education Department, informing him that the school accommodation was insufficient and that they would be required to find 70 additional places. Gepp wrote immediately to The National Society to say that this could not be done by voluntary effort. He felt that a Board was inevitable and that it would be better if there were entirely new buildings, including a teacher's house, on an entirely new site. J S Brownrigg, the new Secretary of The National Society, was not impressed. He wrote to Reverend Houghton, the Vicar of Blockley, in January 1893, saying: "Once before you saved this school. The Vicar writes a very hopeless letter, but I have counselled sharply upon him to make the effort. Can you do anything? Of course we should give a grant."

An exchange of letters continued throughout January and February. "Of all the Church Schools deliberately given up to a Board, never was one more unnecessarily sacrificed, and this hurts me much," wrote Houghton to The National Society in January. Gepp wrote in February: "I have already pointed out that I consider it would be on all accounts undesirable to build on to the present schools. The site is bad. Moreover, a School House must be built. I am not going to give a cottage to a School Board. And, apart from these considerations, I have good reason for thinking that the Department would not sanction any such additions on the present site. I may be wrong. I merely state my opinion."

Whilst Reverend Gepp was having his dialogue with The National Society, Barrington Ward visited Badsey again in January and found that no steps were being taken for a voluntary settlement of the school question. He therefore recommended a Final Notice to be issued immediately, with one month as the period of grace, concluding with the sentence, "A School Board is inevitable."

No action was taken by the deadline of 12th March 1893, and so the parishes of Badsey, Aldington and Wickhamford moved inexorably towards the formation of a School Board. The financial year ended on 31st March 1893, but Reverend Gepp kept the school open until after HMI's annual inspection, which was to have taken place in April, but was actually held on 2nd May. The children of Badsey were then without a school for four months until the Board School opened in September.

The earliest-known photograph of Badsey schoolchildren, taken outside the National School building, about 1890. The girl in the back row, fifth from the left, is Elizabeth Harris, born 1878, who left school in 1892. The staff at that time were Miss Alice Kelland and Miss Kate Fowler.

Schemes for 1899 - 1900.

Approved by M. J. Barrington - Ward Esq.
H. M. I. April 21st 1899.

Recitation.

St. i "The Sailor Boy" (Tennyson) 20 lines
" ii. iii "A New Forest Ballad" (Kingsley) 60 "
" iv "An Order for a Picture" (Alice Cary) "
" v - vi "Selections from "King Lear" 158 "

Class Subjects

St. i. iii (a) Geography. (b) Object Lessons
" iv - vi (a) Do (b) English

(a) Geography.
St. i - ii As per Code
" iii England, Wales, Worcestershire.
" iv - vi British Empire

(b) Grammar.
St. iv Subject. Predicate & Object of a
Simple Sentence. + Parsing of the
Chief parts of Speech.
v - vi Parsing + Analysis of Compound Sentence.
Prefixes. Affixes and formation of
different parts of Speech f

Pages from the Log Book showing the schemes of work of the Mixed Department for 1899-1900, as approved by HMI, Mr M J Barrington Ward. This included "Object Lessons", aimed at stimulating children's powers of observation and expression; models were ordered from an educational supplier to assist in the lesson.

Object Lessons Approved 148

St. i
1. Water. 2. Liquids + Solids. 3. Hard & Soft Bodies. 4. Porous Bodies. 5. Soluble substances. 6. Sugar. 7. Burning 8. Coal. 9. Uses of Coal. 10. A Coal mine 11. Flexible & Elastic Substances. 13. Plastic bodies. 14. Putty 15. The Cat. 16. Dog. 17. Dogs. 18. Sheep. 19. Pig. 20. Cow 21. Horse. 22. Monkey. 23. Rabbit 24. Parts of a Plant. 25. The Root. 26. The Stem. 27. Stems. 28. The Leaves. 29. The Flowers. 30. Corn.

St. ii. iii
1. 2. Starch. 3. Starch foods. 4. Corn 5. Kinds of Corn. 6. Rice. 7. Rice. how grown 8. Maize + how grown. 9. Properties & Uses of Maize 10. Liquids. 11. Mercury. 12. Alcohol. 13. Camphor. 14. The Cow. 15. Milk. 16. Butter and Cheese. 17. Birds & their coverings. 18. A Feather. 19. Birds. 20. 21. Classes of Birds. 22. 23. Birds, Legs & Feet. 24. 25. Air. 26. Fusible substances. 27. 28. Properties of Metals. 29. Copper. 30. Alloys of Copper.

Mr John Henry McDonald,
Headteacher 1894-1913.

3

BADSEY BOARD SCHOOL 1893-1903

The dying years of the Victorian era were an important time for both the village and the school. Badsey in the 1890s was developing at a fast rate with the burgeoning growth of market gardening. The agricultural depression in the latter part of the 19th century had, in most parts of the country, led agricultural workers to forsake the country for new jobs in the towns and cities or abroad. However, in Badsey, the lack of a squire had given the former agricultural workers the opportunity to take over small strips of the former farming land. By the end of the 19th century, the transition from agriculture to horticulture was almost complete, and with it came a new breed of Market Gardeners ready to have a voice in all matters. Whilst the population in most rural areas was declining, the reverse was true in Badsey, and so the necessity to have a good school was never more important.

The School Board

In the nation at large in the mid 1890s, there were still more children attending denominational schools than those provided by the Boards. The transition from a school run on the voluntary system to one run by a Board was not without its problems. The Board was elected by local ratepayers to hold office for three years and seats on Boards were highly coveted. Board members had the power to raise rates, buy land and borrow money to build schools.

The first meeting of the School Board for the United District of Badsey was held in May 1893. Four of the Managers had previously been Managers of the National School: Julius Sladden, Frederick Hooper, Thomas Byrd (who resigned within three months and was replaced by John Poole) and Arthur Savory, who was elected Chairman. Arthur Savory, writing some 30 years later in his book, *Grain and Chaff from an English Manor*, said that he had been persuaded to stand by a deputation of working men. He freely admitted that he had agreed to stand chiefly in his own interests as the largest individual ratepayer in the parish. The Board also comprised three newcomers: John Mason, William John Warmington and Thomas Marshall.

Savory made some fairly patronising comments about his fellow Board members: "We were rather a three-cornered lot: my co-warden; a boot and shoemaker in Evesham, with land in Badsey; a carpenter and small builder; three small market gardeners and myself." Julius Sladden was Savory's fellow churchwarden and he and Savory represented the old established order. The "boot and shoemaker" was Frederick Hooper of Knowle Hill who owned a considerable amount of land; the "carpenter and small builder" was William John Warmington; and the "three small market gardeners" were Mason, Marshall and Poole. Mason was the husband of the former National School Mistress, Miss Wagstaff, who later became Head of the Infant Department, Marshall was later to become landlord of The

Arthur Savory, Chairman of Managers 1893-1899.

Wheatsheaf Inn and Poole was already landlord of The Royal Oak Inn, so all were men of growing influence.

Savory goes on to say: "It was not easy to discover the qualifications of all the members from an educational point of view; some at least represented the village malcontent section, now getting rather nervous as to School Board rates... One, at any rate, was definitely qualified, 'He knowed summat about draining.' The majority were conspicuous as economists in the matter of probable school expenditure, and it appeared later that two, if not three, of the members were unable to write their own names, so that sometimes we could not get the necessary number of signatures to the cheques, when some of the more efficient members happened to be absent." One or two members of the Board during the 1890s were born before 1850, so may not have benefited from the growing movement in education. Edward Wadams was Clerk ("an excellent clerk, a capable man, and well up in the forms and idiosyncrasies of the Board of Education," according to Savory) on a salary of £20 a year.

Early in the Board's existence, one of the economists believed that their first duty was to the ratepayers. Savory corrected him by saying that their first duty was to the children. The disparate members of the School Board sometimes made for volatile meetings. Arthur Savory's method of dealing with any item raised which he considered unimportant, was to appoint a sub-committee to inquire into the matter and report back to the next meeting; usually that was the last of the matter!

Economy became the watchword of the 1890s. Some parishioners, reading of the large sums that the Managers were obliged to spend in response to the requirements of the Education Department and finding the consequent rates a burden, were encouraged to seek election. The newly enfranchised Market Gardeners had a resounding victory at the 1899 triennial election, Alfred Butler, John Mason, John Knight, Leonard White and Walter Blake all polling over 300 votes, with an 81% turn-out. Julius Sladden and Arthur Savory came a poor eighth and ninth in the contest for seven seats. Savory had obviously seen the writing on the wall, as he had been absent from the final two meetings of the old Board. He was upset that he had not been returned but he "was not sorry to escape from the monotony of listening to interminable debates as to whether a necessary broom or such-like trifle should be bought at 1s or 1s 3d."

The new Board, under the Chairmanship of Leonard White, quickly gained a reputation for penny-pinching and there were numerous acrimonious discussions at their meetings, leading on one occasion to a vote of no confidence in the Clerk who was accused of suppressing information. A proposal for his resignation was defeated.

The final triennial election which took place in April 1902 was an exciting event, with 11 candidates contesting seven seats. "We understand that the ratepayers of Badsey are by no means satisfied with the way the school affairs have been managed during the last three years, and it is said that they do not intend repeating the mistake they made at the last election," said a report in *The Evesham Journal*. Henry Stewart, John Idiens, Charles Binyon and William Pethard issued a joint address, favouring economy with efficiency and, on the morning of the election, issued a handbill stating that the self-styled "economical" Board had raised the school rate considerably. The old Board, in strict accordance with their principle of economy, held their committee meetings in the road outside the school, whilst the new candidates met in a house opposite the church. Several carriages, drays and other vehicles brought the people to the poll, and canvassing was keen. Polling took place from 12-8 pm at the school, with the majority of people voting later in the day. In spite of the piercing east wind, a number of parishioners gathered at the school gates to wait for the result which was declared at 9.40 pm. The outcome was a partial victory for both parties, four out of seven members of the old Board obtaining seats, and three of the new candidates being successful. One of these was the young Charles Arthur Binyon, recently arrived in the village, who was to have so much influence at the school for the next 60 years.

The Board School Opens

For four months, from the beginning of May to the beginning of September 1893, there was no provision for education in Badsey. During this period, a few children attended Evesham National School. For example, in June 1893, brothers William and John Bennett, and their cousin, William Hardiman, were admitted to Evesham National School. They stayed for just a short time, withdrawing in September 1893, the reason being "Gone back to Badsey, Board School start".

The first task of the Board members was to obtain an agreement from the Trustees of the National School building that they were prepared to transfer it over to the School Board in accordance with the Education Act. Reverend Gepp, on behalf of the Trustees, signed an agreement for the temporary taking over of the school. The building was in a bad state of repair, with the roof coming through in two or three places. The school was whitewashed and cleaned ready for a new start, and an advertisement placed in *The Schoolmistress* for a Mistress and Assistant Mistress at salaries of £80 and £40 a year.

The Board School came into being on 4th September 1893 with Miss Mary Edgerton as the new Headteacher. Miss Edgerton found the children somewhat unruly and the lower classes (especially Standard I and the Infants) very backward. The apparatus was in a dilapidated condition and there was scarcely any stationery. The desk accommodation was insufficient for all Standard I boys to take drawing at the same time and the needlework was getting spoiled because there was no cupboard or box in which to put it. The stove in the larger room needed attention and some days it was almost too cold to work. It was a constant struggle to get extra staff and thus she was unhappy with the progress of the children.

Despite these problems, the school was soon bursting at the seams as confidence in the new Board School grew. From an average attendance of 73 recorded on 8th September 1893, the numbers increased to 131 by the end of the month, with 135 on the register. It was necessary for Miss Edgerton to refuse admission to nine children and to call for an immediate increase in staff. The two rooms were meant to accommodate a total of 125 children but, during 1894, the average attendance ranged from 121 to 168.

In order to accommodate the overflow of children, Mr Thomas Byrd allowed the Reading Room, situated at the end of a passageway known as The Alley (on land now occupied by part of Poplar Court), to be used for the Infants. Alterations were required before it could be used and approval needed from the Inspector, who wrote: "I have viewed the room from the outside, but I could not get the key, and so could only peep through the windows! It is a large low room, which might perhaps be approved for a few months during the erection of the new buildings – if these people ever build (I have no confidence in their desire to build)!" It was ready for occupation by the end of January 1894 but by the summer months, the conditions were becoming intolerable. Manager Mr Warmington visited one Thursday in June and found the heat most oppressive and the smell from pig-sties very offensive. One day when Miss Edgerton visited she found that several of the infants had fallen asleep. The sooner a new school could be provided the better.

The Need for New Premises

As soon as he took office, Arthur Savory wrote to the Education Department for instructions concerning accommodation requirements. He also wrote to Reverend Gepp asking whether his condition that the school building should not be altered was unalterable. Gepp immediately wrote to The National Society for advice. He was of the opinion that the Education Department would not approve of building on the present site and he himself felt it would be a mistake: "Of course, my refusal to allow additions to be made will be used against me. I shall be accused of 'saddling the ratepayers with unnecessary burdens', etc. But I am quite prepared to do my duty, provided that I am assured of the support of the National Society."

Before making a decision about accommodation requirements, the Education Department requested that a census of the children in the

The first page of the earliest surviving Log Book; Miss Mary Edgerton was the first Head of the new Board School and stayed for a year.

Above: Group of infants at the old school building, 1894. The teacher on the left is Miss A E Crisp, who began teaching at the school in January 1894; on the right is Martha Mustoe, who joined as a Monitress in October 1893.

Below: Group of children at the old school building, 1894. Headteacher, Miss Edgerton, is on the right. Six-year-old John Joseph Warmington, son of School Manager, W J Warmington, is on the front row at the right.

district be taken. Mr Warmington was asked to conduct the census, which revealed a total of 222 children. The Education Department, having reviewed the plans of the old school that had been sent, felt that the accommodation was quite inadequate, and could only properly be recognised for the Infant School, and then only on the conditions that considerable alterations were made. They felt that, under the circumstances, the Board would be advised to proceed at once with the erection of a new school for 250-300 scholars of all ages.

The Board asked the Education Department for permission to build a new school for some of the children adjacent to the present building, connected by a corridor or passage. But the Education Department were adamant that this would not provide adequate provision and plans of the proposed site must be sent by the end of October. The school should be planned so as to be capable of enlargement without difficulty at any time in view of the increasing population. Arthur Savory freely admitted that they employed delaying tactics:

"Many of their requirements we considered unnecessary in a country village and put off the evil day as long as possible with such phrases as, 'The matter is under consideration' or, 'Will shortly be brought to the notice of the Board'." On receiving the plans, the Department sanctioned the temporary use of the National School and said that the Board must fulfil their duties within the time; if not, the Department would dissolve the Board and form another themselves.

The Board thus had little choice. After considerable discussion, it was agreed to build a new school and to find a convenient site as soon as possible.

Acquiring the Land

The Board approached solicitors Messrs Parker & Lord, to see if the Trustees of the late Captain John Lord, a prominent Badsey landowner, would be able to provide a site. However, the solicitors wrote to say that, as the school was a Board and not a Voluntary School, they could not advise them to give a site. After considerable negotiations, the Trustees were persuaded to sell some land for £90. "We concluded the purchase and congratulated ourselves upon the acquisition of a central and in every way desirable site, with a long road frontage, for a very moderate sum," wrote Savory. "On reporting to the Board at our next meeting, the sum appeared large to some of the more simple members, and they were inclined to be dissatisfied until I told them that I was prepared to appropriate the bargain myself and they could find another for the school." That settled the matter and the land purchase went ahead.

Five shillings' compensation was paid to Benjamin Sears and ten shillings to Elizabeth Perkins, the tenants occupying the cottages adjacent to the land, the site of the present-day No 12 School Lane. In addition, a small piece of land was bought from Reverend Gepp, with the assent of the ecclesiastical commissioners. This was a small strip of glebe land, formerly a rick-yard, in area about 440 square yards. This proved to be a very important acquisition as on that site was built the School House, and nearly a hundred years later it was sold for the benefit of the current school.

In April 1894, the Education Department sanctioned the site for the new school and the land purchase was completed two months later.

The Architect and the Builder

From the 1870s, the building rules of the London School Board influenced elementary school construction elsewhere. They were based upon Prussian ideas and aimed to provide a separate room for each class, unlike the schools built earlier in the century which consisted of one large room. In addition, there were separate playgrounds for boys and girls. It was to this basic design that the Badsey school was built.

In January 1894, Mr Edwin Lingen Barker of Hereford was appointed architect. Right from the outset there were problems with his non-attendance at Board meetings. The architect, however, was going through a tough patch. His wife, Eliza, had recently died, leaving him with a family of teenage children. After a long delay, Mr Barker attended the May meeting, and the plans were amended. It was agreed that the building would be improved in appearance if the front block was raised three feet facing School Lane and the windows lengthened proportionately.

Once the plans had finally been approved by the Education Department, advertisements were placed at the end of July 1894 in the two local Evesham newspapers for tenders for the building work. The tender of Mr Frederick Gardner of Bengeworth was accepted. For capital expenditure, such as building new schools, Boards could borrow from the Public Works Loans Commissioners, against the security of the rates. Two loans were negotiated with the Public Works Loan Board: one of £1500 for the school and playgrounds, and one of £500 for a teacher's house, each payable in 30 years at 3½% in half-yearly payments of principal and interest. The School Board rate, to include first payment of loan, was 7d in the pound, and it was expected

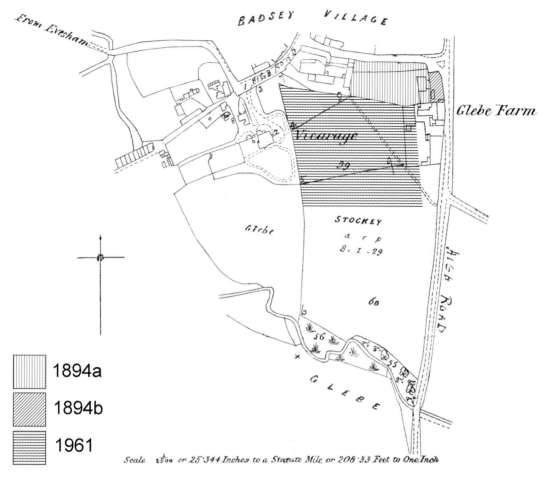

From Evesham

BADSEY VILLAGE

Glebe Farm

Vicarage

STOCKEY
a r p
8. 1 .29

Glebe

HIGH ROAD

GLEBE

| | 1894a
| | 1894b
| | 1961

Scale 1/2500 or 25·344 Inches to a Statute Mile or 208·33 Feet to One Inch

This map of 1894 shows the land purchased for the new school. '1894a' indicates the land bought from Captain Lord's Trustees, '1894b' indicates the land bought from the glebe; '1961' indicates the land bought nearly 70 years later to extend the school site.

that a 7d rate would cover expenses each year.

Meanwhile, plans were progressing for a School House for the Headteacher. Mr Gardner's plans for a seven-roomed house were sent to the Education Department in April 1895. The house was ready for occupation by January 1896.

Opening of the New School

On Friday 21st June 1895, the new school building was officially opened at 3.30 pm by Arthur Savory, Chairman of the Board. The children marched in procession from the old school to the new for the ceremony. Mr Savory declared the school open for the use of the scholars of the three parishes of Badsey, Aldington and Wickhamford and trusted that for many years the school would be a blessing to the children of the parishes. Reverend Gepp also spoke: "The buildings are beautiful, comfortable and healthy, and the children ought to take pleasure in their lessons. I do not know whether they always do, but I hope they will; at all events, there is no excuse for them if they do not." He congratulated the Board on the way they had carried out their work and said that his relations with the Board had been most amicable, which was not always the case when a school had passed from church to state. After the opening ceremony,

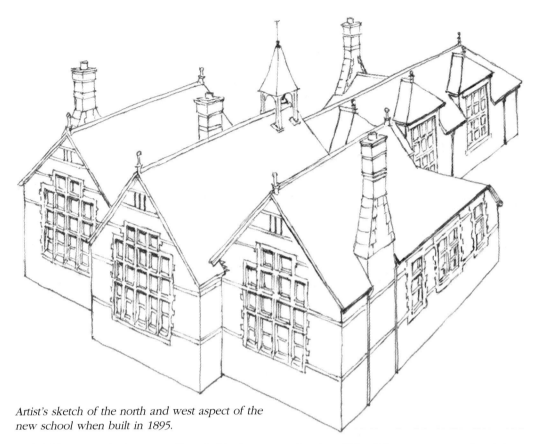

Artist's sketch of the north and west aspect of the new school when built in 1895.

the children marched to Mr Sadler's field where they had tea followed by games. Regular work started in the new school on Monday 24th June. At 9 am, Board members attended, and the Vicar offered special prayers.

Finances

Money was received from a Government Grant, Fees Grant and Drawing Grant, with the latter two grants being incorporated into the Government Grant from 1898. The balance was made up by the ratepayers, with the amount varying according to the rateable value of each parish. Many ratepayers were enraged at the perceived inequities of the system. The population of the three parishes in 1891 was 884. Badsey represented 65% of the population but paid only 43%. Aldington by contrast represented 20% of the population but paid 36% and Wickhamford, representing 15% of the population paid 21%. Aldington and Wickhamford ratepayers were thus subsidising the cost of educating the Badsey children. One assumes that Arthur Savory's view was a

minority: "We did not want a school in our quiet village; it is something to get rid of children when inclined to be noisy, so we did not grumble at a little extra expense."

The Government grant depended on average attendance (hence all Headteachers' preoccupation with attendance figures) and the annual inspection, which was held every April. The following schedule shows how the money was allocated:

1899 Schedule of Grants Allowed

Average: Boys 60.7, Girls 66.4 = 127

Principal Grant	14s
Discipline and Organisation	1s 6d
Singing by Note	1s
Object Lessons and English	2s
Geography	2s
Total 20s 6d x 127 =	£130 3s 6d

Needlework 1s x 66 =	£3 6s 0d
Drawing 1s 9d x 61 =	£5 6s 9d
Pupil Teacher's Grant Art 102	£2
Gross Amount	£140 16s 3d

A "block grant" system of school finance was introduced in 1900 which enabled a wider range of subjects to be taught.

The Headteacher

The first Head of the new Board School was Miss Mary Edgerton who remained for a year. She was extremely frustrated with the inadequate accommodation and teaching staff, and had frequent clashes with her Assistant, Miss Harker. Even after Miss Harker resigned, Miss Edgerton could not be persuaded to stay and the Board decided it would be best to have a Master at the head of the school. An advertisement duly appeared for a Headmaster, and his wife to assist with the infants or lower standards.

In October 1894, John Henry McDonald took charge of the school, with his eldest daughter, Miss Margaret Anne McDonald as Assistant Mistress, thus beginning for the McDonald family what was to be a 50-year association with the school. 44-year-old Mr McDonald, a Liverpudlian by birth who trained at Carnarvon Training College, received a salary of £100 a year, with the additional sum of £10 a year for the rent of a house until the Board was able to provide one. Miss McDonald was appointed on a salary of £40.

On taking charge of the school, Mr McDonald found the order very bad. Whilst the children were clean and capable, the elementary work was very meagre in Standards I and II. He was, however, happy with the work in the Infant room, under the direction of Miss Crisp. With a more efficient staff, he does not appear to have had the same problems as Miss Edgerton. The School Inspector wrote in his report in 1894: "In October the Mistress was replaced by an experienced Master. He seems a capable and industrious Teacher, under whose care speedy improvement may be expected in the condition of the school." In 1902, Mr McDonald received a medal from Worcestershire County Council to commemorate the Coronation of King Edward VII, given to all teachers with 25 years' service.

Early 20th century picture postcard of the school and school house from the east. The chimney on the right was removed in 1926 when central heating was installed and was replaced with a window. The bell-tower was removed in 1930.

BADSEY SCHOOL & SCHOOLHOUSE. B74.

1894.

20

Wk. End²
Oct. 19ᵗ Took charge of these schools on Monday (15ᵗ) and found the order very bad. In the upper and lower Standards the Elementary work is very meagre. The children are clean and capable. Mr. Sladden & Mr. Warmington (Members of the Bd.) visited during the week. Punished two boys on Friday afternoon for theft & lying. Average 137.7
J. H. McDonald.
Certificated Teacher, First Class.

The growing success of the school under the McDonalds was clouded by issues about salary. In January 1898, Mr McDonald felt moved to write to the Board saying that it was over three years since he and his daughter were appointed and during that period they had done their utmost for the welfare of the children and the efficiency of the school, and thus asked for an increase in salaries. The Board were split on the matter and the decision not to increase Miss McDonald's salary was won by four votes to three. Repeated annual requests were unsuccessful. The "niggardly action" of the Board in refusing the increase was the principal clause in the election manifesto of some of the aspiring newcomers at the 1902 triennial election. Nothing was to happen, however, until the school came under Council control.

The Teaching Staff

The teaching staff at the beginning of the Board School years consisted of just one Mistress and one Assistant Mistress, Katherine Harker of Hampton, who had recently finished her pupil teacher training. As soon as Miss Edgerton started, she insisted that more staff were essential. The Board agreed that an Assistant and two monitresses were required. An advertisement was placed in *The Schoolmistress* for an Assistant at £40 a year, and it was left to Miss Edgerton to organise

the monitresses. Much-needed reinforcements arrived on 9th October when Fanny Bennett and Martha Mustoe commenced duties as monitresses. 14-year-old Fanny and 12-year-old Martha had both been pupils at the National School. Little did the young Martha realise that this was to be the start of a long association with the school, culminating in her headship (as Mrs Morris) of the Infant Department of Badsey Council School. The new qualified teacher was 23-year-old Miss Alice Ellen Crisp who had been teaching in Wellingborough but was born and brought up in Bretforton, and was cousin of Elijah Crisp, the Badsey postmaster.

With the arrival of the McDonalds in 1894, a stability settled on the school that had not been seen for many years. Until Miss Crisp's resignation at the end of 1916, Mr McDonald, Miss McDonald and Miss Crisp remained a constant in the fortunes of the Mixed Department.

Further reinforcements arrived when, in 1895, it was agreed to advertise for a Certificated Mistress for the Infants, HMI having reported that this was necessary in accordance with the Code. Mrs Elizabeth Mason who as Miss Wagstaff had been a former Mistress of the National School, was offered the job. The mother of three young sons (her youngest, Thomas, was seven months old when she returned to teaching), she joined the staff just after the school had moved to its new premises. In November 1895, she began keeping her own Log Book, and in July 1896 the Infant Department officially became a separate school, with returns made separately, though under the same Board and accounts. Her brother-in-law, Leonard White, newly elected to the School Board, had made the proposal, thus making the Infant Department entirely distinct from the Mixed Department under Mr McDonald. As far as the children were concerned, however, it did not seem like a separate school – just a separate department in a different part of the building.

During the Board School period, the teaching staff were assisted by Monitresses and Pupil Teachers. When the school became two separate Departments, Martha Mustoe joined the Infants and Fanny Bennett the Mixed. During the course of time, Annie Enstone, May Cull and Lilian Cull were also engaged in the Infant Department and Hilda Butler, Douglas McDonald and Millicent Pethard in the Mixed Department. The Head's son, Douglas McDonald, passed as a Candidate for Pupil Teacher in January 1902. However, in February 1902, Douglas received a month's notice, the Board deeming it "undesirable to employ a boy in a mixed school"!! (Mr McDonald's exclamation marks), and accordingly left on 7th March.

Admissions

The legal starting age for school was five but children were often admitted at a younger age. At the October 1895 Managers' meeting, it was agreed that children under three years should not be admitted into the school until further notice was given by the teachers. But the following year, the Inspector, Mr Barrington Ward, wrote: "The admission of infants appears to have been somehow checked since the beginning of the new school year. Parents should be encouraged to send in their children at three years of age, and the Board will act wisely in directing their Attendance Officer to call at each house in the parish in order to secure the early admission of all infants whose age entitles them to come."

Classrooms

The new school building was built roughly in the shape of a "T". There were three classrooms along the north side which housed the Mixed Department. Miss Crisp took Standard I, Miss McDonald Standards II and III and Mr McDonald the upper standards. The largest room accommodated 68 children, and the rooms on either side housed 44 children each. In the Infant Department, which ran from north to south and was connected to the Mixed Department with a glass-topped passageway, there were two rooms. Divisions I and II were in the large classroom, and "the Babies" in the room next-door, to which there was a connecting door.

New furniture was ordered and visiting Managers in the opening months commented on the rooms being warm and comfortable. In the winter months, candles and candlesticks were used for lighting. In 1896, as the rooms were very dark by the end of afternoon school, Mr McDonald asked the Board to supply a few lamps.

Premises

HMI Mr Barrington Ward visited the new school building soon after it opened and voiced some concerns. Mr Savory was not impressed: "Trouble began with an officious inspector who, on his first visit, complained of the ventilation. An elementary school is never exactly a bed of roses, but we had a lofty building and classrooms, with plenty of windows, which could be adjusted to admit as much or as little fresh air as was requisite. We protested without result, and we had eventually to pull the new walls about and spend £20 on what we considered an uncalled-for alteration." The work was carried out during the Easter holidays 1897.

Within four years of the school being built, the Inspector was already noting over-crowding: "Attention is directed to the overcrowded state of the classroom in which Standards II and III are being taught. The defect must be remedied at once." His visit was followed the next day by a visit from Leonard White, Chairman of the School Board, in order

These two photos were taken in 1898 on the east side of the school. A verandah with a glass roof separated the entrance to the Mixed Department (right) from the entrance to the Infant Department (left). The area where the photos were taken is now part of the interior entrance area of the school.

Above: The Infant Department with Pupil Teacher Martha Mustoe (left) and Headteacher, Mrs Mason (right). On the front row, second from left, is Ethel Barnard. Behind and to her right is her cousin, Harry Crisp and his little sister, Lena (later to become a teacher at the school).

Below: The younger children of the Mixed Department with their teacher, Miss Alice Ellen Crisp, and Pupil Teacher, Fanny Bennett. The door to the Mixed Department can be seen on the right.

to speak to Mr McDonald about the inspector's note in the Log Book. Mr Gardner, who had built the new school, was asked to produce plans for an extension.

In order to build the extension, it required knocking down the external wall at the west end and adding an extension of a further 20 feet. "The building operations have caused annoyance to Standard I and the teacher, the continued hammering to remove outside bricks being almost more than could be borne," wrote Mr McDonald in the Log Book on 23rd March 1900. By 13th April, it had become impossible for Standard I to remain in their room, so they were moved into the Babies' Infant Room. The room was completed by June 1900 at a total cost of £200 for building and furniture.

By June 1901, HMI Mr J C R Days, had concerns about the central room: "The middle classroom is a passage room. A partition should be erected between the two doors." Mr Barrington Ward, visiting four months later, wrote, "The fireplace in the larger classroom must at once be provided with a guard, as the open fire is extremely dangerous. A partition, so often asked for, must be put up in the main room, so that this room may no longer be a passage room." The partition was eventually erected in February 1902.

Playgrounds

The school was built with two playgrounds: one for the girls and Infants to the east and one for the boys to the west. A door connected the two playgrounds, which was kept locked. In October 1896, Reverend Gepp confirmed that he would be pleased to give five guineas towards the expense of building the boundary wall between Glebe Farm and the girls' playground.

The garden at the back of the School House was dug and cleared in 1896 and, at the same time, the land at the front of the school was cleared as well; it was recommended that it should either be turfed or planted with shrubs. The land at the back of the school (where the playing-field is now situated) was called The Stockey, a field with the old furrows and had a footpath running across. In 1901, Manager Mr George Bell, who lived at Stanhope House, Willersey Road, and whose land was at the south-eastern boundary, called attention to the boys getting over the wall from the playground into The Stockey. The Clerk was instructed to write to Mr McDonald and request him to caution the boys and tell them that if they continued the practice, proceedings would be taken against them.

The Curriculum

The curriculum in elementary schools was governed by a Code of Regulations which was issued every year by the Board of Education. The phasing out of "payment by results" in 1890 led to a wider curriculum, but it was not until the introduction of a "block grant" system of school finance in 1900 that a wide range of subjects was recommended for all. The Code defined the core curriculum at various levels. For Infants it was "suitable instruction in Reading, Writing and Numbers; simple lessons on common things; appropriate and varied occupations; Needlework; Drawing; Singing and Physical Exercises". We learn a little from entries in the Log Book. In December 1895, Mrs Mason wrote, "Babies this week commenced word building with two letters." In June 1897, she reported that the greater part of Division II were able to read easy sentences using Royal Readers. The children began learning to write on slates and then moved to paper when they were aged about five. In Infant Departments throughout England, "Kindergarten" lessons became common. These were based on the ideas of Friedrich Froebel who stressed the value of constructive play for the young child. "Kindergarten", a general theory of child learning intended to colour the whole school life of a child, was mistakenly applied as single lessons; nonetheless it led to better infant teaching.

For the children of the Mixed Department, the core consisted of "English, by which is to be understood Reading, Recitation, Writing, Composition, and Grammar insofar as it bears upon the correct use of language; Arithmetic; Drawing (for boys); Needlework (for girls);

lessons, including object lessons on Geography, History and common things; Singing, which should as a rule be by rote and Physical Training." To this core one or more additional subjects could be added.

An Inspector's report of 1897 stated: "The Mixed School is in capital order.... Geography in the upper standards and the neat handwriting of all the scholars deserve special praise." Another year, Geography, Needlework and Singing were all singled out for being of a high standard. It was noted in 1898 that, whilst the children showed ample evidence of intelligence and careful instruction and were in admirable order, "Reading and Recitation might certainly be improved were the children trained to use the aspirate properly. Mental Arithmetic too requires much better instruction." Each year in March, a Drawing examination was held. In most years, the result was "Excellent", which entitled the Board to two shillings per head on the numbers examined. The Drawing exam was not held after 1898 and grants were then paid as part of the Annual Grant.

Children were aided in their learning by a museum, housed in a cupboard, which was started in 1899. A collection of stuffed birds and other items acquired over the years was still at the school a hundred years later. The school also had a harmonium for use in music lessons.

Physical exercise, or Drill as it was called, became more common around the time of the Boer War. The aim was to promote smartness among pupils and, to this end, a Model Course of Physical Training was issued by the Board of Education in 1902 which was largely based on army training methods.

The Religious Issue

The 1870 Education Act had ensured that there was to be "Christian training" in the Board schools, based on "simple Bible teaching". Such lessons were placed at the beginning and end of the day when parents with conscientious objections might easily withdraw their children. A crucial clause declared that "no religious catechism or religion formulary,

which is distinctive of any particular denomination, shall be taught in the school".

In spite of the fact that the Board included some non-conformists, Reverend Gepp was invited to draw up a scheme of religious instruction. Until his departure in 1897, he visited twice a week and supervised religious instruction in the school. The children were prepared for a diocesan examination every March. In 1896, Reverend Canon Houghton was the examiner and was very impressed with what he saw. Reverend Houghton had visited Badsey a few years earlier to try and save the church school from passing to the state; whatever fears he had had then were soon quelled. Likewise the examiner the following year, the Reverend John C Whall, was very positive: "I have been much pleased with my first visit to the Badsey School since it passed under a Board."

Trouble was brewing, however. Many villagers were unhappy with the High Church innovations introduced by the new vicar, Reverend William Price, and the Board was unhappy that he had not gained their permission before setting the date of the examination in 1898. Reverend Price, who was unaware of the procedures, promised to consult in future. When he wrote to the Board in 1899, he was surprised to find that they said it was illegal and contrary to the regulations of the Education Department to hold the exam on a school day and would only permit it to be held if on a Saturday; the children should also be informed that they were not compelled to attend. Furthermore, his visits to school were reduced from two to one as some Board members felt that their children were being taught "a lot of Popery".

Reverend Price tried again in 1900 and wrote asking permission for the Diocesan Inspector to hold a religious exam in the school on Monday 26th March. He stated it was now generally understood that the Department allowed such exams to be held on an ordinary school day. The Board was divided in their opinion, but the final vote was in favour of the examination only being allowed on a Saturday. Reverend Price died suddenly in

March 1903. The school was closed on the afternoon of his funeral. The children lined each side of the pathway to the church porch and subscribed to buy a floral tribute.

Examinations

A Labour Certificate examination was held every April in Evesham for those wishing to leave school before the age of 14. By-laws in force in each district governed the minimum age at which a child could be granted exemption. Initially the Evesham by-laws stated that a child could leave school at ten if he had attained Standard IV; this was raised to 11 in 1894 and 12 in 1900. In addition, a child had to reach the higher Standard V for total exemption. In 1902, a clause was added that a child between 13 and 14 could leave if he had made 350 attendances after five years of age if beneficially employed. The School Attendance Officer had to keep a watchful eye on the unlawful employment of children without a certificate.

Labour Certificates had arisen out of the Factory Act of 1843, the aim of which was to limit exploitation of children in various trades. Usually, around ten children were entered with the majority passing. It was the practice in rural areas for some children, if they passed the examination, to continue at school half-time, returning to school in November. The scheme was never satisfactory although it lingered on until 1918.

Prizes

Whilst there was no formal prize-giving ceremony, prizes were awarded from time to time. In October 1898 the Parish Magazine recorded the following: "A happy suggestion was made by Mr Savory, that a prize should be offered to the children of our day schools, for the best essay written by the children, in order to encourage original thought and composition." The subject selected was "The Harvest" and essays were written by 17 children. The first prize was awarded to 12-year-old Douglas McDonald and the second and third prizes to Arthur Summerton and George Collett. In 1903, for the first time, prizes were awarded for attendance. Those children who were not absent from school more than once in a quarter were given a book; 62 scholars in the Mixed Department received a prize.

Holidays

The School Board was responsible for setting the holiday dates which were often arranged round the agricultural year, with two weeks being granted in June for pea and strawberry-picking and four weeks in September for the harvest. In August 1901, former Manager Mr Savory wrote audaciously to the Board asking if they would arrange the holiday to coincide with his hop harvest. The Board agreed, and even extended the holidays to five weeks when the hop-picking was not finished on the understanding that no children of school age were employed after the end of the holidays. The Log Book, however, reports that a few children were still absent on the Monday working in the hop-gardens.

The school was closed for certain religious festivals – Whitsuntide, Ascension Day and Ash Wednesday – the latter being "one of the days during the year reserved by the Reverend Gepp". A half-holiday was given for the Flower Show each year and a special half-holiday was granted on 24th May 1900 to commemorate the Queen's birthday and the relief of Mafeking. The children had a week's holiday in June 1897 for the Queen's Diamond Jubilee celebrations. A day was often set aside for the summer treat, just before the harvest holiday, and was counted as a holiday.

Attendance

Attendance registers were required to be kept for morning and afternoon sessions. They had to be completed accurately and checked each quarter by a Board member, in accordance with the Code. The first School Attendance Officer, appointed on a salary of £6 a year, was Mr Walter Warmington, brother of School Manager, William John Warmington. It was his job to take legal proceedings against parents. One such person was Ann Willoughby of Wickhamford, who was prosecuted in May

The photographer visited school on 20th June 1900 and took a series of group photos. Children in the same family were placed in the same group so that the cost to parents was not too great. The photos are believed to have been taken at the southern end of the school (now the south side of the Learning and Teaching Area) before the 1928 extension was built.

Opposite above: The Infant Department, with Monitresses Annie Enstone and May Cull on the left, and Headteacher, Mrs Mason and Pupil Teacher Martha Mustoe (later to become the Infant Head as Mrs Morris) on the right. The photo includes the Wilkins twins, Alfred Cecil and Charles William (back row, second and third from left) and Ethel and Fred Barnard (second row, second and third from right). Fred Barnard, aged 3¾, had only been at school for two months when this photo was taken.

Opposite below: The younger children of the Mixed Department with their teacher, Miss Alice Ellen Crisp (seated) and Pupil Teacher Hilda Butler. The photo includes Walter Dore (back row, fourth from left) and Cecilia Barnard (third row, far right).

Above: The older children of the Mixed Department with Headteacher Mr McDonald and his daughter, Miss McDonald. The photo includes John Joseph Warmington (back row, second from left).

1895 for not sending her son Thomas regularly to school.

Bad weather caused the attendance to dip. On 16th November 1894, Mr McDonald wrote, "The weather this week was very bad, and many of the roads were impassable on account of the floods, hence the attendance was poor." Deep snowfalls occurred most winters, causing fewer children to be present than usual.

Anything out of the ordinary also caused absence. "On Tuesday afternoon there were only 135 present, in consequence of a visit to the village of the Fox Hounds," wrote Mr McDonald in December 1894. A football match at Aldington, Bretforton Wake, temperance demonstrations in Evesham, a circus, Evesham Agricultural Show, Sunday School treats, were also excuses to stay away from school. In January 1898, many children were absent to attend the service in connection with the hanging of the new church bells, and in February 1901 for the reopening of Wickhamford Church. In January 1902, the wedding of Miss Cynthia Savory of Aldington Manor, daughter of the former Chairman of Managers, was another reason for absence.

Illness also affected attendance. The children started at a very young age, which proved to be a challenge for some of the less robust. In November 1893, Miss Edgerton recorded that four-year-old John J Warmington (eldest son of one of the newly-elected Managers) "being in a delicate state of health has left until the spring". There are frequent references to coughs and colds and illnesses such as measles, scarlatina, mumps, ringworm, chickenpox, whooping cough. The school was closed twice during this period for several weeks because of illness.

Many children absented themselves to help in the fields for asparagus-cutting, hop-picking, pea-picking and strawberry-picking or, if needed, for baby-minding. Some of the most irregular attenders were the children under five who, during the summer months, were often with their parents in the fields. The School Attendance Officer had to be rigorous in checking the attendances of children, particularly during the hop-picking season. In September 1898, the Clerk was directed to write to Mr Pope of Wickhamford informing him that proceedings would be taken against him if he continued to employ children during school-time.

Concerts

Concerts were given from time to time at the Old School. The Parish Magazine for February 1899 reports: "Two excellent entertainments were given by the children of our schools on 25th and 26th January. Mr and Miss McDonald are to be congratulated on the success of their labours in preparing the children." A concert the following year again met with acclaim: "Two very popular items on the programme were songs given by the school children, which evoked very great applause. They had been very carefully trained by Mr & Miss McDonald, and reflected the greatest credit upon their teachers."

The Caretaker

Mrs Emma Wilson, who had been employed at the National School since 1892, was appointed Caretaker and Cleaner of the new Board school in 1893. She and her husband Edward of Badsey Manor had returned from the States a few years earlier; she was the mother of a young family who attended the school. In 1895, with the much bigger school building, her salary went up nearly three times to £12 a year. It was the Caretaker's task to light the fires each morning which, in winter months, needed to be lit at 7.30 am to get the rooms to a decent temperature. There were complaints if she was late in lighting the fires, as the rooms were still cold when school started at 9 am.

Mrs Wilson also had responsibility for the cleaning of the closets and urinals. On top of all her other duties, this was decided to be too much and, in 1900, the Board agreed to appoint John Knight to clean and empty the closet pans twice a week in summer and at least once a week in winter at a salary of £3 a year. However, at the same time, the Board reduced Mrs Wilson's salary to £10 a year. Given that Mrs Wilson had just acquired the

PUNISHMENT BOOK.

Year 1900

DATE: 1 & Day	NAME OF SCHOLAR	STD. OR CLASS	NATURE OF OFFENCE	PUNISHMENT	SIGNATURE (OR INITIALS) OF TEACHER WHO ADMINISTERED THE PUNISHMENT
23rd	William Nightingale	1	Disobedience	Cane	E. M.
11th 1900	Harry Jinks	1	Throwing stones	Cane	E M
	Walter Harwood	1	"	"	E. M.
	Joseph Porter	1	"	"	E M
	Francis Moore	1	"	"	E. M.
ay 7th 190	James Perkins	1	Taking a ball & chalk from school	Cane	E M
3rd 1904	Walter Smith	1	Whistling in school	Cane	E. Mason
31st 04	John Perkins	1	Bad behaviour in playground	Cane	E Mason
21st	Walter Malin	1	Disobedience	Cane	E. Mason
	George Barnard	1	"	"	E Mason
rd 06	Malcolm Brailsford	1	Whistling in School	"	E Mason

The Punishment Book for the Infant Department. From 1900, it became mandatory for a separate book to be kept in which every case of corporal punishment was entered. The Inspector had to examine the Punishment Book on each visit to the school.

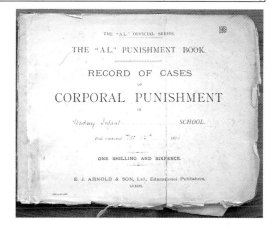

responsibility of an extra room to clean as the result of an extension, she felt aggrieved that her salary had not remained at £12. The Board Managers of the time, renowned for their economy, agreed to increase her salary by just 10 shillings.

The End of the Board School

The end of the Victorian era also marked the death-knell of the Board School. While the larger Boards had worked well, there were too many inefficient small Boards, especially in the countryside, where farmer members were often greedy for child labour. The cost of Board elections and the complexities of administration, where the Department tried to correspond with all 2,568 Boards individually, were other factors in demands for reform. The new County Councils promised a more efficient administrative device. Sidney Webb in *The Education Muddle and the Way Out* (1901), wrote: "What the national well-being demands is that every child, dull or clever, rich or poor, should receive all the education requisite for the full development of its faculties. For every child, in every part of the country, at least a 'national minimum' of education must be compulsorily provided." It was in this spirit that the 1902 Education Act was planned. The Boards were dissolved and replaced with Local Education Authorities. Thus the School Board era came to an end. The final Board meeting took place on 24th March 1903 and the new act came into force on 1st April.

1

1913.

Badsey Council School (Mixed Dept.)

1913
April 1st

I, Frank Edmund Amos, took charge of the above school on this day, (Tuesday, April 1st 1913). The number on roll is ~~203~~ 192 (actual), 183 being present.

Staff.
Frank Edmund Amos, Trained Certificated
Margaret A. McDonald, Certificated
Alice E. Crisp,   "
Jean McD. McDonald   "
Herbert Slaley
Lilian Maud Bird, Uncertificated
                                        F.E. Amos.

Wk. ending
April 4th

The Chairman of the Managers visited the school during the week. Miss M. McDonald was absent during most part of several sessions owing to the illness of her father. The average attendance for the week was 179.3
                                        F.E. Amos

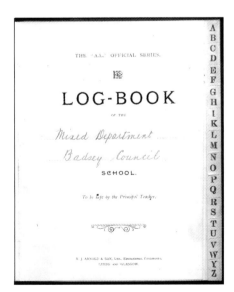

The first page of a new Log Book, started when Frank Amos became Headteacher of Badsey Council School on 1st April 1913.

Miss McDonald and maypole dancers
at Badsey Manor House, 1911.

4

BADSEY
COUNCIL
SCHOOL
1903-1918

The 1902 Education Act established the basic framework of education
administration that lasted until 1944, placing schools under the newly-created
Local Education Authorities (LEAs). The state assumed wide educational
responsibility and constructed an elaborate piece of administrative machinery,
but nonetheless contributed materially in raising the general level of
education.

Almost as soon as the school came under Council control, it was
bombarded by circulars regarding the way that things should be run, in
attempts to impose consistency throughout the county. There were circulars
about salaries, supplies, curriculum; indeed, the whole spectrum of school
life. If the Headteacher needed an item for the school, he had first to ask
the Managers, who would then send in a requisition to County if they felt
the request reasonable. In turn, the Authority took over the responsibility
for repair and maintenance of the buildings. Despite the rather bureaucratic
procedures that were put in place, the establishment of Education
Departments within County Councils enabled elementary education to
progress at a faster rate than under the old School Boards.

The Headteacher

After the sometimes tempestuous times with the School Board, matters were
easier for Mr McDonald under Council control. Frequent requests for an

increase in salary had previously fallen on deaf ears; but the new Managers felt he was an efficient teacher and entitled to be paid the maximum amount for such a position and thus his salary was increased. From 1910, Mr McDonald began suffering greatly from ill-health. To add to his problems, his wife, Margaret, who had not been in the best of health for many years, died in July 1911.

On one occasion, Miss Maggie McDonald took charge during her father's illness, helped by her brother, Douglas, who took charge of Standard IV for a week until a supply teacher could be sent. On two other occasions, a supply Headteacher was sent. It soon became obvious to Mr McDonald that he would be unable to carry on, and so he resigned in March 1913. The Parish Magazine for March 1913 stated: "It is not given to every village to be so fortunate in its schoolmaster as Badsey has been.... We trust and pray that, relieved of the responsibility and anxieties of his official position, he may long be spared to us as a friend and neighbour."

It was not to be, however, and John Henry McDonald died in the early hours of 8th May 1913. The Parish Magazine for June 1913 gave a report of the funeral: "Surpliced choirmen bore the coffin from the School House to the church, school children lined the path as the sad procession passed through the churchyard and afterwards drew up round the grave for the concluding portion of the service, and the funeral was attended by a large and representative congregation many of whom had followed from the School House. By no means the least impressive part of the service was the reverent and sympathetic behaviour of the children above referred to; it was a most eloquent tribute to the character and influence of their late schoolmaster."

Out of 127 applications for the post of Headteacher, 27-year-old Frank Edmund Amos was appointed. Mr Amos had previously taught at the school from 1907-1910 until he left to take up a place at Winchester Training College, so was known to the Managers as an excellent teacher. Back in 1907, however, Mr Amos had been the second-choice applicant. Fortunately, for the future of the school, the other person was found to be unsuitable, and he was offered the job. Mr Amos became Head in April 1913, with 192 on the roll of the Mixed Department and five members of staff. On New Year's Day 1914, he married fellow teacher, Jean McDonald, a daughter of the former Head.

Mr Amos quickly began to stamp his mark on the ever-increasing school, but then the First World War intervened. He was called up in February 1915, and his sister-in-law, Miss McDonald, took charge of the school for the next two years. In February 1917, he was discharged from the Army as physically unfit for further war service owing to wounds received in action. He returned to a bitterly cold school and many children absent through

Sometimes staff were asked to assist at schools in other parts of the Authority. This telegram dated March 1918 came from the Director of Education. Mrs Amos went to take up duties at Wythall School. To get there, she had to get a train to Birmingham, then a train from Moor Street Station to Kings Norton Station, from which the school was about four miles distant.

illness or work on the land. From time to time he was absent because of a facial neuralgia caused by the wound in his head. But slowly, he began to pull things together again, to make Badsey into a school which, during the following decades, was a flagship school for the county.

The Staff of the Mixed Department

Since Mr McDonald had taken over as Headteacher during the Board School years, the staff had remained stable. Mr McDonald taught the top standards, Miss McDonald Standards II and III and Miss Crisp Standard I; they were assisted by three Pupil Teachers or Monitresses. An additional teacher, Mr Amos, was recruited in 1907 to take Standard IV.

Within two years of the school coming under Council control, Miss McDonald's salary nearly doubled. From 1903, professional teachers' organisations put pressure on the LEAs and the Board of Education, not only to improve salaries, but to introduce progressive salary scales, based on a minimum wage. Figures available for 1905 show that the national average salary for a female Certificated Assistant was £82, whilst in Worcestershire it was £65. Miss McDonald's salary had remained at £40 throughout the Board School years, but from 1903 she began to receive gradual increases. Once placed on the county scale in 1905, her salary immediately rose to £75 per annum. At last, Miss McDonald was able to receive a salary which reflected her abilities, and other staff were able to benefit, too.

With ever-increasing numbers, the school was still experiencing staffing problems, exacerbated by changed regulations concerning Pupil Teachers who spent most of their time being trained at a Centre in Evesham rather than on-the-job training in school. Miss McDonald was left with over 80 children to teach single-handedly, so an additional teacher was sanctioned. Miss Lilian Maud Bird began teaching at the school in November 1908, "she having been found as the result of a personal interview to be in every way suitable for the post and having highly satisfactory references". Thus began a long association with the school,

Miss Lilian Maud Bird (later Mrs Woodward), a stern disciplinarian, teacher 1908-1951.

which ended with her retirement (as Mrs Woodward) in 1951.

By the end of 1910, Mr McDonald was feeling the effects of a reduction in staff through the phasing out of the Pupil Teacher system and applied to the Managers for an additional teacher. He still had responsibility for teaching the top standards, a very large class, and consequently he was unable to exercise the necessary supervision over the work of the other classes. The Managers concurred with Mr McDonald and arranged for the Director of Education to visit the school. However, the Director could not be swayed as he felt that the school was sufficiently staffed according to the requirements of the Code. "At the present time there are five groups or classes of children, each containing on average less than 40 children, and there are five teachers," he wrote. He suggested borrowing a teacher from the Infant Department at times of greatest pressure and concluded by saying, "As I understand the village is a growing one, it may be necessary before long to reconsider the question of an additional teacher."

In August 1911, the Clerk was able to write to say that over 40 children had been moved up from the Infants making the numbers considerably over 200. In October, the LEA at last agreed to appoint an additional Assistant Master and Mr Walter Rhys Williams was appointed. He stayed for a year and, on his resignation, was replaced by Miss Jean McDonald, the Head's daughter.

At the start of the First World War, there were six members of staff, but this number gradually reduced as the war progressed. When school opened for the spring term in January 1915, Mr Lewis was absent, having enlisted. A month later, Mr Amos, too, left for the Western Front. Miss Crisp left later in the year after 21 years' service, in order to try and obtain a Certificated post. Both she and Mrs Amos were Certificated teachers but employed as Uncertificated. The LEA had agreed to one member of staff being recognised as Certificated with the appropriate salary and Mrs Amos was selected. Miss Crisp's place was taken by her cousin Elijah's daughter, Miss Lena Crisp, a former pupil and student teacher at the school.

The Staff of the Infant Department

Mrs Mason continued as Headteacher throughout the period. She was assisted initially by two Pupil Teachers, Lilian Cull and Emily Hartwell, who both stayed on as teachers after completing their Pupil Teacher indentures. In order to satisfy the requirements of the Code, a further teacher was engaged in 1910, a job which was offered to Miss Rose Sparrow, a former pupil and Pupil Teacher at Badsey, then teaching at Pershore Council School. At the outbreak of war, there were four teachers in the Infant Department: Mrs Mason, Miss Hunt, Miss Cull and Miss Hartwell. When Miss Cull left in December 1915 to get married, she was not replaced.

Admissions

In 1903, most children entered the Infant Department soon after the age of three, although a few did not start school until the legal age of five. Children were admitted at any time during the term, quite frequently on their third birthday. The normal age of transfer to the Mixed Department was six, but occasionally children were retained in the Infant School past the age of six; these were usually children who were delicate or who had been admitted during the past school year. In 1905, the LEA asked the Managers to consider the question of exclusion or retention of children under five years of age. The Managers felt that there was no educational advantage in admitting such young children and thus favoured exclusion. Furthermore, children under five attended irregularly, which tended to have a knock-on effect on attendance for older scholars. Whilst this was not rigidly adhered to, the percentage of three-year-olds admitted declined from around 70% of the new intake in 1905 to 26% in 1911.

From 1913-1915, the numbers at the top of the school were augmented by the admission of boys from St Christopher's Children's Home. Reverend Lopes had opened a home, firstly at Badsey Manor House, and then at Montpelier (the present-day Badsey Hall). Fifteen boys, ranging in age from eight to 14, were enrolled. The home closed in July 1915, thus reducing the numbers at the school, and most of the boys were sent to a home at Pershore.

Classrooms

At the beginning of the Council School years, there were three classrooms (one of which had been extended to double its size in 1900) in the Mixed Department and two in the Infant Department. There were more teachers than rooms, so some had to share.

The "middle room" in the Mixed Department, which was occupied by Standards IV-VI, had just a simple partition separating it from the corridor between the Mixed and Infant Department. The partition was extended to the ceiling in 1905 after frequent comments from the Inspector and, three years later, glass

Above: Class group about 1905, featuring primarily the Agg, Barnard, Brewer, Crisp, Keen and Marshall families. As in previous years, it is assumed that family groups were put together for the purposes of the photograph, in order to minimise the cost for parents.

Back row: -, -, -, -, George Marshall, -, -, -, -. Second row: Nellie Marshall, Cecilia Barnard, -, -, -, -, Mr McDonald. Third row: Miss Millicent Pethard (Pupil Teacher), Hilda Brewer, Ethel Barnard, Nellie Agg, Rose Brewer, Lena Crisp, -, -, -, Miss McDonald. Front row: Fred Barnard, -, George Brewer (holding slate), William Keen, Steve Brewer, -, Harry Crisp. The man standing behind Miss Pethard is unknown. There were no male members of staff at that time and, whilst the school did train two male Pupil Teachers, they were not at the school during this period.

Below: The older scholars of the Mixed Department, about 1912. Mr Williams is on the left and Mr McDonald (seated) and Mr Staley are on the right.

was added to allow more light to the infants' room across the passage. The room, built to accommodate 54, quickly became too small. Edward Williams, who took temporary charge of the school during Mr McDonald's absence in 1912, was not impressed by the overcrowding in the school and wrote: "Average attendance is in excess of the accommodation and the work, especially in Standard IV and upwards, is much hampered thereby. In Standard IV, nearly each desk is occupied by three instead of two children."

Ventilation was a concern, particularly in the middle room. The end of May 1913 was extremely hot, and several of the lessons were taken in the playground owing to the heat and stuffy condition of the classrooms. In September 1913, Mr Amos noted that the ventilation of the middle room was very defective, the air in the room during the week being most offensive, though doors and windows were open. 77 children were crammed into the room on that particular day; by the following year, the numbers had risen to 89.

In the Infant Department, galleried classrooms, which had been the fashion in Victorian times, still existed, but they were no longer considered suitable and their removal recommended. The gallery in the larger room was removed and replaced by dual desks in 1908, but the one in the smaller room was retained as it was felt to be more conveniently constructed and less steep than the other. But this, too, was removed in 1911 at the order of the Director of Education. The new desks were much more suitable, as HMI had recommended as early as 1904 that "the desks in the 'baby' room should be altered so that they may be *perfectly flat* (for convenience in writing and Kindergarten lessons)."

A return for 1913 revealed that there were then 297 children on the register, 227 living in Badsey, 45 in Wickhamford, 23 in Aldington and two in Bengeworth. The residents of Wickhamford were keen to have a school of their own, a suggestion which the Managers felt worthy of consideration in view of the overcrowding at Badsey. The LEA held an Enquiry at the school in December 1913. The decision was made to build a school at Wickhamford, but then nothing happened. In 1914, HMI Mr Cartwright brought the matter of overcrowding to the attention of the Board of Education and Mr Priestley, the Chief Education Officer for Worcestershire, was asked to submit a return to the Board of Education. This gave the Board cause for concern as it highlighted the severe overcrowding. In March 1915, the LEA issued a Public Notice stating their intention to provide a new Public Elementary School for not more than 100 children in the parish of Wickhamford; but then no more. The war-time restrictions must have prevented this scheme from ever getting off the ground. Certainly, four months later, the Director of Education visited Badsey to discuss the issue of accommodation and there was no mention of a school for Wickhamford and, because of the restrictions, no alterations could be made at Badsey. As a temporary measure, no children were promoted from the Infant Department at the end of the school year. Thus the Mixed Department consisted of Standard II and upwards, each teacher retaining the same children, but taught as a higher class.

Premises

Soon after coming under LEA control, a letter was received asking for a report on the state and condition of the schools and asking for observations. From then on, the County Architect made his annual survey and requested particulars of any works or repairs which the Managers wished to see done during the ensuing year. The repairs were supposed to take place each year during the summer vacation, but occasionally the work overran and sometimes no maintenance was done due to lack of funds.

In 1909, a major overhaul of the toilets, or "out-offices", as they were often referred to, was undertaken, in order to comply with new Board of Education regulations. The School Medical Officer had sent a report setting out the improvements which he considered necessary to the closets and urinals. The main

17th April 1912, Mr Binyon's telescope, taken on the occasion of an eclipse of the sun.
Left to right: -, Miss Lilian Cull, Miss Emily Hartwell, Miss Maggie McDonald, Miss Maud Bird, Mr John McDonald. The photo was taken by School Manager, Charles Binyon.

changes consisted of replacing the existing pail closets with trough latrines, providing an automatic flushing tank for the urinals and new wash-basins in the cloakrooms, repairing the brick pavement outside the closet doors, and rearranging the water pipes with a view to preventing the flooding of the rooms which occasionally took place.

Playgrounds

Ten years after the school was erected, the playgrounds were in a very bad condition and repairs had to be undertaken most years. New gravel was put down, gates and entrances repaired and the west boundary wall, which was in danger of

After the eclipse, the children were asked to write an essay on the subject. First prize was awarded to 12-year-old Nancy Crisp who described the phenomenon:

"It started at 10.50 am, reached its maximum at 12.08 pm, and ended at 1.28 pm. We saw it through a piece of smoked glass, and other different contrivances, such as telescope reflections, eye-lenses, pricking of a pin through a piece of white cardboard, etc. When the eclipse was at its height it seemed to grow dusky, everything seemed peculiar, and in some places the hens began to roost, and the birds stopped chirping. The temperature began to go down, and at 12.08 it was very low, according to the temperature of the day. Mr. Binyon was kind enough to bring his telescope for us to see the eclipse quite plainly, and I think he had no little trouble in getting it ready. Also he brought his camera and we had our photographs taken, and though I thank him for it, and, am thinking of buying mine, I think without that I could remember it (the eclipse) quite plainly."

collapsing into the adjoining gardens, was rebuilt. A drain in the boys' playground did not allow the water to flow away quickly enough, the result being that, after heavy rain, that playground was flooded. The playgrounds became very muddy and, as a consequence, the rooms dirty.

It was not until 1912, after heavy rains in December 1911 had resulted in the playgrounds being almost entirely submerged and there was serious concern for the health of the scholars, that Mr Priestley, the Director of Education, gave permission for a portion of the playgrounds to be asphalted and the necessary improvements to the drainage of the playgrounds carried out at the same time.

The Curriculum

In 1904, the Board of Education's Code defined the purpose of a public elementary school as forming and strengthening the character and developing the intelligence of children: "to fit themselves, practically as well as intellectually, for the work of life". To this end, teachers were "to implant in the children habits of industry, self-control, and courageous perseverance in the face of difficulties". Hand in hand with changing official attitudes were improvements in the textbooks produced which became more varied and interesting.

In 1905, a *Handbook of Suggestions* for elementary teachers appeared. Teachers were now given freedom to show initiative in syllabus and method. Its thoughtful preface declared "each teacher shall think for himself, and work out such methods of teaching as may use his powers to the best advantage and be best suited to the particular needs and conditions of the school. Uniformity in details of practice … is not desirable even if it were attainable." This was a momentous change from the old order.

Evidence of the type of essay a child might be given in Composition may be seen in the report of an Inspector who visited in 1907 and set the following subjects for composition:

1. How to take sole charge of a baby from 5 am to 5 pm
2. Your boots

3. Your dress
4. A piece of land (40 x 20 yards). What use would you make of it?
5. Description of wall in front of you.

Drawing, which had previously only been studied by boys, was also taught to girls from 1905. The Inspector, writing in 1906, was pleased to note the change: "Needlework is well done and it is satisfactory to note that Drawing is now being taught to girls as well as to boys. Slates should not be used for teaching Drawing in Standard I." A visit from the Drawing Inspector gives an idea of the work undertaken. He saw the drawing of the whole school, which included Freehand, Scale, Geometry and Design. He gave as a test for Memory drawing, "A pair of Scissors" for the girls and "A garden fork" (boys Standard IV) and "A wheelbarrow" (boys Standards V-VI).

Mr Amos was keen to encourage Art and, soon after his arrival, asked for sanction to frame several specimens of the children's drawing and painting for hanging on the school walls. The LEA, however, did not share Mr Amos' enlightened attitudes, and replied rather dismissively: "… sanction cannot be given for an expenditure of £1 1s 0d in framing specimens of the children's work. It is doubtful whether the work is worth framing and if money is to be spent in this way, it should be found locally." The Managers, though, had every confidence in Mr Amos, and the matter was brought up directly with the Director of Education who happened to be visiting the school the next day on another matter. Mr Amos got his frames!

In 1905, the LEA first suggested that manual instruction and use of tools for boys, and cookery for girls might be introduced; but the first mention of Badsey children receiving such instruction was in October 1910, when seven boys attended a Woodwork class. Each year from then on, the upper class boys attended the Centre at Evesham on one afternoon a week. From September 1914, 18 girls started a Cookery Course at Evesham. An LEA circular of October 1916 advised on the importance of letting the boys begin their woodwork instruction as soon after their eleventh birthday

Scholarship paper, 1910. The Headteacher selected the most able 11 and 12-year-old children to take a written examination in English, Arithmetic, Geography and History. There were four papers amounting to 7½ hours altogether. The results of this, together with a report from their current Headteacher and an oral examination conducted by the Headteacher of the secondary school, decided whether they would be given a free place at secondary school.

WORCESTERSHIRE EDUCATION COMMITTEE.

Examination for Secondary School (Entrance) Scholarships.

SATURDAY, MAY 21ST, 1910.

ARITHMETIC.

Two hours allowed.

You may do as many questions as you can. Marks will be given for legible and intelligent setting down and for shortness and directness of method as well as for the correct answer.

1. Multiply the difference between 72 guineas and £13 8s. 7½d. by 79.

2. A greengrocer sold 9 tons, 4 cwts, 5 stones of potatoes at £5 13s. 4d. per ton; what was the total amount realised?

3. (a) A field, measuring 14 acres, 3 roods, 17 sq. poles, 5¾ sq. yds. is divided into 4 equal parts; find the area of each part.
   (b) Simplify $18 - 4 \times 3 + 2 \div 2$.

4. The following items were purchased by a lady, who tendered £3 10s. 0d. in payment and received 6s. 8½d. as change; what error was made?
   - 5½ yards of silk at 7s. 6d. per yard.
   - 3¾ yards of lace at 5s. per yard.
   - 9 pearl buttons at 3s. per dozen.
   - 2½ yards of lining at 5d. per yard.
   - Sundries 1s.

5. (a) Nineteen amounts of £99 17s. 6d. each have to be added together; do this by the shortest method you can.
   (b) A scholar wrote down one "dekametre" instead of one "decimetre." What was the extent of the error in yards?
   (Give the answer to 3 places of decimals. Note 1 metre = 39·37 inches).

6. Required the value of x.
   $x : ·06 :: 4·05 : ·3$.

7. A train is 80 yards long and takes 2½ seconds to pass a signal post; how many miles per hour is it travelling?

P.T.O

WORCESTERSHIRE EDUCATION COMMITTEE.

Examination for Secondary School (Entrance) Scholarships and for Rural Secondary School Scholarships.

SATURDAY, MAY 21ST, 1910.

ENGLISH.

One and a half hours allowed.

All candidates should answer the question in Section I. and not more than 2 questions from Section II. and 2 questions from Section III.

SECTION I.
Composition.

Not more than half an hour must be given to the essay.

(1) The Death of King Edward VII.
or (2) A Farmer's life.
or (3) The bravest deed you ever heard of.

SECTION II.

1. (a) Give the feminines of "nephew" and "hero."
   (b) What are the diminutives of "globe" and "goose"?
   (c) Write out the prefixes and affixes in these words:— Government, warlike, permit, conform.
   (d) Write one sentence containing a figure of speech.
   (e) Supply the relative Pronoun which is omitted:— He . . . . thou lovest is sick.

2. Write out the substance of the following passage in your own words:—
   Mine be a cot beside the hill;
   A beehive's hum shall soothe my ear;
   A willowy brook that turns a mill,
   With many a fall shall linger near.

3. Analyse the following passage:—
   (a) Merrily, merrily, shall I live now
   Under the blossom, that hangs on the bough.
   (b) Off shall the pilgrim lift the latch,
   And share my meal.

4. (a) Copy the following, and fill in the blank spaces with any words which you think are derived from the same root as the verb:—

WORCESTERSHIRE EDUCATION COMMITTEE.

Examination for Secondary School (Entrance) Scholarships.

SATURDAY, MAY 21ST, 1910.

GEOGRAPHY & HISTORY.

Not more than four questions should be answered in each Section.

SECTION I.
Geography.

One hour allowed.

1. On the outline map of England supplied to you mark:—
   (a) The chief coalfields.
   (b) Seven large seaports.

2. Draw a sketch map showing the positions of the chief mountains and rivers in any one of the following countries:—Scotland, France, S. America, India.

3. Where are the following industries carried on:—Fruit growing, slate quarrying, growing of early spring flowers, glove-making, copper-smelting, boot-making?

4. Describe any methods used in your School for keeping weather records. What winds generally bring rain to your district and why?

5. If you look at a map of the Bristol Channel you will find one large port on the South side and several large ones on the North side. Give reasons for this difference.

6. Name two towns built by the Romans. Why did they choose these particular places for the building of towns.

7. What part of England is known as the principal chalk region? What are the chief occupations of the people in this locality.

8. Compare the surface, climate, and occupations of the people of Durham with those of your own county.

9. A hundred years ago Crewe, Devonport, Llandudno, Cardiff and Scarborough were small villages. To-day they are prominent towns. Give your reasons for their rapid growth.

10. Describe any one of the following journeys:—
    (a) Up the Rhine from its mouth to its source.
    (b) From Hull to Dublin by train and boat.
    (c) From Liverpool to Japan (going westward).

P.T.O.

WORCESTERSHIRE EDUCATION COMMITTEE.

Examination for Rural Secondary School Scholarships.

SATURDAY, MAY 21ST, 1910.

NATURE KNOWLEDGE & GEOGRAPHY.

SECTION I.
Nature Knowledge.

One hour allowed.

Answer not more than four questions.

1. Describe the flower of the Sweet Pea or Daffodil. Illustrate your answer by drawings.

2. Name four common trees and say how you would know them (i) in summer and (ii) in winter.

3. Why do leaves wither when they are cut from a plant and are exposed to the sun? How could you prove your answer to be correct?

4. In what kind of places would you find five of the following wild plants growing:—Vetch, ferns, silvery weeds, poppy, ivy, gorse (furze), anemone, yellow flag (iris), mistletoe, butterwort.

5. What are the uses of roots to plants? Name four roots used by man as food.

6. Describe any wild bird and say where you would expect to find its nest. What are the eggs like?

7. Which of the following are the farmer's enemies:—Snails, earthworm, beetles, greenfly, caterpillars, daddy-long-legs (crane fly), and slugs? What methods does he use to get rid of any two of the enemies.

P.T.O.

as possible in order to enable the largest number of boys to obtain a full two years' course. However, throughout the war, the boys were only able to do Woodwork sporadically, according to the availability of an Instructor.

In February 1914, an LEA Circular asked the Managers whether they felt the subjects taught were the most suitable, bearing in mind the occupations likely to be followed by the children in after life (a matter which had been brought before the LEA's attention by the Pershore District Education Committee). Fortunately for Badsey, the school had an enlightened Head and Managers and they were unanimous that, in view of the varied occupations followed by the children after leaving school and the advantages to them of an all-round general education, no alteration should be made to the curriculum.

In 1911, a flag-pole and fittings for physical exercises were acquired and, once the playground had been asphalted, it became easier for drill to be undertaken. In November 1912, the Inspector wrote: "Physical training is well taught and the girls especially went through their movements with freedom and precision. The timetable should provide for three lessons a week of 20 minutes in this subject."

Examinations and Scholarships

Until the first decade of the 20th century, the vast majority of Badsey schoolchildren, in common with children throughout the country, did all their schooling in one elementary school, leaving either at 14, or 12 or 13 if in possession of an exemption certificate (so the cleverest children left school the earliest). Only the very few whose parents could afford a secondary education went on to somewhere like Prince Henry's Grammar School in Evesham.

However, Balfour's Education Act of 1902 paved the way for change by increasing the provision of secondary schooling. The first reference to scholarships appears in the Managers' Minute Book of March 1906 when it was noted that the Head Master had received a form about County Scholarships. Three

children were entered for the County Scholarship exam that year. In September 1906, Mr McDonald reported that Thomas Mason (youngest son of the Infant School Head), Tom Warmington (son of Walter Warmington, landlord of The Bell Inn) and Laura Cull (daughter of Ruth Silvester, a former Mistress of the old National School) were now in attendance at the Grammar School.

From 1907, it became a requirement that all grant-aided secondary schools had to offer at least a quarter of their places free to children from public elementary schools. Thereafter the highly competitive "scholarship examination" became a crucial moment in the lives of elementary pupils. But, although secondary education was becoming available to a growing band of bright children from poorer homes, the main beneficiaries were the offspring of the lower middle classes. Sometimes, indeed, children from poor homes could not afford to take up the scholarships they had won.

Prize-Giving

The first prize-giving took place in April 1903 and the prizes were distributed by the Chairman of the Managers. Initially the prizes were just for attendance but, from 1908, the LEA allowed the school more discretion in awarding prizes. It was agreed that in each Department prizes were to be awarded for attendance, punctuality, cleanliness and industry. The prizes were obviously intended to be inclusive rather than exclusive, as shown by the following amounts claimed in 1912, which seem to indicate that all the children in the school received a prize: Mixed Department, 185 children at 3d per head, Infant Department, 89 children at 2d per head. The prizes were books or paint-boxes and were usually presented at a prize-giving just before the school broke up for the Christmas holidays. The County Council continued to provide money for prizes until December 1914, but then war-time restrictions meant that this was no longer possible. However, from December 1917, Mr Binyon provided prizes on the same scale as the County Council.

Labour Certificate for 12-year-old Cecilia Barnard. The normal school-leaving age was 14, but children who passed an examination showing proficiency at Standard V were allowed to leave early. They also had to present their birth certificate to prove eligibility. Eleven children entered for the labour exam in 1905 and all passed. The others were: Hilda Brewer, Lily Crisp, Margaret Harwood, Gertrude Hinds, Edith Perkins, Emily Roberts, Eva Wasley, William Agg, Alfred Hiscock, Henry Cox.

Sometimes special prizes were awarded for compositions. In June 1910, Edith Ballard (described in the Admissions Register as a "painstaking and clever girl") won a prize given by the Director of Education for a composition on "Australia, its Physical Features and Productions".

Holidays

At the beginning of the Council School period, school holidays were still built around the agricultural calendar but, by 1906, the school year began to take the shape of the one we know today. In addition, the school was closed for whole days or half days because of special events. One of the highlights of the year was Badsey Flower Show which in those days was held on a Wednesday, and so the children were granted a day's holiday. An article in the Parish Magazine of August 1904 says: "The Badsey children now look forward to the Flower Show year by year and probably regard it as an institution nearly as old as Christmas." In 1908, the LEA introduced new rules whereby, if attendance was over 90% for four consecutive weeks, the school was entitled to a half-holiday. In Badsey, this was used to advantage to have a half-holiday on the day of the Evesham Mop Fair. From May 1910, the Managers decided to give a holiday on Ascension Day, as many children had absented themselves in previous years.

The school was closed on the occasion of parliamentary elections. The Managers tried to arrange for the poll to be held at the old school to avoid having to close, but they were not successful. We learn from the Log Book that in 1906 the children were very excited all week at the prospect of the General Election, but they were not allowed to wear party badges during school hours.

Attendance

Attendance figures are available for the Mixed Department from the school year ending 1907 to the school year ending 1918. During this period, the numbers fluctuated from 176 on the books in 1907, with an average attendance of 164 (93%), to a high of 209 in 1915, with an average attendance of 201 (96%); however, by the end of the war, attendance had dropped to 87%. 8th October 1906 was a red-letter day in the Infant Department when every child on the books was present. Headteachers of this period continued to be obsessed by attendance figures as the school grant was calculated according to the average attendance. Children who achieved 95% were awarded a certificate and those with 100% attendance gained a medal. In 1906, Frances Moisey and Henry Jinks both received a book as well as a medal for two years' perfect attendance.

The weather continued to have an effect on attendance, on occasion necessitating closure. The LEA had no definite rule as to the proportion of absentees necessary before a school could be closed on account of inclement weather; but generally, a school was not closed unless the attendance was less than 50% and the ordinary work seriously interfered with. Heavy snow at the end of March 1916 meant that very few children assembled at 9 am, only 70 out of 176 in the Mixed Department, and 16 in the Infants. As water was coming through the roof in three separate places, Mr Binyon visited the school and took the responsibility of closing for the day. The Director was notified of closure by postcard. In January 1918, again because of deep snow, Mr Binyon took the decision to abandon the morning meeting. As the school was closed for two days because of snow, the school would not make 400 openings unless they opened on a Saturday, so a Saturday in February was designated.

Special local events – a Sunday School tea at Wickhamford, Bretforton Wake, Broadway Races, a church choir trip, a confirmation service, a circus in Evesham – were also

reasons for missed attendance.

Attendance was affected by "half-timers", who left school in the summer months to work in the fields. They were able to do so until the 1918 Education Act abolished the system. The problem was exacerbated during the war. Pressure on the LEAs to exempt children from school attendance for child labour was so extensive that the Board of Education stipulated conditions for this exemption so as to prevent exploitation. From March 1916, children aged 11 and over could be released for occasional work on the land for a period not exceeding a monthly average of three days a week. This legitimised what, in practice, had already been happening and many market gardeners took advantage of these provisions.

In March 1917, Mr Amos received notice from the Director that any child of 12 years or over could be exempt from attendance provided that a written statement was forwarded from the employer stating that the child was to be employed on the land and that the parents were agreeable. By the following week, this resolution had already begun to affect the average attendance. By the end of April, many more parents had taken advantage of the County Council's resolution. This made work in the upper classes difficult as the children put in their attendances on different days.

The health of the children suffered during war-time as Miss McDonald wrote in June 1916: "Attendance lowered more owing to several children being away under doctor's orders, suffering from general debility. Many children are very sleepy and tired owing to insufficient sleep. They are up much later at night-time than they should be, but have to get up early in the morning (Daylight Saving Bill)."

The School Health Service

Ill-health was a major issue. In the first decade of the 20th century, the school was closed on seven occasions because of scarlet fever, measles, mumps, or diphtheria. The first closure was in 1904 owing to a sudden outbreak of scarlet fever. The Managers made arrangements for the school to be thoroughly

Above: To celebrate the Coronation of King George V, June 1911, the children were given a week's holiday and a special event was held at Badsey Manor House. Some of the children dressed up in costumes of the British Empire.

Below: As part of the Coronation celebrations, the girls put on a display of country dancing. The maypole dancers wore white dresses with red, white and blue sashes.

Alfred William Sparrow was one of 28 children (out of about 100) in the Infant Department who achieved 95% attendance for the year 1906-07.

cleaned and whitewashed after the month's closure. The Aldington children were excluded for a further period and attendance continued at a fairly low level, particularly in the Infant Department, for the rest of the term, as the disease lingered on. Scarlet fever broke out again in mid-August, and the Managers took the decision to close the school two days early for the harvest holiday. By the time school reassembled in September, there were just a few lingering traces of scarlet fever, with still a couple of families being excluded because of danger of infection.

In 1906, a diphtheria epidemic spread through the village. The school closed in May and reopened in June, but new cases of diphtheria continued to appear. Julius Sladden, Chairman of the Managers, wrote in the Log Book, "Attendance very unsatisfactory on account of parents keeping their children at home, alleging fear of diphtheria, am reporting this to authority at Worcester." It was not surprising that parents took this action, as two

children died: four-year-old Norah Grove and six-year-old Frederick King.

Throughout the Victorian and Edwardian period, epidemic disease posed major threats to the lives and well-being of the nation's children. The poor state of health was brought to light when a great many men being recruited for the Boer War were deemed physically unfit. Thus reform of child welfare was high on the agenda of the Liberal government which came to power in 1906. One of the great advances in social history was made in 1907 when a clause in a Bill made medical inspection of children an LEA duty and allowed powers of treatment; out of this grew the school medical service. In Worcestershire, four doctors were appointed in 1908 to undertake the duties they were obliged to carry out under the Act. Routine medical inspections were held at the approximate ages of five, eight and 12, and mothers had the opportunity to meet the doctor and ask questions. Education of parents in health matters was one of the key aims of the school health service.

The first medical inspection at Badsey took place in July 1908 and, from then on, the Medical Officer visited every autumn to examine the children. The LEA provided a weighing machine and height standard for each school. A classroom in the Infant Department was usually used for medical inspections. It is not known what the outcome of the first medical inspection at Badsey was but nationally, the first school doctors' reports of 1908 were a horrifying catalogue of disease and defect. 70% of children were "dirty", some were found sewn into their clothes, parasites were a problem and defects of eyes, throat and teeth were common, as was malnutrition. There was a regular system of inspection by "the nit nurse", who was also on the look-out for ringworm and "scald head".

A national survey of 1913 conducted by the Chief Medical Officer pinpointed the principal problems which the inspections had revealed. Out of six million children attending elementary schools in England and Wales, he estimated 50% suffered from injurious decay of their teeth, 10% suffered from a serious vision defect, 10% were unclean in their bodies, 5% suffered from defective hearing, 3% suffered from suppurating ears, 3% had adenoids or enlarged tonsils, 2% had tuberculosis, 1% had heart disease, 1% had ringworm. By the eve of the First World War, a radical shift had occurred in attitudes towards child welfare. The health of the elementary pupil had become a matter of public concern, and initiatives were being taken on a variety of fronts to assist those who were now perceived as the nation's future.

Meal-Times

Most children went home for their midday meal, but those who lived too far away, took a packed lunch of bread and cheese. Fred Mason, who lived at Wickhamford and consequently was unable to go home, recalls that he had his lunch in a satchel which he hung on his peg, but sometimes the lunch would be stolen (poverty still being a major issue), so he had to hand it in and collect it again at midday. During the long lunch-break of almost two hours, they were left to roam the village. Frank Caswell, the blacksmith, was often their first port of call. Another favourite pastime was loitering outside Badsey Manor House, watching the German prisoners of war returning for lunch. A third place they frequently visited was the Cider Mill where they would occasionally be given a drink of apple juice.

Concerts

The beginning of the 20th century saw the start of participation of events with other schools. For example, in 1905 and 1906, a Festival of Village Choirs was held at Evesham. Concerts were put on from time to time and were held at the Old School, such as one in February 1911, a children's operetta entitled *Cinderella's At Home*. The Parish Magazine gave a full report: "The very greatest credit is due to Ida Dore and all her little colleagues, as well as to those who trained them or otherwise assisted in the production of the piece. Only those who have had to do with the musical training of children can properly appreciate the character of the task so pluckily undertaken and so successfully performed by Miss Bird and Miss Sparrow."

Getting to School

All the children walked to school whether they lived close by or as far afield as Aldington or Wickhamford. Fred Mason, who lived at Pitchers Hill, recalls getting to school: "On my very first day at school, as a young lad of five, Miss Nancy Pethard took me to school. After that I had to fend for myself. I and some of the other children from Wickhamford would meet up and walk together. My main pals were Edgar Southern and Jack Styles. We started at

A measles epidemic caused the school to be closed in February 1905. When school was due to reopen on 27th February, the Sanitary Officer was present. Many children were still absent and those from infected houses were instructed to stay away. The Medical Officer thus sent a telegram to advise closure for a further week.

POST OFFICE TELEGRAPHS.

8 am, messed about on the way, and would get to school by 9 am. There were very few cars, just horse and drays, so there were not the dangers that there are today. Very occasionally, severe weather conditions such as snow or floods would prevent us from getting to school. On the way to school, we would drop off the milk cans at Elm Farm, the farm belonging to John Mason [husband of Mrs Mason, the Infant School Head], and then on our way home from school we had to collect the milk. We usually went by the road, though occasionally went past the church and along the footpath; this was usually in summer when we could paddle our feet in the brook. Each side of the road (Golden Lane) was a fruit farm belonging to Wickhamford Manor. I remember we used to stand and watch small groups of German soldiers working there during the war. One day, as we stood there watching, one prisoner came out and gave us a penny each; I will never forget that moment, and often wonder what happened to him."

Most of the staff lived locally, but there is evidence that some were beginning to come from further afield. Mr Walker stayed for only two terms in 1910 because of transport problems. The Log Book reports: "Mr Walker arrived at school at 10.15 am having a breakdown on the road and having to wait for a train." The same thing happened the following week and, soon after that, he relinquished his post, having obtained a post nearer home. Miss Hunt, who joined the Infant Department in 1912, lived at Worcester but lodged with her relatives at The Poplars during the week, to minimise the travelling. When she first started, we learn from the Log Book that the Managers gave Miss Hunt permission to arrive at school a little late on Monday mornings, as the train service did not permit her to be at the school in time for the opening at 9 am.

The Caretaker

The Caretaker throughout this period was Mrs Wilson. When the Director of Education visited in December 1907, he was concerned about the cleanliness of the school, and he felt that the job was too much for one person to cope with. Accordingly, George Hardiman was offered the job of window-cleaner. Mrs Wilson's salary was increased to £16 a year as it was felt she could not be expected to carry out her work at a satisfactory standard at the low salary paid her. The services of Mr J Knight, who had been employed as Sanitary Cleaner, were dispensed with in 1909 when the toilets were improved. In 1914, the LEA laid down further stipulations about the level of cleaning in schools, and the Caretaker's salary was increased accordingly to £20.

In 1914, there was again an issue about the temperature of the classrooms, which were sometimes as low as 36°F and 38°F at 9 am. All the rooms were far too cold for children to sit in until morning recreation. A letter signed by a number of parents, was sent to the Managers complaining of the coldness of the schools, so Mrs Wilson was advised that she must ensure that the fires were lit in adequate time.

The Managers

The first meeting of the newly-appointed Managers for Badsey Council School met in May 1903. Four Managers were appointed by the County Council, one by Badsey Parish Council and one by either Aldington or Wickhamford Parish Meeting. Four out of the six Managers had been members of the previous Board and Mr Julius Sladden, who had been defeated at the Board election in 1899 after nearly 20 years' service as a Manager, returned triumphant to be elected as Chairman, a post he was to hold until his death 25 years later. It was during this period that Charles Binyon became greatly involved with the school, visiting on a regular basis and offering advice and support.

There was sadness when Manager William Pethard, a prominent Market Gardener, died in July 1908, aged 42. Just four months later, his only daughter, Lucy, died. Mr McDonald wrote in the Log Book on 13th November 1908: "Lucy Pethard, Standard VII, was buried on Tuesday. She was in school on 3rd July. Her father died on 5th July, since which date she

These photographs are all taken in the garden of the Sears' house in Badsey Fields Lane, where the children practised after school. Mrs Beatrice Sears, whose three children attended the school at that time, coached the children, together with Miss Bird.

Above: Participants in a children's concert, about 1916. Irene Sears and Helen Barnard are the main characters. Evelyn Crane, pupil 1916-1923, remembers her part as a fairy dressed in a white satin frock trimmed with tinsel, carrying a tomato cane covered with silver paper for a wand. She sang a little ditty which started, "I am Fairy Content, this is Fairy Goodwill, and this is Fairy Fun as you see." Her friend, Evelyn Barnard, was very jealous as she wanted to be a fairy rather than a flower girl!

Above: The girl in the hat holding a doll, left of centre, is Lilian Rose Keen (born 1907) who, on leaving Badsey School, went to Prince Henry's Grammar School and then returned to Badsey as a student teacher.

Back row: Marjorie Allard, Beatrix Sears, Helen Barnard, Irene Sears, -, -, Lucy Mustoe.
Front row: -, Ruby Hatch, Gertie Bennett, Blanche Collett, Stella Crisp, Alice Brooks, Stella Bowley.

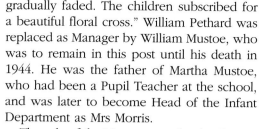

Dear Miss Bird,

Very pleased to hear from you last week, and to know that you arrived home safely. This is the Old School, Badsey, do you recognize it? I could not get one of the new Schools, will send you one later if I can. There are some fresh cases of diptheria. Another of the Stewarts (which makes four altogether now) and Lily Careless, I think these are all as yet but there are several with 'sore throats'

This postcard of the old school (one of a series of picture postcards of the village in Edwardian times) was sent to teacher Miss Bird, who had gone home to Smethwick, when the school was closed in 1909 because of diphtheria. Two children died during the epidemic: eight-year-old Florence Jane Brewer (daughter of the baker) and five-year-old William Douglas Sparrow.

gradually faded. The children subscribed for a beautiful floral cross." William Pethard was replaced as Manager by William Mustoe, who was to remain in this post until his death in 1944. He was the father of Martha Mustoe, who had been a Pupil Teacher at the school, and was later to become Head of the Infant Department as Mrs Morris.

The role of the Managers under the County Council was quite different to their role under the School Board. Everything was controlled by the Education Committee at the centre. Each year, their estimate of expenditure for the forthcoming year was sent to the County Council. The LEA set the limit for expenditure on books, apparatus and stationery which, for 1904, was 2s 9d per child in the Mixed school and 2s 6d per child in the Infant School, with needlework and drawing materials extra.

The First World War

The first indication of the First World War having an impact on the life of the school was in September 1914 when Miss Bird was absent from school for one day attending hospital in connection with the Red Cross Society. Meanwhile, the girls in the upper class spent their Needlework lessons getting shirts and socks ready for Worcester Regiments.

Children were expected to "do their bit" during war-time. An egg collection for wounded soldiers was made, flags were sold and children were encouraged to collect plants and fruit. Over 500 lb of dandelion roots were collected in April 1917 and 1918 for drug manufacture. In September 1918, Mrs Amos took some children blackberrying and over ½ cwt was sent to the jam factory.

The impact of war in Belgium witnessed an influx of refugees to England; a small hostel was set up in Badsey at what is now the Spar shop. In January 1915 the first Belgian refugee was admitted: six-year-old Maria van de Wyngaert who attended Badsey School until her family left the village in August 1915. In

Sir Julius Sladden (1847-1928), Manager for over 40 years and Chairman 1903-1928.

October 1915 another refugee family moved to Badsey. The children, Simon, John and Joseph Verbeeck, attended from 1915-1917. Jim Brailsford (pupil 1915-1924) sometimes played with the Belgian children and remembers that there had to be a watching guard on the door to prevent Joseph, the youngest boy, from running away from school.

Schools, like society, were drenched in propaganda. Biased textbooks explained the war to the young and Empire Day became more prominent. In 1916, on the authority of the Director, a half-holiday was given on 24th May, Empire Day. In the morning, special lessons were given to each class in which Empire Day was particularly alluded to in connection with the war and compositions on the subject were written. At 11.30, the classes were marched into the playground, where they saluted the Union Jack, sang patriotic songs, concluding with "The National Anthem".

In total, 23 former scholars and one member of staff, Mr Lewis, lost their lives during the First World War. Mrs Mason was afflicted with tragedy when her second son, Lieutenant George Mason, was killed in May 1917. George was a former pupil of the school and was engaged to his childhood sweetheart, Cecilia Barnard. The Amos and McDonald family, too, suffered a loss when their nephew, Arthur Henry Logan McDonald, who had grown up with his grandparents and aunts at The School

House, was killed in August 1917.

Thankfully, for the good of the school, Mr Amos was himself spared, but at a cost. In June 1918, he was absent from school for several days owing to the wound in his shoulder flaring up again, and he continued to suffer for years afterwards from old war wounds. But the school was about to enter one of the most successful periods of its history, helped by changes in attitude after the First World War. A major act of August 1918 proposed a school system "which shall get rid of all class distinctions and privileges", bringing to each child "the training – physical, mental and moral – of which he is capable". Although many of the Act's proposals soon foundered in the economic crisis, its spirit set the tone for the work of post-war reformers, and for good Headteachers such as F E Amos to make a real difference.

Belgian refugees, M & Mme Verbeeck with Simon, John and Joseph. The children went to school in Badsey for two years.

The school and school house from School Lane. Note the war-time presentation shell just behind the railings, which was erected in 1922, funded by the Badsey War Savings Committee. Julius Sladden, the Chairman of Managers, rode round the village on the traction engine which delivered the shell. The shell was removed for scrap metal during the Second World War.

Headteacher, Frank Amos, 1920.

5

BADSEY COUNCIL SCHOOL – THE INTER-WAR YEARS

As the First World War drew to a close, the people of Badsey had their own problems to contend with. The influenza pandemic which was spreading throughout the world had reached the Vale. The school had been closed since the middle of October and only reopened on Armistice Day. Many of the children were still not well enough to return to school, and were unable to participate in the holiday granted on the afternoon of 12th November to celebrate the cessation of hostilities. But, slowly, the school began to pick itself up after the hardships of the war, and entered perhaps what may be seen as the golden era of its history. And this was primarily down to the inspirational leadership of Frank Amos who, together with School Manager, Charles Binyon, produced a school of excellence which was highly regarded throughout the county.

The Headteacher

After Mr Amos' return from the war, he dedicated himself to making Badsey a first-class school. He was given the opportunity on more than one occasion to go for promotion but he preferred to stay at Badsey. Mr Amos was a man who commanded instant attention. He was a strong disciplinarian but the children had great respect for him. He had lost the use of one eye as a result of his war wound and consequently the children never knew if he was looking at them or not; and he had a deep war wound on the side of his head, which would become even deeper if he was angry.

The School Inspector, Mr H A Jenkin, had nothing but praise for his headship, as this report of 1934 shows: "The Headmaster, who has held his post for more than 20 years, has succeeded in investing his school with character and individuality. Discipline is sound, the manners of children are good, interest in school work is well maintained .... Altogether the Headmaster has every reason to feel proud of what he has accomplished for his school and for the welfare of his village."

Frank Amos was well respected by the County Education Office and, as Badsey was considered a showcase school, the Director of Education frequently sent visitors to see the school and work. These included an Indian gentleman who was returning to Kashmir to reorganise education, and a group of missionaries studying at Avoncroft College, Offenham. In 1931, the Inspector, Mr Jenkin, brought two teachers from Greenhill Private School in order that they might see the methods adopted at Badsey for teaching

Mrs Jean McDonald Amos.

Arithmetic and other subjects.

Staff of the Mixed Department

Throughout this period, Mr Amos and Miss McDonald provided great stability at the top of the school. For most of the time, there were six members of staff for seven standards (a few of the most able children were in Standard VII; they learnt alongside Standard VI but were given separate lessons occasionally by Mr Amos). The classes were off a long corridor, beginning at the east end with Standards VI and VII, Standard V next-door, Standard IV, Standards II and III combined and lastly Standard I in the new classroom. In each classroom, the children sat two to a desk, about five rows by four, with the teacher facing the whole class. Each desk had a lift-up lid in which books, paper and pencils were kept. The troublemakers were placed at the front of the class.

Many elderly residents of the village today have vivid memories of their teachers and rooms during this period. Miss McDonald, who took Standard V, was a great favourite with the children. A short lady with glasses, she was also responsible for Needlework in the school, and was a good musician. A large picture of her father, former Headteacher, Mr McDonald, hung on the wall. There was also a big scroll chart with all the Kings and Queens of England from 1066 which was unrolled and learnt by heart, a relief map of the Evesham District and a large case of stuffed birds. When Miss McDonald retired in 1939 after 45 years' devoted service, she was greatly missed. Her sister, Mrs Amos, was equally well-liked. Mrs Amos took a break from teaching when her daughter, Margaret, was young, but returned to full-time teaching in October 1930 when her daughter was 11. Margaret, who had been taught at home, started at the school in April 1930, where she remained for two years before entering Malvern Girls' College.

Mr Sealey taught at the school from 1923-1932 and was responsible for sport; he was known as "Sir", was Clerk to Badsey Parish Council, and was very involved in village affairs. He was replaced in 1932 by Mr Page.

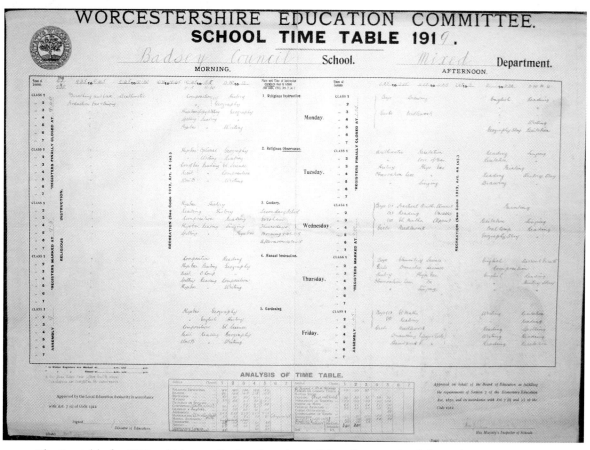

The timetable for 1919, which was displayed on the wall for all to see. Until the early 21st century, it still hung on the wall of the Headteacher's office. It is now stored at the Worcestershire Record Office.

Miss Graham (later Mrs Westbury) taught Standard I from 1928-1934.

And then there was Miss Bird, a very smart woman, who was a strict disciplinarian. She was not popular, deemed unfair and ruled by the ruler. As was common in many schools in those days, she resorted to hitting, pinching and throwing chalk (or worse) as a means of punishment. She wore red leather shoes with a little bar across, and would trot along with a pile of books under her arm. It was quite a shock moving to her class after the caring attitude in the Infant Department.

In 1928, the Managers wished to appoint an additional teacher, as recommended by HMI, to allow Mr Amos more time for the general supervision of the school, which he was not able to do under existing circumstances. This was not achieved until 1932 when Mr Bill McKanan-Jones, a dynamic Welshman, was appointed. Mr McKanan-Jones

took Standard IV and was responsible for Art. He used to give the boys the cane, but spared the girls. If the girls were talking, he would put them behind the blackboard and write "Gossip Corner".

The provision of an extra member of staff was short-lived, however. Warnings came in November 1933 when the LEA said it would need to make reductions in the teaching staff in order to make economies in education expenditure. Fortunately, the Mixed Department did not have to make anyone redundant as Mrs Westbury (née Graham) resigned after her marriage and no one was appointed in her place.

In an earlier decade, the only indication of problems was when the staff of the Mixed Department resigned en masse in May 1920, action which was replicated in many other parts of the country. A new national scale of salaries for teachers had just been introduced,

Class photographs of the whole school were taken in 1924 including these four pictures.
Standard I. Back row: James Pitman, Hubert Crane, Edwin Grove, Thomas Bennett, Thomas Major, Reginald Chamberlain, John Walker. Middle Row: Benjamin Green, Basil Hall, Ronald Hicks, Frederick Robbins, George Halford, Arthur Griffin, Arthur Dore, Harry Welch. Front row: Irene Sandford, Mary Marshall, Hilda Reeves, Gwendoline Moisey, Sybil Manners, Kathleen Hall, Joan Chamberlain, Joan Enstone, Dorothy Keen, Joan Cockerton, Margaret Bott, Beryl Hall.

Standard III. Back row: Percy Taylor, Evelyn Cockerton, -, Percy Waldron, Betty Grove, Alice Knight, Dorothy Sandford, Betty Woodward, Fred Waldron, Cyril Jelfs, Margaret Moisey. Middle row: -, Richard Huxley, Fred Jones, Albert Sutton, Clifford Hall, John Bradley, Arthur Hall, Fred Taylor, -, -, Louis Salter, Olive Hartwell. Front row: Gladys Cave, Jack Dore, Margaret Mustoe, Frederick Roberts, -, Gladys Southern, "Holly" (Holloway) Reed, Clarice Butcher, Tommy Sadler, Rosie Howe, -, Nellie Salter.

Standard V. Back row: Frank Knight, Ronnie Tovey, -, Ken Cull, George A Grove, -, Ernie Stewart, Sylvia Barnard, Jim Harwood, Ethel Jelfs, Cecil Collett. Middle row: Gertie Hartwell, Ruby Manners, Kathie Cole, Vera Crane, Lucy Crane, Enid Hardiman, Dorothy Pitman, Bert Sears, George E Grove, Florrie Taylor, Les "Buster" Mustoe, Evelyn Agg, Irene Sadler, Norah Wheatley. Front row: Bill Sandford, Frank Styles, Jack Salter, Molly Dore, Esme Sparrow, Molly Evans, Zillah Crane, Zena Crane, Teddy Butcher, Billy Cole, James Hancock, Emily Knight.

Standard VI. Back row: Douglas Sandford, Jack Styles, -, Reg Pitman, Jim Brailsford, Stanley Hatch, Bill Churchill, Charles Crane. Middle row: -, Frances Knight, Ethel Moisey, Jack Malin, Ernest Shelley, Doris Haines, Muriel Griffin, Kathleen Cave, Doris Savage, Lilian Mustoe. Front row: Cecil Butcher, Charles Heritage, Cynthia Southern, Edie Greening, Peggy Haines, -, Doug Pethard, Fred Mason, -, Philip Sparrow, -.

but Worcestershire LEA resisted the introduction of the Burnham Scale because it did not want to bear the expense of paying "to scale". Apart from the Scilly Isles, it was the only LEA which refused to pay the minimum level. The school was due to reopen on 31st May after the Whitsun holiday, but the following comment was written in the Log Book by Mr Binyon: "Closed the school until Monday 7th June on account of resignations of assistants." School did open as planned on 7th June. The staff withdrew their resignations as the County Council had altered their previous attitude with regard to pay-scales.

Staff of the Infant Department

Mrs Mason was still in charge of the Infant Department immediately post-war, but her heart seemed no longer in teaching after the death of her son in the war. She decided to retire in September 1922.

The Infant Department then went through a period with several changes in Head Mistress. Firstly, Mrs E D Thompson, who stayed for a

Artist's impression of the central classroom, with glass partition, which enabled Mr Amos to patrol the corridor daily and check on what was happening. Blackboards were in common usage throughout the 20th century but have now been replaced by whiteboards.

year, then Mrs Martha Morris who, as Martha Mustoe, had been both a pupil and pupil teacher at the school. Mrs Morris resigned her post three years later. Mrs Frances Kissack of Paignton, South Devon, was appointed to replace Mrs Morris as Head Mistress. Mrs Kissack suffered greatly from gastritis during the spring term 1927 and was absent for some time but the Inspector was nevertheless happy with the progress being made. 1928 was a difficult year for Mrs Kissack as one teacher, Miss Hunt, was off sick for over six months, and Mrs Kissack's mother died at the start of the autumn term. She finally resigned at the end of November 1928, and was replaced by Mrs Morris, who returned for a second stint of headship. Mrs Morris' father, Mr Mustoe, one of the Managers, was a frequent visitor and gave sweets to the children.

Throughout the various changes in Headteacher, Miss Hunt and Miss Hartwell were the two Infant teachers until Miss Hunt resigned in 1930. She was succeeded by Miss Evelyn Barnard, a former pupil of the school. Miss Barnard joined at a difficult time when the country was hit by depression. Economies had to be made and, in December 1933, the Managers were asked to name a teacher for transfer. On the basis of "last one in, first one out", Miss Barnard, who had been sent on supply to Sedgeberrow, was regretfully found an alternative post at Cleeve Prior School, which meant that the Infant Department was left with just two teachers: Mrs Morris and Miss Hartwell.

Miss Hartwell was a very popular teacher. The young Margaret Amos, who was taught at home during her early years and used to watch from the School House garden, has vivid memories of her bringing out the children into the playground, and singing such songs as "Poor Mary's a'weeping", "The Farmer wants a Wife" and "The Good Ship Sails on the Alley-Alley-Oh". Miss Hartwell was a real stalwart and trained generations of Badsey schoolchildren.

The Inspector's reports reflected well on Mrs Morris, as this one for 1930 shows: "This is a happy little school, the condition of which is very creditable to the Head Mistress and her assistants. The children are very bright and responsive and eager to do their best." The report for 1933 says: "There is nothing but good to be said about this school – of the teaching as well as of its results."

Mrs Morris was ill for much of the autumn term 1936 and a temporary Head took charge. Mrs Morris returned to school in January 1937 but decided to resign her post at the end of the year on account of ill-health. The decision was taken by the Director of Education to merge the two Departments, appoint an Assistant Mistress in the Infant Department, and make Mr Amos Headteacher of the whole school. Miss Norah Smith, who was to remain at the school until 1975, joined the staff of the newly-merged departments in February 1938.

Admissions

Whilst some children did not start school until the official starting-age of five, many parents sent their children at the age of three or four. Throughout the 1920s, the numbers of three-year-olds starting represented about half the new intake. This continued until 1934 when there was a change in policy and no more three and four-year-olds were admitted. Some four-year-olds were admitted in 1936 and 1937 but in 1938, when the Infant Department merged with the Mixed Department to form one school, children were no longer admitted until they had reached their fifth birthday.

During the inter-war period, because of its excellent reputation, many parents from outside the parishes of Badsey, Aldington and Wickhamford sought to send their children to Badsey. A few came from Evesham but the majority (54 during this period) came from the Littletons.

Premises

By the end of the First World War, the school was suffering desperately from overcrowding. In May 1919, the Director of Education and the County Architect visited the school in order to view the buildings with regard to enlargements. They agreed that an extra classroom was necessary; but building work did not commence until five years later. Due to financial constraints and the large backlog of building work across the county as a whole, Badsey had to wait its turn. At last, in November 1923, when matters were at breaking-point, the LEA gave the go-ahead, but building work did not start until August 1924.

The start of the autumn term was delayed by a week because of the building work. Great difficulties were encountered for most of the term in carrying on the ordinary work of the school whilst the builders were in and out. The mid-term holiday, which was meant to be one day only, to make up for lost time at the beginning of term, also had to be prolonged, on the orders of the Director of Education who visited the school. As there was no easy means of notifying parents, the children assembled on the due start-date and then had to be dismissed.

By the end of November 1924, the extension was able to be used for the first time. During the next week, the various classes moved to their fresh quarters as the rooms were prepared and the furniture arrived. The new classroom accommodated 50 children, for whom 25 dual desks were provided. As a result of the enlargements, the school was then recognised by the Board of Education as providing accommodation for not more than 238 in the Mixed Department and 106 in the Infant Department.

At the same time, a Headteacher's office was added and the large west room made into two separate rooms. For many years, the Inspector had stressed the need for a partition. In the absence of a more permanent solution, a curtain had been erected in 1918. However this did not prevent Miss Lena Crisp from being absent from school on at least two occasions due to loss of voice attributed to teaching continually against another class. Mr Binyon made a comment in the Log Book in September 1923: "In the long room, three different classes are being taught under great difficulties."

The new classroom was heated by hot water pipes, unlike the rest of the school which was heated by coal fires. In 1926, hot water heating apparatus was installed throughout the school and an outside boiler built adjacent to the new classroom. School was again delayed in opening because of the work which necessitated holes being made in all the walls, the floors being taken up in several places, and alterations made to cupboards, in consequence of the installation of the heating apparatus pipes.

Not long after, further major building work occurred at the school. The LEA decided to build a Practical Instruction Centre at Badsey. At first it was proposed to utilise the old school for the purpose, but by June 1927 the LEA planned to build at the current school. The Managers recommended that the Centre should be built at the south end of the Infant School building. Work took place during the summer term. The building was completed by July 1928 and the boys were able to have their first woodwork lesson there on 27th July. In February 1936, gas was supplied and a gas cooker and boiler fitted.

Once the Handicrafts Centre was built, it was also used for concerts and parties, and was sometimes let to outsiders, being an attractive venue for social functions. But not all hirers were deemed suitable. An application in 1929 from "The Roosters' Dance Band" was turned down on account of the irresponsibility of the applicants. But a month or two later, the Girls' Friendly Society were allowed use of the school for their weekly meetings. One wonders what riotous antics members of the Royal Antediluvian Order of Buffaloes got up to at a party in January 1934. It was necessary for the Clerk to write to the Secretary of the Local Lodge concerning damage to the Centre caused by their party.

Electric lighting was installed at the school and the School House in 1929, electricity having recently been made available in the parish. Such was the novelty of having electric lights that the children used to hope for a dull day so that the lights could be switched on.

Playgrounds and Playing-fields

In 1920, the school acquired a small piece of land when the land adjacent to the School House, belonging to Mr Victor Cockerton, was put up for sale. The Managers thought it desirable that it should be acquired for possible future school use. Mr Amos was allowed to occupy the piece of land, conditional on his rent being increased and, if at any time the garden of the School House was required to be occupied for playground purposes, then the rent would be proportionately reduced. The land was never used for that purpose and remained part of the School House garden, but 70 years later it proved to be a very prudent investment when the land was sold.

One of the sheds in the Girls' playground was an ink-shed. Bob Butler was the Ink Monitor when in Standard VI. Every Friday afternoon at playtime, he collected up the long-framed inkwells and took them to the ink shed where the ink-cans were stored. Here he filled up the inkwells, put them in a rack and left them until Monday morning, whereupon he collected them and put two at each double desk.

As early as October 1920, the Managers had suggested raising the boundary fence between the school property and Mr A E Jones' property, but the LEA had refused to sanction this. However, in 1932 it was decided that, in order to protect the property adjoining the boys' playground, the provision of a wire netting fence was necessary. This did not deter the children, however. One of the school rules was that no solid balls were to be used in the playground, and no climbing the walls to retrieve balls. Boys being boys, they wanted to get their ball back, so whoever kicked the ball over had to go and get it. Lionel Knight recalls that this involved going out of the boys' playground, into School Lane, then down a footpath which led zig-zag fashion and came out opposite Sands Lane. This took about five minutes, and woe betide any boy caught by Mr Amos!

In a corner of the boys' playground was a painted map of all the counties. Common playground games for boys were conkers, tag, marbles, cigarette cards, leapfrog and "Jack on the Mopstick", the latter game being one

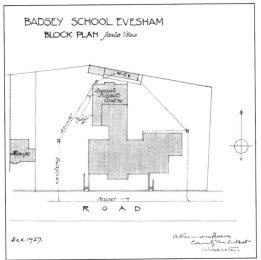

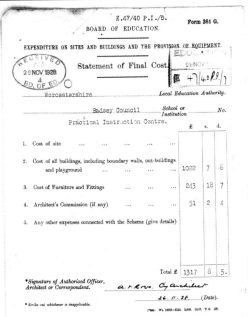

Plan showing the new Handiworks Centre built in 1928 and a statement of its final cost.

which would surely be banned today! It involved two teams of about eight. The largest boy stood against the wall whilst the others bent in front of him. The opposing team then had to jump on to someone's back, the idea being to get all the team on the other's backs. The team that got the most on won the match.

The girls played mainly tag, whip and top, hopscotch and skipping. Skipping was done with long ropes, with up to a dozen girls joining in. A favourite game was "Sheep, sheep, come home," which involved a long run from the railings to the wall and often resulted in badly grazed knees.

The Curriculum

The Badsey area with its market garden development and patterns of land use was a rich resource and Mr Amos made good use of the local environment in the school curriculum. First-hand observations, made by Welsh graduate, Evan Llewelyn Harry in 1929 for his MSc dissertation, tally closely with the memories of former scholars recalling their schooldays more than 70 years later.

High standards of Arithmetic were expected, with the emphasis on mental arithmetic. Local material was used to illustrate general arithmetical principles wherever possible. For example, calculations were based on so many pots of cabbages at so much per pot, and losses through disease of crops.

In the upper standards, the boys studied Surveying whilst the girls did Needlework and Knitting. In the early days, Mr Amos always wore knickerbockers and the top class girls kept him well supplied with diamond-patterned turnover-topped stockings.

From 1928, Woodwork and Cookery classes were held in the new Handicrafts Centre which was also used for classes by senior pupils from six other parishes (prior to this the children had gone by coach to Bengeworth Old School and Offenham College). Miss Holmes was the Domestic Science Teacher. Mr Collett, who taught Woodwork, was impressed with the high standards at Badsey because the boys' knowledge of mathematics and drawing enabled them to do better work. Lionel Knight still has strong memories of the smells in the Woodwork room which were very pungent – there was no need to be a glue-sniffer!

Mr Amos was a keen historian, and so history played an important part in the curriculum, with Mr Binyon being invited to school regularly to give lectures on local history, supported by the original documents from the Church. For other aspects of history, children were encouraged to paste newspaper

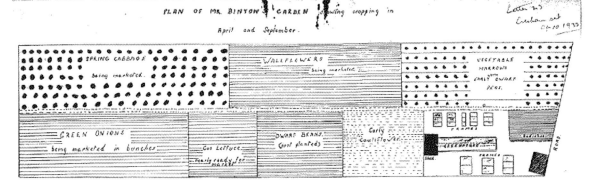

FIGURE 1.

APRIL.

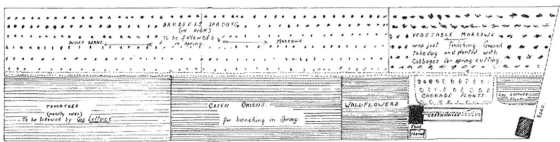

FIGURE 2.

SEPTEMBER. / Drawn by B.B. Bayliss.

Mensuration and surveying were introduced in the higher standards for boys, and pieces of land and the village roads were measured and plotted, which assisted pupils to understand geometry. This scale drawing of the Chairman of Managers' garden (on the site of the current-day Binyon Close) was done by Berwick Bayliss in 1933.

cuttings appropriate to the theme of their lessons into their books.

English Language and Literature were also important. Evan Harry wrote: "More stress than is fashionable at present is laid on grammar. This is chiefly due to the peculiar dialect of the neighbourhood. Youngsters are often particularly weak in English, but they improve very much before leaving school." Books and poems written locally were studied and some of the older children were taken to those places to see what inspired the poets.

Geography and Geology were studied together, with a local approach undertaken, the Cotswold and Bredon Hills affording an excellent contrast in topography to the low-lying Vale. Nature study was conducted with the aid of the flora found in the neighbourhood. For example, in June 1926,

Mr Amos and Mr Binyon took the older boys on a Nature Study Expedition to Weston sub Edge Woods; the next day they were given time to paint the seedlings of trees which were found. Maps of the distribution of market garden crops at different times of the year were made and the standard of artwork throughout the school was high. Evan Harry wrote: "It seems almost incredible that such a high degree of excellence in artistic attainments is possible in children of school age."

Prior to the 1944 Education Act, religious education was not required to be taught by the Board of Education, but it was an LEA requirement. "It is commonly assumed that council schools, not subject to visits by the village vicar, do less scripture than those that are visited weekly by the vicar," wrote Harry. "Unhampered by church supervision, the

Architectural drawing of the Norman doorway at Badsey Church, by Berwick Bayliss, 1933, done with the aid of set square, compass and ruler. Some of the older children were often taken by Mr Amos and Mr Binyon to view fine examples of architecture.

schoolmaster plans a good scripture course. His pupils have never to be primed full of useless information for the vicar's weekly visit."

In April 1933, the children of Badsey School had the honour of participating in research for Rothamsted Experimental Station in Hertfordshire, which was a centre of research into the history and development of agriculture. The aim of the Director of Rothamsted, Sir John Russell, was to inform the public about agricultural matters and one way he did this was by BBC radio talks. He planned a series called "What the Counties Do" with letters from schoolchildren describing their daily life and work. Sir John approached local school inspectors for suggestions of schools to contact and, as a result, Badsey School was chosen. The letters, 48 of which survive, were written with great clarity and were often surprising, funny or moving. On 19th May 1933, most of the senior children and Standard III had the opportunity to listen to Sir John Russell's broadcast, courtesy of a radio set lent by Mr W Sadler. Sir John read extracts from their letters and mentioned their school and many of their names. In June, at the request of Sir John Russell, further letters were written to Canada describing life in an English village for broadcast purposes there.

Physical Exercise

In January 1920, Mr Amos began a Football Club, with the full support of the Managers. It was felt that a start should be made in this direction, even though organised games were not recognised by HMI as officially part of the school curriculum until several years later. By February 1920, they were ready to start competing against other schools, the first match being against Bretforton. At the start of the second season in September 1920, two elevens (the Greens and the Red and Blacks) were formed instead of just one, and a school league for the District was in the course of formation. At 3.30, one afternoon a week, 24 boys from Standards IV-VII were taken along to the new Recreation Ground on Sands Lane

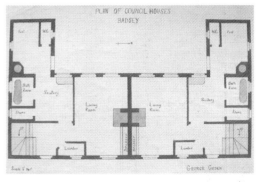

These plans were drawn by 12-year-old Charles Malin and 13-year-old George Geden in 1921, the year that the houses were built. The plans are of Nos 3 & 4 Synehurst; Charles' family had just moved into No 3.

9, Council Houses
Badsey
Evesham
11th April, 1933

14.

Dear Sir

I live in Badsey which is in the Vale of Evesham My father is a market gardener I go to Badsey Council School We have fourteen in our family My father is pulling onions and my mother is tying them. My sister and I go to help to pick plums in the summer also gooseberries and currants which are black and red. Father also has a lot of asparagus and daffodils. He sends his produce to Evesham market which he takes in a horse and cart. We also send gillies to market which my sister and I help to pick We pick beans and peas in the summer for my father. My mother and my big sister help to do all the things that I do I tie onions and pick daffodils which are grown on the ground.
      I remain,
      Yours Truly,
      Hilary Crane (Aged 9.)

Letters written by two of the youngest children who submitted letters to the Rothamsted Research Institute describing life in a market gardening community. Note the classic style of Badsey handwriting. Reproduced by kind permission of the Lawes Agricultural Trust and Mrs Hilary Jobson (née Crane) and Mrs Dulcie Cleaver (née Jelfs).

Class photo showing some of the young letter-writers: Dulcie Jelfs, Irene Barnard, Evelyn Keen, Hilary Crane.

Lindwood Villa
Badsey
Evesham
11th April 1933

3.

Dear Sir,
      My father is a market gardener who lives in Badsey. I go to Badsey Council School. There are six of us in the family I do lots of things to help on the ground Sometimes I tie onions. My other brothers help on the ground at nights in summer time. My father grows onions, leeks, gillies and vegetables and a lot of other things. My father grows different plants in the different seasons. It is very pleasant here in the summer time. Sometimes I take the tea up to father so that he can stop after tea. In the winter he comes home to tea and does not go back after My father has about four acres of ground He sends his plants to London I think it is very nice to be a gardener though it is hard work
      I remain
      Yours Truly
      Dulcie Jelfs. (Aged 9).

86

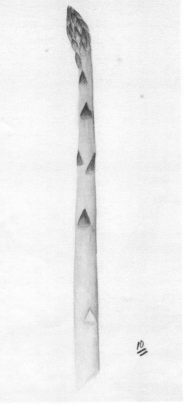

I like the way you have tried this leaf

Beryl Hall.
1932.

Harebell

Badsey had a high reputation for art as these drawings done by 13-year-old Beryl Hall show. Pastel drawings of cultivated market garden crops, wild flowers, trees and shrubs were all popular subjects. Paintings done by Badsey children were used at a Nature Study Summer School for Teachers in 1929.

for organised games. The Badsey boys quickly proved themselves and in April 1921 were the first winners of the Evesham & District Schools' League, winning by a margin of 13 points. Shortly after, they entertained the "Rest of the League" team to tea in the school. A match was arranged and the visitors were defeated 5-1. Badsey retained the cup for several years.

In the 1930s, one of their main opponents was Grove House School, Stratford on Avon. Every Friday afternoon Mr Amos put up the team-sheet for those playing on the Saturday. Lionel Knight and three of his mates had an arrangement. They would take turns each week to ask to go to the toilet just before home-time to see who had been picked for the team. It took some time before their teacher eventually realised what was going on.

The girls, meanwhile, had Drill taken by Miss McDonald. They also did country dancing in the playground to a gramophone player, and a few of the boys also took part. Netball was introduced in 1935.

Examinations and Scholarships

In the 1920s, examinations were held at the end of each term, with the examination held in March being particularly important for promotion purposes. But from 1932, when the start of the school year changed to September, exams were only held in July and December. From 1927, school reports were issued each December, so that parents gained an indication of their children's progress.

From the 1920s, the top class took part in an essay-writing competition for the League of Nations Union. Miriel Field, Standard VI, was awarded 1st Prize by the Evesham & District Branch for an essay on "How Quarrels have been settled in the past and how they should be settled in the future". She was emulated by her younger brother, Frank, who was the winner in two successive years. In 1931, Kate Brailsford was the recipient of ten volumes of the *Children's Encyclopaedia* which formed the first prize for the best essay on "Ovaltine" in the Counties of Gloucestershire, Worcestershire and Herefordshire.

The majority of children stayed at Badsey

School until they were 14, with a few leaving earlier because of Labour Certificate exemption, which lingered on for a few years after the war. April 1922 was the last time that children left with Labour Certificates. From then on, they had to stay at school until they were 14. A few stayed slightly longer, such as Esmé Jelfs who remained for a few months after her 14th birthday in order to take an examination to enter Domestic Science College in Gloucester.

Some children did leave Badsey School before the age of 14. These were children who had passed the scholarship. The First World War had sharpened social ambition and many parents were keen for their children to receive a grammar school education. But there was a shortage of free places and many children were refused a free place, despite passing the examination. In 1924, the number of free school places was doubled, thus easing the situation slightly.

In the inter-war period, Badsey had a good reputation for producing Grammar School pupils and Mr Amos tried to enter as many able students as possible for the scholarship. However, even if awarded a free place, not all children took up the offer because there was still a considerable amount of expense with fares, uniforms and equipment, or perhaps they were needed in the family business.

Because of the continued success of Badsey pupils at Prince Henry's Grammar School, Mr Amos was, from time to time, invited to the Prize-Giving. In 1924, Gladys Brewer obtained the chief prize, two other pupils obtained the form prizes for being top of their respective forms, and two other pupils obtained special subject prizes. Gladys Brewer was by that time back at Badsey as a student teacher, undergoing a year's training.

Evan Harry, who conducted a survey of previous Badsey scholarship winners, had this to say: "The children entering are particularly successful. In 1921, 1922, 1924 and 1927, children from this school won the highest prizes that Evesham County School has to offer. On termination of the secondary school course,

Badsey Council School Football Team, 1928, champions of the Evesham District Schools League 1927-28. They won all 8 games, scored 40 goals, and let in 8 goals.
Back row: Mr Frank Amos, Wilfred King, Arthur Stewart, Arthur Hall, Frank Field, Albert Bott, Frank Southern, Ronald Knight, Leslie Mustoe, Mr V C Sealey. Front row: John Dore, Cyril Jelfs, Percy Taylor, Lawrence Smith, Clifford Hall.

The two Badsey School teams, the Greens and the Red and Blacks, 1931. Jack Haines (back row second from right, pupil 1924-1934), went on to become a local soccer legend. He played professional football for West Bromwich Albion, Bradford and Swansea, and was capped for England. He played only once, but scored two goals against Switzerland in 1948.

Back row: James Parker, Herbert Crane, Jack Hartwell, Jack Haines, Donald Wasley. Second row: William Woodward, Kenneth Ellison, George Crane, Ronald Hampton, Berwick Bayliss, Leslie Mitchell, Ernest Sadler. Third row: Douglas Malin, Louis Jelfs, James Wheatley, Sidney Halford, Frank Salter, Jim Sadler, Denis Hartwell, Harry Field. Front row: George Robbins, William Salter, Frank Field, John Walker, Ronald Reed, Reginald Hardiman.

Netball Team, 1938, on the occasion of a match at Evesham Council Girls' School. Back row: Eileen Jelfs, Barbara Harris, Joyce Heritage, Doreen Hall, Nesta Moisey. Front row: Helen Hartwell, Margaret Stanton, Joan Wheeler.

the children are free to take up any vocation they like. They become surveyors, teachers, accountants, architects, journalists, salesmen, lawyers, clerks and three have entered the university. Two of the university entrants have taken their degrees. One of them is a chemist in the firm of Lever Bros, representing them in Sierra Leone. The second holds an engineering degree and has a responsible position with an engineering firm. The last is well on the way to a degree in the classics." The last-mentioned person was George Edward Churchill who did not gain a free place at the Grammar School because of shortage of places. Instead he entered Worcester Cathedral School, then became an undergraduate at Hertford College, Oxford; he later became Director of Education for Northamptonshire.

Prize-Giving

The annual prize-giving ceremony had been resumed towards the end of the war through the generosity of Mr Binyon who provided prizes on the same scale as was formerly given by the LEA before the First World War. He presented book prizes to two children in each class, for progress and good conduct. From 1927, in addition to those from Mr Binyon, prizes were also awarded by the Seward Trust and other Managers. Mr Amos and Mr Binyon made a trip each year to an educational suppliers' company in Birmingham in order to buy the books for prize-giving.

Once the Handicrafts Centre was built, the Prize-Giving became a grander affair. Carols and songs were sung by the First and Second Classes and the National Anthem terminated proceedings. In the 1920s, the prizes were normally presented by Mr Binyon but, by the 1930s, guest speakers were invited. In 1931, Miss Wedgwood of Stanton, who was greatly interested in education and social work and who was an old friend of Mr Binyon, presented the prizes. At the prize-giving in 1934, Mr Amos' sister, Miss E H Amos, late Headmistress of Halford Road School, Fulham, was present. One year later, Mr Binyon's brother, the poet Laurence Binyon, came. Doreen Ballard recalls having to recite a poem. It was one of Binyon's own poems, about two children dancing to a barrel organ, so it was particularly scary for the young Doreen to recite it in his presence.

Holidays

The school, in common with schools everywhere, was closed all day on Friday 18th July 1919 in connection with the local Peace Celebrations. Every child attending the school from the parishes of Badsey and Aldington was presented with a mug in commemoration of the Signing of the Peace. The mugs were provided from public subscriptions.

The Evesham Mop Fair had not taken place during the war but was resumed in 1920. A number of children were absent so, for two years, the Managers granted a half-day holiday. From 1924, instead of taking a half-holiday, school assembled at 1 o'clock and lessons taken earlier in order that no attendances were lost.

In the inter-war period, Badsey Flower Show was a very grand affair and always took place on a Wednesday in July. The school was a major participator in the show, and so a holiday was granted on that day in order to allow the children to attend. The children spent many hours preparing paintings, drawings, writing, woodwork, sewing and knitting for the show, and were allowed extra time to complete their work. The children would go miles to collect a variety of wild flowers for the displays.

Fred Mason's first prize certificate at Badsey Flower Show, 1920.

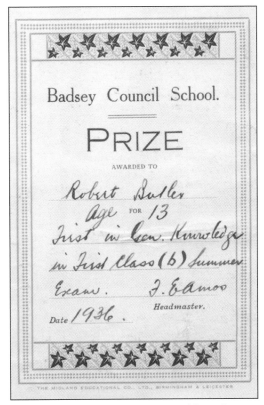

13-year-old Robert Butler won a Bible as first prize in General Knowledge in 1936.

Village events such as the Chapel Sunday School outing merited a closure, certainly at the beginning of the period. In 1921 and 1931, Mr Amos performed the role of census enumerator. The Mixed Department was thus closed on census day. Royal weddings also occasioned a holiday. A day's holiday was given for Ascension Day; in 1929, it was reported that over 130 children attended the service voluntarily. Until 1924, a holiday was given for the Asparagus Show.

In 1933, the Director of Education wrote to suggest that all schools in the district should take their holidays at the same time, and his letter contained suggested dates for holidays. The dates were basically in accord with the holidays that pertain to this day, though the summer break tended to be for four weeks. The Managers, who had previously been responsible for setting holiday dates, gave their general approval to the suggestions.

On the instructions of the King, the school was closed for three days in May 1935 for the Silver Jubilee celebrations. Singing, Dancing and Physical Training displays were given by the children one afternoon, watched by about 400 people. Doreen Ballard, who was at the school from 1928-1936, recalls the splendour of the occasion when she took part in the country dancing, dressed all in white with a beautiful sash. Seating accommodation was brought from Littleton & Badsey Growers and Messrs Cadbury's Canners Company, Blackminster, by the LBG lorries. All the staff were present to superintend the children and to assist in the tea which followed. Each child was presented by the Rural District Council with a Jubilee Mug.

The Infant Department was closed on the afternoon of 28th January 1936 for the funeral of King George V but the Mixed Department remained open. In accordance with a circular letter from the Education Office, each school made its own arrangements for suitably commemorating the funeral of His Majesty, King George V. With the approval of the Chairman, Mr Amos arranged with the Vicar for a special service solely for the schoolchildren to be held at the end of the morning session.

Attendance

Poor attendance was often caused by bad weather. On one day in January 1919 only 47% of children were present. Mrs Mason wrote in the Log Book: "Most of the children were absent with bad coughs, the weather too was very cold with snow or rain making it very difficult for little children to attend school from a distance." In March 1920, heavy snow, several inches deep, caused the attendance to drop: "A very snowy morning, only 20 children present and those children were carried to school by their parents," wrote Mrs Mason. Mr Binyon advised that the Attendance registers were not marked and that the children should not return to school in the afternoon. In September 1927, owing to the exceedingly heavy rains causing the roads in the vicinity to be flooded, Mr Amos was obliged to cancel the attendances of 28 children who left school early in the afternoon and were taken by dray through the flooded area.

Illness also affected attendance. Epidemics occurred of measles in October 1921, January 1929 and January 1932, whooping cough in February 1922 and scarlet fever in 1930, all resulting in closure. The 1929 measles epidemic was particularly severe. When the school reopened at the beginning of February 1929, the health of the children had not returned to normal. "The attendance this week has been worse than any week I remember," wrote Mr Amos on 15th February 1929. The Medical Officer visited the school three days later and ordered its closure again owing to the prevalence of measles and influenza amongst the children. Mrs Brookes and Mr Sealey were also struck with influenza, and Mrs Morris in the Infant Department.

In September 1923, for the first time in Mr Amos' ten-year headship, all the children were present on one day. This happened again in September 1932, when all 207 children of the Mixed Department were present.

School Health Service

Improvements in the school health service continued after the war. The number of Medical Officers was increased, and a full-time dentist and part-time oculist were employed. The first mention of a dentist and oculist visiting the school was in 1921. The school doctor and nurse had to be present when teeth extractions were required, in order to administer the gas.

There were regular visits from the school nurse, who would advise on such matters as the exclusion of children because of the condition of their hair, ringworm, scabies or impetigo. Children found to have ringworm of the scalp were required to wear caps. The School Nurse would often visit the homes of children who had been excluded for medical reasons.

The Medical Officer also visited. In July 1923, there is a record of vaccinations taking place for the first time; 88 children whose parents had given consent were vaccinated. A classroom in the Mixed Department was initially used for the medical inspection, with the children being taught in the playground. When wet, they had to work in the passages and other rooms, or be sent home. In the Infants, the smaller room was used, so the three divisions of infants had to be taken in the Main Room. The problem of accommodation for medical inspections was resolved in 1924 when a store-room was altered.

If a child suffered seriously from pulmonary complaints, heart trouble or anaemia, the Medical Officer might suggest a temporary stay at the Open-Air School in Malvern. The concept of the open-air school was started in Germany in 1904 but then spread to other parts of Europe. In 1914, a private open-air school was opened on the eastern slope of the Malvern Hills, and was taken over by Worcestershire LEA in 1920. Instruction was given entirely in the open air and children normally stayed at the school for one term of 12 weeks. The first record of Badsey children attending the open-air school was in 1924 when 11-year-olds, Sylvia Hall and Ellen Grove, went for a short time.

Meal-Times

There were no school meals provided so those from further away took a packed lunch, which they ate in the bike sheds. One child who lived at Aldington was taken home each lunch-time on the back of her mother's bike. Miss Graham, who came from Worcester, took her lunch in a white cake box and usually had pieces of flan with peaches and cherries – mouth-watering luxuries for most of the

Miss Graham's Class, Standard I, 1931. Back row: Frank Barnard, Esmé Jelfs, Barbara Harris, John Sutton, Horace Wheatley, George Keen. Second row: Miss Graham, Olive Parker, Joan Wheeler, Monica Haines, Marjorie Jelfs, Mona Collett, Mary Gosling. Third row: Nesta Moisey, George Perks, Lewis Welch, Jack Taylor, Lionel Knight, Geoff Hall, Walter Warmington, Frances Jelfs. Front row: Queenie Merriman, Dot Wells, Kathy Hemming, Helen Hartwell, Cynthia Padfield, Wilf Major, Norris Days.

children. At the beginning of each meal the children sang:

> Be present at our table, Lord,
> Be here and everywhere adored.
> These mercies bless and grant that we
> May feast in Paradise with thee.

And at the end:

> We thank thee Lord for this our food,
> But more because of Jesus' blood
> Let manna to our souls be given,
> The Bread of Life sent down from Heav'n.

Milk was provided mid-morning. In the 1920s, Connie Wixey came round with the milk in a pony and trap. She had a big can with half pint and one pint measures which she dipped into a churn and put into the school jug. In November 1934, a Milk Scheme was introduced with each child paying a halfpenny a day for a third-pint bottle of milk. On the first morning of the scheme, 161 children in the Mixed Department participated. The bottle had a cardboard top in which a straw was placed, and the children often placed their bottle on the radiators to warm.

Outings

The first school outings at Badsey took place in the late 1920s. In the wake of the Hadow Report of 1926, *The Education of the Adolescent*, which reported on secondary education outside the grammar schools, Mr Amos and Mr Binyon embarked on a programme of activities aimed to widen the horizons of their senior scholars. The first educational visit was to Swindon Great Western Railway Works in December 1927, when Mr Amos and Mr Binyon took a party of 19 boys. From 1928 onwards, Mr Amos, Miss McDonald and Mr Binyon regularly took a group of children to an organ recital at Worcester Cathedral, given by the cathedral organist, Sir Ivor Atkins.

From at least 1932 onwards, the children of the top classes went with Mr Amos to see a Shakespearean play at the Stratford Memorial Theatre which included *As You Like It*, *The Merchant of Venice* and *Henry V*.

Extra-Curricular Activities

Following on from the first Hadow Report of 1926 which had looked at secondary education in elementary schools, a second Hadow Report on the primary school in 1931 was more radical in tone. School was to teach children how to live. Learning was best based on "the experience, the curiosity and interests of children themselves". This eloquent Report became the basis of modern primary practice. Novel teaching devices appeared in schools. The British Film Institute sponsored educational films, which could be hired (with projector) for school use or, as in the case of Badsey, the children were taken to the cinema.

Music played an important part in the life of the school with Miss McDonald at the helm, training her pupils to high standards. Once the Handicrafts Centre was built, concerts were held at the school. Proceeds from the concerts went towards buying a piano, a gramophone and records for Country Dancing and paying expenses of children attending the Musical Festival. From 1932 onwards, Mr Amos and Miss McDonald took some of the Senior children to the Schools' Evesham & District Musical Festival at the Public Hall, Evesham.

One custom observed at Christmas was the Post Box. In a large red Post Office sack, the children posted cards and little presents addressed to their friends. These were handed out on the last afternoon amidst great excitement. Father Christmas visited the Infants and distributed toys, oranges and sweets. Carols were sung and a party held in the Handicrafts Centre.

In February 1924 a Rural Libraries Scheme was started in Worcestershire and Mr Amos acted as the village librarian with the library being housed in the school. All the books sent from Headquarters were lent out the first night and further books were hastily sent for.

Getting to School and Road Safety

The majority of children at Badsey Council School walked to school, but by the 1920s, some were beginning to cycle. In 1928, bike sheds were built in the playground. There were 15 spaces which were allocated according to distance from school. Lorna Bayliss, who lived at Middle Littleton, has vivid memories of frozen hands and feet and thawing them on the pipes after the long cycle ride. Margaret Amos, the daughter of the Headteacher, remembers that in winter the children who walked would arrive with great big scarves tied across their backs and their gloves tied on with string so they did not lose them. In winter, the Bowers Hill children would walk all the way by the road, but in summer, they walked across the footpath from Pear Tree Corner.

One family travelled by car from Wickhamford, but that was the exception. An attempt was made in 1924 to arrange for the conveyance of children living at Wickhamford, particularly for the winter months, but the LEA said they could not sanction such expenditure at that time. The matter was again brought up in 1931, but once more nothing happened. It took until 1939 before a bus was provided, but this was short-lived because of the intervention of the war.

Amongst the staff, Miss Aldington, who taught at the school immediately after the First World War, rode a motor-bike from Offenham, as did Mr Page in the 1930s who came from Stow-on-the-Wold. Miss Holmes, the Cookery teacher, came by car, and Miss Graham came by train from Worcester.

In June 1930, a fatal accident occurred outside the school playground which resulted in the death of Ronald Summers from Wickhamford, aged 4¼. Ronnie had only

started at school in May. The accident occurred during the interval between morning and afternoon sessions. Ronnie had remained at school during the interval and he and some others were playing on a pile of chippings off the school premises on the other side of School Lane. He slipped and fell under a beer lorry which was delivering to the pub. Many of the children were in the playground and had to be dragged away from the railings. The memory of the accident has never left the elderly residents of the village who were at school at that time. Mrs Morris, the Infant School Head, was extremely upset. In the Admissions Register under "Cause of Leaving", she simply wrote "Left", as if she could not bring herself to write a different word.

In those days, teachers were not responsible for the children during the midday break. The accident highlighted the need for some special provision being made for care of the infant children who took their midday meal at the school during the interval. The LEA recommended that Mrs Morris should communicate with all parents of infants under five years of age attending the school and who partook of their midday meal at the school, and request that some arrangements be made for supervision of them during the midday interval.

As a result of the tragic accident, it was decided to provide safety gates at the two entrances to the school premises. It seemed at first that this request would not be complied with, but Badsey Parish Council took up the

Performers in the "Living Whist", 11th September 1928, held in Abbey Park as part of Evesham Gala Week. The children, directed by Miss McDonald, dressed as playing cards and played a game of whist to music. Under the direction of a herald, they were "shuffled" and "dealt". They were then "played" in a proper game by two ladies and two gentlemen, whose living cards were concealed from each other by canvas screens. The players included Ron Knight (King of Clubs), Vera Sadler (Queen of Clubs), Jack Dore (Jack of Clubs), Pat Mustoe (Two of Clubs), Arthur Emms (Knave of Hearts).

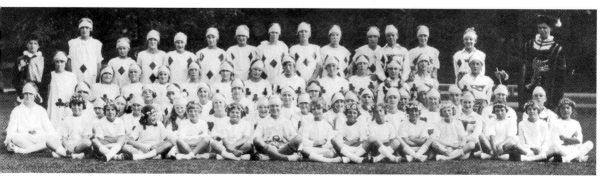

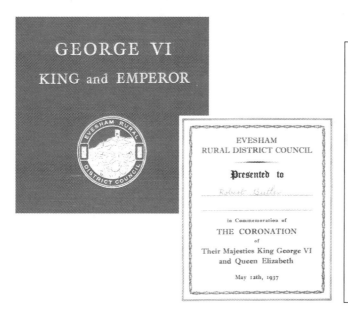

FOREWORD

THE Evesham Rural District Council are presenting you with this book which will tell you
the story of our new King—George VI.

You will read about the King as a boy, of his life
in the Navy and Air Force, of his tours of the Empire
and of his work in recent years. And, in reading, you
will get to know and understand something of the very
difficult task the King has to do, and of the spirit in
which he is doing it.

You will learn of his interest in humble people,
of his Boys' Camps and inspections of mines and
factories, and of his ready sympathy with all workers.

In the last chapter you will find a description of
the coronation in Westminster.

We hope you will keep this book to remind you of
this year's great event and that you will realize something of the duties of citizenship as you grow up,
so that you may play your part and take your share
of the responsibilities which are the lot of all of us.

C. A. BINYON, *Chairman of the Council.*
C. H. GARDINER, *Clerk of the Council.*

Evesham Rural District Council chose to mark the occasion of the Coronation of King George VI in May 1937 with a book for each schoolchild. The book was customised for Evesham children with a special foreword by C A Binyon and C H Gardiner, the former being both Chairman of Evesham Rural District Council and Chairman of Managers of Badsey School. A gold-embossed emblem of the Council was printed on the front of the book.

The school was closed for three days in 1937 to celebrate the Coronation of King George VI. A big tea-party was held in the Girls' Playground and a programme of sports was held. Mr Amos' garage is at the centre back and the bike sheds to the right, set against the southern boundary of the school. Beyond the boundary is Glebe Farm, demolished in the 1960s. Many of the tables are set out where the present-day Hall is now situated.

cause. The barriers were finally erected by the start of the autumn term 1935, five years after little Ronnie died.

The Caretaker

Mrs Wilson remained in post until retirement in 1929 after 38 years' service. At the age of 65, with increasing duties and advancing age, she felt it was time to call it a day. During the last decade of her working career, with the extensions in 1924 and 1928, the work had increased considerably and her salary rose from £20 to £54 by the time she retired.

Mr & Mrs Cecil Keen of Badsey were appointed as Joint Caretakers in place of Mrs Wilson. Cecil Keen was popular with the children and always had a twinkle in his eye as he stoked up the boiler.

The Managers

The inter-war period was a very stable period for the Managing Body, with very little change in personnel. In 1926, the Chairman of the Managers, Julius Sladden, had the honour of having a knighthood conferred on him by the King. A half-holiday was granted on 1st April to commemorate the occasion. On the death of Sir Julius, Mr Charles Binyon was unanimously elected Chairman, a position he was to hold for the next 30 years. The son of a clergyman, educated at St Paul's School, London, and brother of the poet Laurence Binyon, Mr Binyon devoted his adult life to the welfare of Badsey. He was well-loved in the village and it was largely because of Mr Binyon and Mr Amos that the school was so successful in those years.

The End of the Elementary School

In the 1930s, Worcestershire County Council was caught up in educational reform. The government had decided that the old system of elementary education, with boys and girls staying at the same school until the age of 14 was not good enough. The Hadow Report of 1926 had suggested a complete reorganisation of schooling: "primary" up to 11 and "secondary" up to 15, the proposed minimum leaving age. Alongside grammar schools,

Charles Arthur Binyon, OBE (1874-1963), Chairman of Managers 1929-1959.

"modern schools" were to be developed for the average child. These proposals were officially approved, but delayed in practice. The massive economic depression in the early 1930s crippled educational progress.

The new scheme meant an expensive programme of building new senior schools. In September 1933, the Managers received a copy of the Statutory Notice of intention of Worcestershire LEA to erect a Senior Council School at Evesham for about 400 children. A year later the LEA sought the co-operation of the Badsey Managers in the provision of the best possible Senior School in Evesham, by agreeing to the reorganisation of Badsey School as a junior school for children up to 11 years of age. The Managers felt that, while agreeing with the principle, they thought it would be unnecessary for children over 11 years of age to attend from Badsey, in view of the excellent accommodation and efficiency of the Badsey school.

By September 1935, the decision had been taken to erect a Senior Council School at Blackminster in the Evesham Rural District. Nothing more was said on the subject in the Managers' Minutes because it was basically a *fait accompli* that the school would lose its children aged 11 and over in due course.

Meanwhile, storm-clouds gathering over Europe heightened the sense of uncertainty. School closed for the summer holidays on 28th July 1939 with the knowledge that things might never be the same again.

Artist Michael Barnard has dedicated this sketch to Miss Norah Smith who was in charge of Red Cross lessons and who died in January 2004. The lesson times can be seen on the board on the left. Some children are trying out their gas masks; others are being patients whilst having bandages and splints applied. The rest are making camouflage nets by tying strips of cloth on to the nets. The finished product resulted in heavy drapes for use by the army as camouflage for their vehicles. Note the strips of adhesive on the school windows to prevent shattering in the event of an air raid.

Medal awarded to John Bird in March 1944 as his contribution to the Book Recovery Campaign organised by the Ministry of Supply through the LEA. The children were rewarded with a paper medal to hang around their neck with the appropriate rank according to how many books they collected. Badsey collected 2,500 books in the first week and over 5,000 the following week. The final results showed that Badsey School had collected the greatest weight of books of any school in the Evesham Rural District, the total being over 1¼ tons; Blackminster Senior School came second with 1 ton.

In 1930, the school bell turret was found to be unsafe and was taken down. In 1940, Mr Amos gave the disused bell to Dick Caswell, the Badsey Fire Chief, to be used for parish purposes during war-time, but it was never put into operation.

6

BADSEY COUNCIL SCHOOL 1939-1948

Momentous events both locally and nationally meant that 1939 marked a watershed in the history of Badsey School. Two events that year were of huge significance: on 1st September, the school became designated as an Infant and Junior School for children up to the age of 11 and, on 3rd September, the Second World War broke out. To a lesser extent, but also a disruption as far as the children were concerned, one very longstanding member of staff retired, and two staff transferred to the new senior school at Blackminster.

The Outbreak of War

Badsey Council School opened for the autumn term on Monday 28th August 1939. The senior children of 11+ years (65 in number) were due to attend the new senior school at Blackminster, commencing Tuesday 5th September, and from 1st September Badsey Council School was to function as an Infant and Junior School. But the crisis unfolding in Europe meant that it was uncertain what would happen. Mr Amos, writing in the Log Book on 31st August, indicated that he did not know what would happen if war broke out and a state of emergency was declared.

By the next day, matters were clearer. All over Britain "Operation Pied Piper" was launched and schoolchildren were evacuated for fear of air bombing in cities. Plans had been given to LEAs in 1938. The country was divided into evacuation, neutral and reception areas. Badsey, as a reception area, prepared to receive the evacuees who were transported from the cities to vaguely-known destinations in the countryside. Throughout the country, one and a half million people were moved in three days, in a "triumph of preparation, organisation and discipline". Evacuation Day was an important event in the history of World War II.

Thus it was that a group of Birmingham children arrived at Evesham Station on 1st September and were put on a bus, the girls being sent to Bretforton, the boys to Badsey. The Badsey contingent comprised 71 children, mainly from the Handsworth New Road Senior Boys' School, together with Mr J F Goode, Headmaster, and his staff of 11 assistants and four lady helpers. They were taken to the old school building (now the British Legion) which was used as a community centre and were allocated lodgings.

The opening of the new Senior School at Blackminster was postponed and Badsey School was closed until further notice. Consequently, Mr Page and Mr McKanan-Jones, the two teachers due to be transferred to Blackminster, reported at Badsey for duty as usual. All the staff, including newly-appointed Mrs Beatrice Howells, were on duty to assist in the evacuation, rationing and billeting of the Birmingham children, teachers and helpers.

Badsey School Reopens

Badsey School reopened on 11th September. Blackminster School also opened, so the 65 Seniors were transferred to Blackminster. In cordial agreement with the Headmaster of the Handsworth New Road School, Mr Amos decided to amalgamate the classes where possible, Birmingham children being taken into Badsey classes where age and availability proved advisable. This was considered a better plan than working a two-shift system.

The school was in a position to accommodate the large influx of evacuees because the school now took children only up to 11 rather than 14. Until Blackminster School was able to take the Birmingham secondary-aged children, they were taught at Badsey by their own staff in former classrooms vacated by the Badsey children and were not entered in the Admissions Register. The former Handicrafts Centre, which was to have been used as a Hall for music and physical training, and another classroom, were allocated to the Birmingham secondary classes. By 5th

---

EVACUEE PROFILE

Stanley Hayes, aged 12

"I was a pupil at Handsworth New Road School. We assembled at the Community Hall and were allocated lodgings. There were only three left at the end, and I was allocated to Mr & Mrs Wasley who lived at Aldington. We arrived two days before war was declared. On the Sunday morning, we assembled at what is now the British Legion and were taken to church. We were in church when war was declared and the Vicar made an announcement. Sometimes I would walk by the brook to get to Badsey School. I still keep in touch with Mr & Mrs Wasley's daughter."

Stan Hayes, right, with fellow evacuee, Bob Grainger and his landlady, Mrs Illot Wasley, with whom he lodged at Aldington.

February 1940, it was possible for the senior children evacuated from Birmingham to start attending Blackminster Senior School but the junior evacuated children remained in attendance at Badsey. Of the 71 children who had been evacuated in September, 31 transferred to Blackminster and nine remained at Badsey; the others had gone back to Birmingham.

In addition to the official evacuees from Birmingham, 31 private evacuees were entered in the school register in September 1939. These were children from all over the country (London, Birmingham, Bristol, Portsmouth), whose parents had made arrangements for them to live with friends or relatives in the country. Many did not stay for long, however, returning to their homes often within a matter of days. Evacuation had proved premature. The Phoney War intervened and bombs did not, in fact, drop for a further 11 months after evacuation took place.

The private evacuees included the Eckles family from London who came with their mother, Vera Crane, who had been born and brought up in Badsey and still had many relatives in the area. Another private evacuee was Donald Jones from Birmingham whose father, Albert Jones, had played for Badsey Rangers before the war and arranged for Donald and his mother to stay with the Corbett family.

Soon after school opened in September 1939, a Board of Education Inspector called to see how the arrangements for the evacuated children were working. Mr Amos was able to give a very satisfactory account of all the matters, educational and social, connected with both the evacuees and the Badsey children. The Director also called and saw the mixed classes of evacuees and Badsey children all working very happily and comfortably. Later in the month, the BBC visited the school and recorded some of the activities of the evacuated children, which was broadcast on "The Home Front – Evacuees in the Country".

In the summer of 1940, a second wave of evacuations occurred owing to the intensification of the war. In June, 13 girls from

a Barnardo's Home arrived accompanied by their guardian, Miss M Lord, and were mainly billeted at Wickhamford. Throughout June, more evacuated girls from Barnardo's Homes were admitted. The senior Barnardo's girls, who had attended Mossford School, Barkingside, were taught separately by their teacher Miss Haward, who lodged with the Martin family at Wickhamford. In October 1941, Miss Haward received instructions to return to Ilford. As no other teacher was sent in her place, the Managers decided that as Badsey School was now providing accommodation, teaching staff, materials and apparatus for them and as Mr Amos now had the responsibility for their education, the children should be entered on the school roll. They were thus absorbed in the various classes and treated as ordinary scholars resident in the village. Mr Amos felt that this step was very good from an educational point of view as the children were of varied ages and it was a difficult task for any teacher to take them all together as one class. The Barnardo's children remained in the area until the end of the war, but most by this time had transferred to Blackminster.

Annual returns, together with evacuation statistics, were sent to County Hall. By September 1942, nine official evacuees remained (though there were still a number of private evacuees), the rest having gone home or transferred to Blackminster. "Trickle evacuation" continued throughout the war; children returned home when the bombs weren't dropping and fled again when they were.

War-Time Special Measures

Badsey was fortunate in that it was well away from the theatre of war. But this did not mean that the children were exempt from air raid practice or from carrying gas masks. At the outbreak of war, in accordance with a directive from the LEA, an Air Raid Scheme was devised and practised.

> *In the event of an air raid warning occurring, or of an actual raid occurring:*
> **(1) In School hours.**
> *Each teacher will see that each child has its gas mask ready, and that all the children get near the walls and/or under the desks to gain as much protection from any flying glass or splinters that might come through the windows.*
> *Regular practice must be given in this as arranged for each class in order that it may be done speedily and without noise, commotion or panic.*
> **(2) Immediately before or after school hours, or during the mid-day interval (applies to children in the playground).**
> *All children, immediately, are to enter their own classrooms and to take up positions previously assigned to them.*
> *All teachers, who are available, are to go to their own classrooms to supervise. Places assigned to the various groups are as follows: Birmingham children in Rooms E and H shelter under desks. 2nd class Infants to go into the Stock Room. 1st class Infants and Standards I, II, III and IV to stay in their own room and get under the desks as arranged.*

Mr Amos was the Chief Air Raid Warden for the Parish of Badsey. The Managers tried to arrange for a telephone to be installed at the school, as a joint arrangement between the Air Raid Precautions Department and the County Education Department; but the LEA's policy was to provide telephones only at Senior Schools, so would not sanction the installation.

Badsey children were fortunate that they never had to participate in a real air-raid procedure but, on the night of 17th December 1940, there was a heavy air raid in the neighbourhood and many children were absent the next day; those present were tired and listless. A considerable number of bombs were dropped on the Vale of Evesham, particularly during 1940 and 1941, but luckily Badsey escaped, the nearest one being in the north-west of Aldington parish.

By and large, however, the war seemed fairly distant. During the summer holidays of 1941, many children went to see the wreckage of a Hampden aircraft which had crashed in an orchard at Golden Lane, Wickhamford, after hitting tall trees. The following year, on 31st August, an Armstrong Whitworth Whitley bomber crashed in a field at Bowers Hill.

The children were always very keen to contribute to the war effort. Collections were made at various times during the war for organisations such as Aid to Russia Fund, Aid to China Fund, Waifs and Strays Society, Earl Haig's Poppy Day Fund. "Wings for Victory" week occurred in May 1943 and savings were taken both morning and afternoon all week, each class competing against the others. Altogether a total of £870 was collected. In May 1944, a special week for the War Savings Campaign, "Salute the Soldier", was held. Collections were made twice daily and the amount raised from the children's savings was £556. The target of £1 per head (£200) was more than doubled. Rose hips were collected in 1943 at the request of the Government, 3 cwt being collected in total.

In November 1939, for the winter period, the school times were changed to 9-11.45 in the morning and 1-3 in the afternoon in order to allow extra time in the daylight for the

Artist's impression of schoolchildren greeting the Dunkirk soldiers, June 1940. 200,000 British troops were evacuated from Dunkirk, and dispersed all over the country. One day in early June, many arrived in Badsey. Note the Spitfire flying overhead; many aircraft were built at West Bromwich and it would have been in transit to an airfield.

caretakers to clean the school before dark and before the "blackout". However, with the resumption of Summer Time on 25th February, the former timetable came back into force. The times were revised again in March 1941, in response to a circular from the Director of Education. The Ministry of Transport had urged the Board of Education to agree to the commencement of school throughout the country at 9.30 am instead of the usual 9 am in order that no children should use trams, buses and trains at the times war workers were needing them. Though schools such as Badsey were not affected, it was thought better that all schools should conform to the one time. Consequently, from mid March, morning school was from 9.30 to 12.30. Throughout the war, timings were continually revised, according to the latest directive.

The Headteacher

Mr Amos' final years as Headteacher were perhaps the most difficult of his career with the outbreak of war coinciding with an enormous change in educational structure. He and Mrs Amos retired in October 1944 and were much missed by their many pupils, past and present.

Mr H Walter, a London County Council evacuated teacher, was transferred from Redditch to be the temporary Head until the new Headteacher was available to take up his post. The person appointed was Ronald Henry West from Luton, who started on 29th January 1945, a day when deep snow had fallen and many children were absent. His tenure of office was short, however. He was seconded for service to the staff of Cooper's Hill Training College, Egham, Surrey, under London County

July 1943, Jean and Joan, aged 9. Jean Poole (top) was an evacuee from Dr Barnardo's Home in London and started at Badsey Council School in October 1940, two months short of her seventh birthday. She lodged for most of the war with the Martin family at Wickhamford, whose younger daughter, Joan (below), was just three months younger. Over 60 years later, Jean and Joan still correspond with each other.

Council. Worcestershire LEA undertook to keep his job open for him until his return, but he left in July 1946 and never returned.

Maurice Harvey was appointed temporary Headteacher of Badsey Council School in September 1946. Mr Harvey was familiar with the school, having taught there for a short time when he came with the evacuees from Handsworth New Road School, and his own children, Pamela and Richard, had been pupils at the school. His appointment was eventually confirmed as permanent five years later once it was definite that Mr West would not be returning.

The Teaching Staff

With the opening of the new senior school at Blackminster in 1939, Mr Page and Mr McKanan-Jones transferred to the staff at Blackminster. Miss McDonald, after nearly 45 years' service, retired on 31st August 1939. "The School will greatly miss her valued services as she has been my chief assistant for the past 26 years," wrote Mr Amos in the Log Book. Although officially retired, Miss McDonald was more than happy to step into the breach if her services were required during the difficult war-time years. Less than a fortnight after retiring, because of the crisis brought about by the start of war, she was back in school giving voluntary help in teaching and clerical work.

In addition to Mr Amos, the staff at the outbreak of war comprised Mrs Amos, Mrs Howells, Miss Bird, Miss Smith and Miss Hartwell. No teacher had been appointed for Standard IV and, had it not been for Miss McDonald's assistance, followed by help from the Birmingham teachers, the class would have had to have been left to its own devices. Mr Harvey, from Handsworth New Road School, took Standard IV for most of the year, but on moving to Blackminster, the class was again left without a teacher. "This class has to be left as I find it, utterly impossible to be teaching this class myself all day and at the same time doing the numerous jobs pertaining to a Head's work in a school of this size," wrote Mr Amos in September 1940. Mr Amos was ill for ten days in October 1940 and again, voluntarily and without any remuneration, Miss McDonald undertook the teaching of Standard IV during her brother-in-law's absence. Also, when her sister, Mrs Amos, was absent for a few days in 1941 and 1942, she took her place without payment.

An additional teacher was appointed in February 1941 who was allowed to remain at the school as long as the number of pupils exceeded 200. The person appointed was Mrs A B Jones, who was subsequently replaced by Miss Burns and then Miss Hatton.

Miss Bird, after 33 years of teaching at the school, married during the Christmas vacation 1941-2. She continued teaching for a month as Mrs Woodward and then ceased teaching at the end of January 1942. She was replaced by Mrs Castle and then Miss Heath. On Miss Heath's departure in November 1944, Mrs Woodward joined the staff again as a temporary supply teacher, having done short periods of supply in the intervening years, and was later made permanent.

At a time when there was less stability in the teaching staff in the older age-groups, Miss Smith, who taught the older infants, and Miss Hartwell, who took the new intake, provided a comfortable introduction to school. Miss Smith was beloved by all her young charges and Miss Hartwell, who had long been a favourite with generations of Badsey children, proved to be very patient with the evacuee children. One little boy of eight could not read or write at all. He was brought into Miss Hartwell's class of five-year-olds and, after a time, he was soon reading; the wonder on his face when he had learnt this skill was a joy to behold.

Admissions

Children entered school shortly after their fifth birthday and left at the age of 11. In November 1944, a petition was sent by Wickhamford parents for an Infant school at Wickhamford. The following March, the School Attendance Officer called to make enquiries regarding children attending from Wickhamford, but nothing further came of this.

Classrooms

With the departure of the children aged 11 and over, Standards V-VII no longer existed. In 1942, the class numbering system was changed with the top class (previously Standard IV) becoming Class 1. There were four classes in what was now the Junior Department, and two classes in the Infant Department.

As the senior children had departed, there was no further need for the Handicrafts Centre, and the equipment was transferred to Blackminster. Initially, the Centre was used to house the secondary school evacuees from Birmingham before they were transferred to Blackminster, but then it was used as a hall and gym.

Premises

The minimum of maintenance and building work took place during this period. After the war was over, however, an architect spent two hours at the school in October 1945, making a survey of the school buildings with special reference to the requirements of the Education Act 1944. The internal decoration of the school proceeded, room by room, and plans were set in motion to build a kitchen.

Card given to John Bird (pupil 1938-1944) on Empire Day. From the early years of the 20th century, and becoming more prominent during war-time, British schoolchildren began to celebrate Empire Day, 24th May, the date of Queen Victoria's birthday.

Playgrounds and Playing-Fields

As with the buildings, little maintenance work occurred during the Second World War. In February 1945, the Managers felt it important to call the attention of the LEA to the condition of the playgrounds which were considered in some places to be dangerous. The following year, the LEA agreed to resurface the playground and the Physical Training Organiser spoke of the possibility of obtaining a field. It was to be 16 years, however, before the vision of a playing-field was finally achieved.

Because of the building of a kitchen at the school, the resurfacing of the playground was delayed. The repairs to the playground surface started in August 1947. The school was delayed in opening because the work was incomplete. The school reopened a week later under difficult conditions with both playgrounds still under repair and not available for use. Both morning and afternoon breaks were omitted and joined on to the dinner hour. Children who took a packed lunch were taken each day to the recreation ground by two teachers. One week later, one playground was available for use, playtime being taken in two sections to avoid accidents with Juniors and Infants. But the Managers were unhappy with the work that was carried out, and the resurfacing had to be repeated the following year.

The Curriculum

Once the school had become a primary school, with the children of the top three classes being educated at Blackminster, certain elements of the curriculum, such as Woodwork, Cookery and Geometry, disappeared.

The core subjects of the curriculum carried on as normal with the tried and tested means that Mr Amos had introduced since becoming Head in 1913. After the implementation of the 1944 Education Act, changes began to take place in the primary school curriculum which were taken forward by the new Headteachers. For example, in June 1945, the County Drama Adviser visited the school and outlined his ideas of dramatic expression and creative work with junior children.

Schools' broadcasting was being expanded and, to be able to tune into the programmes, the school acquired its own wireless in April 1940.

As a result of the 1944 Act, religious education was made compulsory in every school for the first time, the only part of the curriculum actually set down by law. Furthermore, "the school day ... shall begin with collective worship on the part of all pupils"; thus the religious assembly became familiar in the school experience. Yet, in reality, the school world, like society about it, was to be increasingly secular in post-war years.

Examinations and Scholarships

Throughout the Second World War, Badsey children continued to do well in the secondary selection tests. The last group of children to be admitted to Prince Henry's Grammar School under the "free place" scheme was the cohort of 1944, which included ten-year-olds Terry Sparrow and Brian Jennings, plus seven 11-year-olds. The rest of the children went to Blackminster Senior School, except for the few whose parents paid for them to attend the grammar school.

Arrangements were made for the evacuated children to take the secondary schools' entrance examination of their home area in Badsey. Thus Pamela Harvey (daughter of future Headteacher Maurice Harvey, who had come to Badsey with the Handsworth evacuees) took the Birmingham Entrance exam and Helen Eckles, who lived with her aunt, Mrs Emms (née Crane), took the Metropolitan Evacuating Area examination. Both girls passed and started at Prince Henry's Grammar School, Evesham, in September 1944, together with Valerie Davies, one of the Barnardo's girls.

By 1945, as a result of the 1944 Education Act, all places were free at the Grammar School. Children were selected by means of the "11+" as it quickly became known.

Prize-Giving

A prize-giving was held as usual in November 1939 but, because of war-time restrictions, it was the last one for six years. Mr Goode,

Headmaster of Handsworth New Road Senior Boys' School, presented the prizes. All the Managers were present, including 98-year old Mr Mustoe. Mr Amos congratulated Mr Mustoe on being able to be present at the function and also thanked the Managers for their support in his attempts to run the school on sound educational lines during difficult times. Mr Binyon spoke of the school's progress and achievements, mentioning the sorrow they felt in the great loss to the school of Miss McDonald's services and recalled the difference in the attitude and outlook of the Managers at the present time compared with that of the time when he was first appointed Manager of the School.

The first post-war prize-giving ceremony was held in December 1945. Prizes were comparatively few in number owing to the high prices of books, and were entirely provided by the Managers. The format was the same as for the pre-war years, with Mr Binyon presiding, songs by various classes, parents of prize-winners being invited, and a tea for Managers at the end of the ceremony. A House system was introduced in 1946, to encourage children to perform well in work and in sport, and to get points for good behaviour. The houses were named after local hills: Cotswold, Malvern, Bredon and Abberley.

School Hours and Holidays

At the beginning of 1946, the school times were fixed at 9.15-12.15 for the morning session and 1.30-4 for the afternoon session. In the case of the afternoon session, the bell was rung at 3.55 to give time for the children from Wickhamford to catch the bus at 4 pm.

The Mop Fair and the Flower Show were suspended during war-time. On the occasion of the post-war revival of Evesham Mop, the school was closed early on the first Friday in October 1945 to obviate unnecessary absence, but this was the last year that special arrangements were made. Likewise, the Flower Show was revived in 1947, but it had moved to a Saturday in 1937, so there was no need for a day's holiday.

A special half-holiday was granted on 31st March 1943 when the children were given the afternoon off to commemorate Mr Amos' 30 years as Headteacher of the school. The school was also closed for two days, 8th and 9th May 1945, which were national holidays for thanksgiving and celebration of the Allied Victory in Europe. A holiday was granted on 20th November 1947, at the request of King George VI, on the occasion of the wedding of the heir apparent, Princess Elizabeth.

Attendance

Within a month of war breaking out, a chickenpox epidemic had spread through the village. This was followed by very severe weather in January and February 1940 which accounted for poor attendance. "The most terrible winter weather that we have ever experienced has caused a very bad attendance during the past week," wrote Mr Amos on 2nd

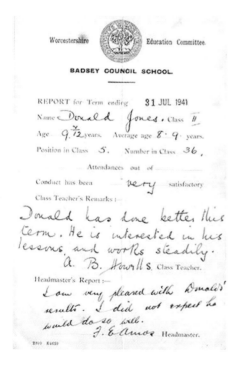

School report for Donald Jones, a private evacuee. Donald Jones' daughter had no idea that her father had attended school in Badsey until after he died, when the school report came to light.

February; about 40% of the children were absent. Mrs Howells was unable to get to school on Monday and Mr Harvey could not get there until Thursday owing to the state of the roads and railways. Mr Amos, who prided himself on the excellent attendance records of the school, noted, "Owing to epidemics and the terrible weather, the attendance for the past two quarters has been very poor, only 88% and 85% respectively instead of the more usual 95%."

In order to achieve the compulsory 400 openings during the school year 1939-1940, the Easter vacation was taken in two parts. As the school had been closed for six days at the outbreak of war, and Easter occurred very early in 1940, school resumed on Wednesday 27th March 1940. The Easter vacation was continued at the beginning of April once a new school year had been started.

On one day in January 1942, 119 children were absent because of heavy snowfall or mumps, attendance being just 41%. On an equally bad day in January 1945, Mr West, the new Headmaster, had a bad start. The attendance was down to 49% and Mr Binyon, the Chairman of Managers, visited the school, concerned about attendance.

Whilst there were some extremely harsh winters during the war-time years, the school appears to have been closed only once because of the weather. This was in January 1941 when less than half the children attended owing to the heavy snowfall, and those who came had their milk at 11 o'clock and then went home. Closures did occur three times during this period, however, either because of boiler problems or lack of fuel.

School Health Service

During the war the normal doctor, nurse, dentist and oculist visits were maintained. Mr Binyon often assisted by undertaking the weighing and measuring and testing of the eyes of the children to be medically examined. Physically, children benefited from the expansion of medical services in war-time. Fear of epidemics following bombing led to diphtheria vaccination of nearly seven million children, which soon reduced deaths. Joan Martin recalls that they were marched, class by class, to Blackminster to have the inoculation.

Meal-Times

During war-time, as in previous years, the majority of children went home for their midday meal, except those who lived some way distant from the school. From February 1945, those children who stayed for lunch were given a cup of cocoa. This was a precursor to the provision of midday meals. The previous year, preliminary talks had begun taking place about providing meals and the alterations that would be necessary at the school. Plans were drawn up in 1945 for a scullery, with rooms and classes being rearranged to make the Hall (the former Handicrafts Centre) into the Dining Room and the classroom next-door into a scullery.

To begin with, in order to get the scheme up and running, meals were provided only for those children who lived at a distance. On 27th March 1946, 52 children from the outlying areas received a midday meal. Miss Lloyd of the Worcestershire County Council staff and Miss Storey of the Blackminster Central Kitchen, were in charge of arrangements. By November, the school meal service had been extended in scope and included all children who wished to take midday meals at school. Roughly three-quarters of the total children in school were present at the first school meal when Badsey children were included. Meals were cooked off-site at the central kitchen at Blackminster School and delivered daily in large aluminium containers.

Work at last began on the scullery in January 1947. As the contractors were still at work at the beginning of the spring term, the Hall was not available for PE activities and no school meals could be served in the Hall until the end of the month.

Blizzard conditions in March 1947 meant private transport had to be arranged to transport the school meals, obtained through the kindness of Littleton & Badsey Grower officials. Even that was not possible by the end of the week, and so no school meals were provided.

Outings

Generally speaking, school trips were not a possibility during the war. However, in April 1945, shortly before the end of the war, the school choir was able to attend a Musical Festival held at Worcester, organised by the County Federation of Women's Institutes for Women's Institutes and School Choirs.

In May 1946, the school's first-ever residential trip took place at Wilderhope Manor Youth Hostel, near Much Wenlock in Shropshire. Mr West and Mrs Woodward, together with two adult assistants, went for five days with a party of 23 children from Class 1. Miss Smith was in charge of the school during the Headmaster's absence. Mobility during war-time had been very restricted so for children who had never previously been to school in peace-time, a trip to Shropshire, with the opportunity to stay away from home, seemed like going to the ends of the earth.

Extra-Curricular Activities

The first school Harvest Festival was introduced by Mr West in October 1945. A large collection of produce was received and was distributed among all the hospitals in Evesham. The decorations and arrangements were made by Mrs Woodward and Class 1. The Managers and former members of staff attended. The Harvest Festival has been an annual event in the school calendar ever since.

In July 1946, a music festival was held at Blackminster School. An Infant and a Junior choir, each of 30 children, attended. This was the start of an annual event that was to last until 1971.

No mention was made of Christmas festivities during Mr Amos' final years at the school, but in 1944, under the temporary Headteacher, Lower School and Upper School Christmas parties were held. Christmas parties were a regular feature from then on and, in 1945, under Mr West, a Christmas concert was given consisting of plays, songs and dances prepared by various classes of the school. The

Above: May 1946, top class children on an outing to Stokesay Castle, Shropshire, during a four-night trip to Wilderhope Manor Youth Hostel.

Below: Another outing in May 1946. Mrs Woodward (formerly Miss Bird) at Stokesay Castle with the 12 girls who went on the trip to Shropshire. Back row: Mrs Woodward, Brenda Tomkins, Angela Smith, Emmeline Sheward. Middle row: Hazel Barrand, Jean Jelfs, Greta Cole, Lynda Hewlett. Front row: Sheila Griffiths, Gillian Bennett, Betty Johnson, Jane Collett, Shirley Evans.

children concluded the term by assembling for a Carol service.

Getting to School

For years there had been no provision for the Wickhamford children to get to Badsey School but, early in 1939, a bus was provided. This was short-lived, however, because as soon as war broke out, the bus was stopped and they had to walk. Joan Martin, who lived at Pitchers Hill and had started at school in the summer term of 1939, recalls that her mother was not best pleased as the bus was stopped without notice and she had to stop her work and accompany them to school to explain why they were late. After that, the children walked on their own, but occasionally, if the weather was bad, Joan's father would take them to school as he was a Market Gardener and had petrol. He had a little Morris 8 and all the children used to crowd in, perhaps eight or nine of them. Mr Amos used to remark, "Mr Martin, I don't know how you get all those children in."

At the end of the war, attempts were made to provide a bus from the school after the afternoon session for taking the children to Wickhamford; but the LEA's response was that the children lived well within the legal distance for walking to and from the school, so they would not make any provision. However, a bus to and from Wickhamford was in operation by the beginning of 1946, as the school times were fixed specifically to coincide with the bus timetable.

Most of the staff lived locally, but Mrs Howells lived in Worcester and came by train and bike. Don Hartwell, a former pupil of the school, was working by this time at Littleton & Badsey Station, and would get her bike ready for her when she got off the train and, on one occasion, mended a puncture.

Non-Teaching Staff

The caretakers during most of this period remained as Mr & Mrs Keen. Under a new scheme introduced in January 1948, Mr Keen was appointed sole caretaker.

Mr Amos had no clerical assistance during his time at the school, but this was remedied under Mr West's headship. Representation was made to the LEA, and it was agreed that provision could be made on a part-time basis in connection with school records, distribution of milk and school meals. The first assistant is unknown, but when Mr Harvey became Headteacher, his wife performed the tasks.

Managers

During a period of great change, the school benefited from having a stable Managing Body. Mr Binyon had been a Manager since 1902, Mr Mustoe since 1908, Mr Swift since 1921, Mr Knight since 1929, and Mr Jones and Mrs Carter since 1934. Mr Mustoe celebrated his 100th birthday on 19th October 1941 and was sent a letter of congratulations by the children. Mr Mustoe died in August 1944, aged 102. In his will, Mr Mustoe bequeathed four religious pictures to the school. He was replaced as Manager by Mr Samuel Johns, a former old boy of the school.

The End of the Council School

Social reform became a secondary consequence of the war. It was "a time for revolutions, not for patching" noted Sir William Beveridge. In this spirit, the Board of Education planned a reformed education service. R A Butler, the President of the Board, prepared a White Paper, "Educational Reconstruction", out of which emerged the Education Act of August 1944. The President now became Minister of Education and was given more power to direct and control development. LEAs were reformed to minimise their differences; each LEA had to survey local need and submit reorganisation plans to the Ministry. Thus, in January 1947, the Managers were sent a copy of the Education Development Plan for the Evesham District, which said that Badsey Council School should be maintained as a mixed primary school providing for a one-form entry of juniors and infants of age-range 5-11.

Mr Harvey and some of the girls'
hockey team 1967 (left, Yvonne Syril;
bottom, Jane Parriss).

7

BADSEY COUNTY PRIMARY SCHOOL 1948-1975

Primary schools were formally established by the 1944 Education Act and in April 1948 the name of the school changed to Badsey County Primary School. As far as the children were concerned, this had little impact, but the old order of things was changing and, in the post-war reconstruction, changes began to be made nationwide. When the school opened for the summer term on 13th April 1948, Badsey County Primary School had 195 children on the roll. Over the next 25 years, the number was to rise by 50%.

The Headteacher

Badsey County Primary School began its life with Maurice Harvey as Acting Headteacher. His position as Headteacher was not made permanent until January 1951. During his tenure, he had the honour to be appointed President of the County Board of the NUT in 1961 for a year. During the 1960s, Mr Harvey had periods of illness during which time Miss Smith was in charge of the school. After a second heart attack in June 1967, he decided to retire at the end of the year. Miss Smith did not wish to take on the responsibility of Acting Head so an external person, Mrs J Dipple, was appointed to the post of Acting Head during Mr Harvey's absence in the autumn term.

The person who replaced Mr Harvey was Hugh Chaplin, formerly Headteacher of Madresfield School. Mr Chaplin took over the headship of Badsey County Primary School in January 1968 with 287 children on roll, the highest number in the school's history to that date. During his headship, he was for a time President of Evesham & District Association and Vice-President of the County Federation of Headteachers. Mr Chaplin, too, suffered from ill-health during the final years of his tenure, which necessitated a supply Headteacher for a term, but he was able to return to work for a few more years before retirement.

Teaching Staff

The staff in the first years of the County Primary School were, in addition to the Head: Mrs Woodward, Mr Jackson, Mrs Howells, Mrs Hodgetts, Miss Smith and Miss Hartwell. By 1950, an extra teacher was required. This was agreed to, and Miss C Hughes, an emergency-trained teacher, was appointed to take Class 4. Mrs Hodgetts, formerly teacher of Class 4, started work in the Hall with a newly-formed Transition Class. (A shortage of teachers nationwide had been foreseen in war-time, and an emergency training scheme was launched in 1943, which produced about 35,000 teachers by 1951.)

The school saw several changes in 1951. Firstly, Mrs Howells, who had joined the staff at the start of the war, retired. Then, at the end of the summer term, the school said goodbye to Miss Hartwell and Mrs Woodward (formerly Miss Bird) who, between them, had a combined service of over 90 years. Other staff came and went, but the teachers who were at the school for ten years or more during this time included Mrs Eileen Peet, Mrs Julie Williams, Mrs Sylvia Gorin and Mrs Phyllis Churchill. In the later years of the County Primary School and leading into the First School years, Mrs Jean James, Mrs Pat Gorin, Mrs Joyce Watkin and Mr David Dodridge were long-serving

members of staff.

Under the terms of the new Burnham Report, a hierarchy of senior posts within schools was introduced, attracting extra funding. From 1956, the school was entitled to the post of Deputy Headteacher, the allowance being £80 for a man or £64 for a woman (equal pay for men and women was not achieved until the 1970s). Miss Smith was given the job but the Managers were unsuccessful in their claim for a further "graded" post. The issue concerning graded posts rumbled on until 1967. Due to a misinterpretation in the District Clerk's Office, it was discovered that a graded post should have been awarded to the school in 1964. Mr David Miller, the teacher of the top class, was awarded a graded post as from 1st April 1967. But it had come too late. He had already been offered and accepted a graded post at a school in Redditch as from September. The person who succeeded him was Mr George

Opposite above: School staff, about 1954-1956. Back row: Mr Norman Owens, Miss Norah Smith, Mr William Hunt. Front row: Mrs Eileen Peet, Miss Pat Barnard, Mr Maurice Harvey, Mrs Beryl Osborne, Mrs Sylvia Gorin.

Opposite below: School staff, April 1969. Back row: Mr Tony Barry, Miss Norah Smith, Mrs Phyllis Churchill, Mrs Pat Gorin, Mrs Joyce Watkin, Mr Stan Banks. Front row: Mr George McGowan, Mrs Jean James, Miss Cheryl Price, Mr Hugh Chaplin.

Left: Mr Harry Hilton Jackson ("Jacko"), who taught at the school 1948-1953. He had served in the Forces during the war and loved recounting his war exploits. David Miller (pupil 1948-1950 and later a teacher), hero-worshipped him. On arriving home from school his father would say, "Well, son, how did old Jacko win the war today?"

Above: Class 1, Mrs Williams' class, 1963. Back row: Mr Maurice Harvey, Heather Davis, Brian Knight, John Pipcin, John Meadows, Christopher Jordan, Alan Clements, Hazel Whiting, Gillian Redgewell, Richard Austin, Mrs Julie Williams. Second row: Anita Bowley, Melvin Hall, David Webb, Paul Halford, John Hewlett, Godfrey Nicholls, Stewart Hilland, Barbara Lord, Martin Bent. Third row: Isabelle Gresty, Gillian Sutton, Roger Hartwell, Nigel Beasley, Ronald Knight, Julie Brown, Rosalind Grinnell, Jane Begley, David Smith, Mary Braby, Carol Marshall. Front row: William Griffiths, Anthony Bennett, Stephen Hemming, Clifford Davies, Christopher Cox, Philip Sutton, John Hall, William Daffurn.

McGowan, whose wife, Marion, later taught at the school, and whose children attended the school, son Alistair later becoming a famous television personality and impressionist.

The staff maintained a strict discipline regime in the early years of the County Primary School. Corporal punishment continued at the school until the mid 1960s, with the Headteacher's cane reserved for the worst offenders. Will Dallimore had occasion to remember the cane when Mr Harvey took exception to a piece of "rude" poetry he had written. This obviously did not dampen his literary ambitions as he is now the sponsor of the Literature Cup at Badsey Flower Show! One teacher was renowned for using a plimsoll across the back of the legs to instil discipline and enforce law and order. John Hewlett recalls an occasion in the early 1960s when she

Opposite above: Class 2, Mrs Peet's Class, 1963. Can you spot the future Headteacher? Back row: Mrs Peet, Margaret Tyszkow, Lynn Sharpe, Chris Haile, Richard Underhill, Linda Plant, Diane Norledge. Second row: Leslie Jinks, Richard Syril, Timothy Spragg, Pauline Brazier, Janet Allchurch, Michael Clements, Ian Smith. Third row: Ronald Anderson, Sally Hewlett, Cheryl Watts, Roger Keen, Elizabeth Wheatley, Penny Nicholls, Jonathan Hardiman. Front row: Diane Bennett, Graham Keen, Glyn Dennick, Peter Lord, Angela Dallimore, Wendy Moran, Jacqueline Hardwick.

Opposite below: Miss Smith's Class, 1963. Back row: Linda Turley, Susan Knight, Susan Brazier, Ian Hardwick, Jennifer Pipcin, Robert Lake, Alan Padfield, Philip Gresty, Shirley Stewart, Miss Smith. Second row: Karen Woodcock, Martin Osborne, Stephen Jones, Lyndon Bowley, Rosemarie Ellison, Jane Parriss, Celia Nicholls, John Merriman. Third row: Rachel Jones, -, Stephen Lippett, -, Stephen Webb, Jackie Begley, Jane Goldstraw, -. Front row: Patty Sutton, Denise Hewlett, David Wheatley, Kim Strangwood, Andrew West, John Dallimore, David Turner, Shirley Camden.

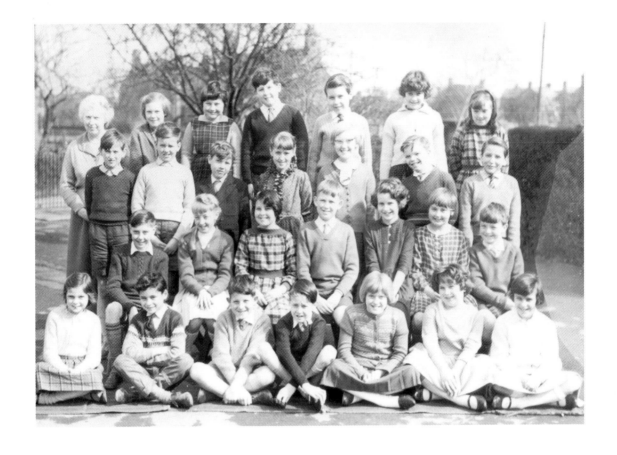

lined up a dozen boys for treatment with the slipper after a session of stuffing new-mown grass up jumpers and down shirts got out of hand! Whilst corporal punishment was not officially banned in English schools until 1986, Badsey, in common with the majority of primary schools, relinquished the cane some 20 years earlier.

Admissions

By 1949, with 225 on roll, the school was beginning to feel overcrowded. In those days, there was no specific published admissions number but the County Inspector's advice was that numbers per class should not exceed 40 if possible, giving a total of 240 in six classes. If numbers increased and the accommodation became difficult, an additional classroom should be requested. The national birth-rate had been in decline before the war but this situation changed with the post-war "bulge". Crowded schools were a problem everywhere, with classes of over 40 being common well into the 1960s; certainly at Badsey there was at least one class with 46 children.

The issue of overcrowding was compounded by the fact that 50 new houses were being built at Green Leys. The Assistant Director of Education visited the school in November 1953. Whilst he agreed with the desirability of having an additional classroom, he felt that Badsey did not have first priority at that time, but the position must be watched in view of local housing development. By the following year, the need for an additional classroom was recognised as the most urgent case in the district.

In 1954, with 270 on roll, Mr Harvey had to refuse admission to at least 15 children whose families lived out of catchment. For some years, it had been the practice for some children from Cleeve Prior, Evesham, Honeybourne, Sedgeberrow, Offenham and the Littletons to attend the school. For the next six years, a ban was imposed on admission of children from outside the normal catchment area.

By 1960, the post-war baby boom was beginning to recede and the passing out of one of the "bulge groups" in the Junior School

1965, Mrs Goldstraw and her newly-opened nursery with two of her own children and three neighbouring children: David Goldstraw, Sally Hardiman, Jane Goldstraw, James Hardiman, Judith Hardiman.

and consequent drop in numbers, meant that there was even a consideration of staff reduction. By 1964, however, more new houses were being built resulting in increased numbers and Mr Harvey again had to restrict new admissions to catchment-area children. The numbers continued to rise, exceeding the 300 figure for the first time in the summer term 1970. The LEA kept a watchful eye on the school situation in relation to possible future growth of the village, but by then plans were already afoot to change the age-range of the school, thus deferring the issue.

Children were admitted to school on attaining the age of five, mid-term admissions being allowed. It was not until September 1958 that "rising fives" were admitted (children who were to attain the age of five in the forthcoming term). As children were not able to start school until they were five, there was a crying need for an improvement in nursery education. The Plowden Report of 1967 highlighted two factors: a growing appreciation, learned from psychologists, of the vital importance of the infant years on a child's intellectual development, and the ever-growing tendency for married women to go out to work. Mrs Pat Goldstraw (née Barnard), a former pupil and teacher at the school, had already perceived a need and started a nursery school in the grounds of her home at Chalcroft, Old Post Office Lane (a site now occupied by houses at the end of The Lanketts). For over 20 years it catered for the needs of the pre-school child.

Classrooms

The school was bulging at the seams and other work-places had to be utilised, which in the 1950s included the parish room at the side of the old Vicarage. The top class girls used it for Needlework, whilst two classes used it when they had to vacate their rooms in preparation for dinner. The garden of Field Cottage, opposite the old Vicarage, and home to Norbert, Christopher and Clara Tucker, was used occasionally for Art classes in the late 1950s and early 1960s.

In 1966, Mr Harvey vacated the School House prior to his retirement the following year. As the house was not needed as a residence until Mr Chaplin started in 1968, it was used for extra teaching accommodation. Mrs Pat Gorin recalls doing artwork with the boys in the School House. There was nowhere to display the work, so she used to hang it from the picture rails in the bedroom.

The Plowden Report of 1967 surveyed progress in primary school education since the war. The most important advance was a reduction in the size of classes, ensuring that primary school children were taught in classes of fewer than 40 pupils. It was in 1967 that an unofficial group of parents banded together to put pressure on the Managers concerning the issue of overcrowding. The Managers were able to reassure the parents that they were aware of the overcrowding and had been continually pressing for extra accommodation and that approval had been given for an extra classroom. In the event, two mobile classrooms were acquired, thus placating all concerned. They were erected on the school field and brought in to use in February 1968. These were seen as a temporary measure, but they continued in use for the next 25 years.

Because of lack of classroom space and the need to reduce class sizes, Mrs Pat Gorin, who began working at the school in 1967, did not initially have responsibility for a class. Instead she took groups of children and taught them in an open area off the Hall, where the office is now situated. This area was partly enclosed in 1969 when a wood and glass screen was fitted to exclude draughts. In December 1973 the area was closed off completely to make an enclosed room for use as a library, student teacher practice groups, medical inspections, and work with small groups of children.

Premises

When peace came in 1945, there were immense problems with putting the 1944 Education Act into effect. The 1945 Building regulations set ambitious standards: kitchens, specialist rooms and playing-fields were now essentials. By contrast, a 1948 survey described inadequate buildings left from the past: "two-storey red-brick buildings, whose architects, uncertain as to whether their model schemes should be a church, a barracks, or a railway-station, created something solid, serviceable and ugly."

The Assistant Director of Education met the Managers in April 1955. Whilst he agreed that a school of Badsey's size should possess a school hall and that the school needed the extra accommodation, he could not promise when the work would be carried out because of more urgent cases in the county. Work eventually began in January 1958. The whole of the playground used by girls and infants was placed out of use. Entrance to the school was confined to the boys' playground and during the building operations all the children played together in the boys' playground. The new extensions comprising Hall, Kitchen, Infant toilets and Staffroom were completed in October 1958 and were officially opened at the Prize-Giving Ceremony the next month, when all the school was able to be in attendance.

Having acquired the new extension in 1958, which included infant toilets, the Managers felt that the boys' and girls' toilets (which were still the original external block built when the school was erected in 1895) ought to be rebuilt

Performers, 1962. Back row: Roger Keen, Robert Bindoff, Peter Lord, Paul Harvey, Michael Jones, Richard Underhill. Front row: Elizabeth Wheatley, Diane Norledge, Jacqueline Hardwick, Susan Hewlett, Elizabeth Hall, Wendy Moran, Pauline Brazier, Sally Hewlett, Anne Morcombe, Cheryl Watts. Note the original boundary wall with a breach to the right permitting access to the newly-acquired playing-field. Three years later the wall was lowered to 15" and covered with a smooth cement finish to form a seat. The present Head plans to remove it altogether.

Successful candidates in the 11+ exam, 1965, who went on either to Prince Henry's Grammar School or the technical stream of Evesham Secondary School. Back row: Mark Norledge, Betty Cleaver, Simon Page, Stephen Churchley. Front row: Sara Kitcher, Clara Tucker, Valerie Davies. Note the lowered boundary wall and fixed agility apparatus to the left.

and converted to an internal sanitary block, but money was not forthcoming. The unsatisfactory nature of the situation was brought home in January 1963 during one of the coldest winters on record. The playgrounds were full of deep snow-drifts preventing any outdoor play and, apart from visits to outside toilets, the children were in school all day including the dinner break.

Further representation was made to the LEA for the provision of indoor toilets both from the point of view of hygiene and weather conditions. The response was initially in the negative, but at last approval was given for a Junior toilet block which was completed in September 1965 at the rear of the Main Hall.

Meanwhile, the fabric of the rest of the school was allowed to deteriorate. During the war, little or no maintenance had been carried out, and for the next 40 or so years, the continuing theme was lack of money for annual repairs.

Playgrounds and Playing-fields

During the summer holidays 1948, both playgrounds were resurfaced and were in much better condition having fallen into bad repair during the war years. In the post-war years, an increasing volume of traffic meant that safety precautions had to be put in place in the school playground. Delivery vans entered the east playground via gates in front of the School House and it became necessary to place a notice on the gate warning drivers that permission must be obtained before entering the playground in school hours.

In 1953, money was made available by the Ministry of Education from a Coronation Grant of £25 to provide seats in the boys' and girls' playgrounds. Four teak-wood seats were fixed in the boys' playground and three in the girls' playground. With the balance of money left over, a clock for the Hall was provided.

In the meantime, negotiations for a playing-field progressed slowly. At a Managers' meeting in April 1949, it was agreed to ask the LEA to designate the land at the back of the school on both sides of the public footpath for educational use. In the Worcestershire Development Plan, 1951, 3.5 acres of land were designated for compulsory acquisition under the Town and Country Planning Act 1947.

By January 1957, the portion of land to the north of the footpath, amounting to 0.47 acres, had been acquired. A further 1.87 acres of land, to the south of the footpath, was bought in January 1961, thus making a total of 2.34 acres. Land originally designated to the west was never acquired and a strip of land to the extreme east was also left for building houses on Willersey Road. The vendor was Mrs W J Smith, the daughter of Mr V Cockerton who had begun the original negotiations with the Authority. The public footpath which crossed the land was closed, the ground was levelled and grass seed was sown during the October half-term holiday. "The weather has been ideal for the task and the soil was in a fine tilth," wrote Mr Harvey. "No appreciable rain has fallen for many weeks. A few hours after the seed was sown a steady rain persisted and over half an inch of rain was recorded." Thus, by the time school reopened on 6th November, there was an excellent germination of grass seeds resulting in a fine green carpet of grass on the new playing-field.

Curriculum

An HMI report of 1950 commented that much of the teaching and some of the schemes of work followed traditional, rather formal lines, and that the selection examination influenced the outlook of the school unduly; but many aspects of the work were deemed very satisfactory, notably Religious Instruction, Music, Drama, Arithmetic, Needlework, Choral Speech and History.

Teaching continued along fairly formal lines

Mrs Williams and class, 1961, displaying skirts made for the Flower Show: Ann Sutton, Bess Priest, Penelope Betteridge, Irene Thomas, -, Ann Meadows, Yvonne Smith, Anne Butler, Rosemary Tucker, Rosalind Bannister, Judith Byron. Until 1969, Needlework was taught as a separate subject but from then on it was taught as a class topic in an integrated approach to Art and Craft without separation of boys and girls.

until the late 1960s. The Plowden Report of 1967 espoused child-centred approaches and the concept of informal education, together with flexibility of internal organisation, was introduced. Other factors also contributed to a more humanist approach: the liberal attitudes of the 1960s, full employment, relative affluence and a decline in the inspectorial role of HMI. As a result, Badsey's teachers (particularly the younger ones fresh from the training colleges of the 1960s), in common with schools everywhere, began to explore new methods of teaching. "Creative writing" in English written work, experiments in mathematics and the adoption of discovery methods in elementary science studies became common.

In 1970, the school acquired its first television, with rental funded by the Parent Teacher Association (PTA). There was a growing number of programmes for schools which were used to enhance the curriculum.

Physical Exercise

One of the factors of post-war education was the physical well-being of schoolchildren. Once the school had its own playing-field, it was possible to hold a school sports day, the first one being held in June 1962. The weather was fine and a large gathering of parents and other visitors together with Managers were able to enjoy the 33 events which took place. A special House Trophy for Athletic Events was provided by the Chairman of Managers, Mrs D Carter, and was won by Abberley House. In order to stimulate competition, a House system had been introduced in the dying days of the Council School, and became pre-eminent during the County Primary School years. There were four houses, named after the surrounding hills: Cotswold, Malvern, Abberley and Bredon.

The football team continued to do well, winning the majority of its matches against schools such as Bretforton, Bengeworth and Swan Lane. There were also House Matches. The girls played hockey, playing against Swan Lane or The Littletons, and were normally unbeaten. Throughout the 1970s, Mrs James was the hockey coach. One match against

Littleton in September 1971 resulted in a 19-1 victory for Badsey.

In May 1958, fixed agility apparatus consisting of gym bars, parallel bars and climbing frame was installed in the playground. To begin with the outside apparatus was restricted to class Physical Training lessons, but when the children were familiar with its use, an extension of use was permitted. Many considered the equipment to be dangerous, but it was not removed until 1981.

Swimming lessons at the pool on Common Road, Evesham, were introduced from 1957. Later, swimming instruction took place in a school pool behind the Roman Catholic Church in Evesham. Mrs James, who taught at the school from 1967, and Mrs Harvey, the wife of the former Headteacher, assisted with swimming.

Examinations

Following the 1944 Education Act, the children in the top class sat the Secondary Selection

Report for Robert Bennett, 1967. The report form had changed little in 40 years, the main amendment being in 1963 when the LEA asked for "Position in Form" to be removed.

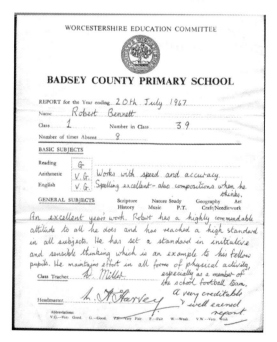

Top: Swimming lesson at the old Evesham swimming pool, Common Road. A board on the side of the pool gave the water temperature – generally about 12°C as the pool was not heated. The changing rooms, a long row of exterior cubicles running down the side of the pool, can be seen on the left-hand side. The teachers never entered the water but instructed from the poolside. "I never did learn to swim. I wonder why?" remarked Will Dallimore, a pupil at the school from 1955-1961.

Middle: Hockey Team, 1972. Staff at back: Mr Hugh Chaplin and Mrs Jean James. Back row: Michelle Ford, Marilyn Bennett, Sally Bindoff, Angela Hughes, Sharon Westmacott, Anna Olender. Front row: Sandra Taylor, Nicola Cleaver, Liz Goldstraw, Sylvia Stewart, Veronica Dore.

Below: Football Team, 1966-67 Season. Staff at back: Mr David Miller, Mr Maurice Harvey. Back row: Tim Franklin, Moray Porter, Robert Bennett, Malcolm Turley, Peter Jepson, Stephen Knight, Robert Hemming. Front row: Raymond Harris, Stephen Sunley, Colin Smith, James Hardiman, Clifford Gottfried.

Examination (commonly known as "the 11+") in February for entry to the Grammar School in September. There was also selection for the technical stream at the County Secondary School in Evesham. Those children who were unsuccessful went to Blackminster.

The Managers noted in May 1960 that they were pleased to learn that seven children had been selected for admission to Prince Henry's Grammar School. However, they were curiously silent when the results were not so good. In the early 1950s, the number of children attending the Grammar School ranged from 20% to 28%, but things took a downward turn from 1958 when only 12% passed and then 8% the following year. The results in 1960 represented 14%, hence the Managers' favourable comments. The results varied a great deal during the 1960s, reaching a low point in 1964, when only two children out of a year-group of 45 attended the Grammar School.

The final year of the 11+ examination was in 1972. The county was moving towards comprehensive education with no selection. As an interim measure, in 1973 and 1974 there was an unselected intake to Blackminster School at age 11, prior to the changeover in 1975 when the school became a First School and pupils transferred at 10 to Blackminster.

Prize-Giving

Each November or December, the Annual Prize Day was held, with a guest of honour presenting the prizes. In the 1950s, these included Mr George Churchill, Director of Education for Northamptonshire, and a former pupil of the school, Mr Ronald West, a former Headteacher at Badsey, and Mrs Laurence Binyon, Mr Binyon's sister-in-law and widow of the well-known poet.

The Annual Prize Distribution which took place in 1958 was held in the new school hall on 26th November. Mr Harvey, in his report, pointed out that it was 30 years since the last extension. "The provision of the new hall does not in any way make this a better school," he said in his address. "It does, however, give all of the children and staff the opportunity to

Above: Village clubs and individuals gave House trophies: Mrs Carter, Chairman of Managers, presented a trophy to be awarded on sports day; former pupil, Gladys Barnard, who played hockey for England, donated a cup for hockey; there was also the Sears Football Cup and the Badsey Cricket Club trophy.

Below: A typical Prize-Giving programme, 1965.

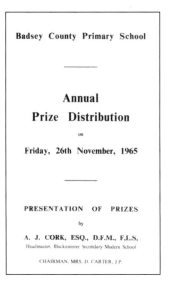

Badsey County Primary School

Annual
Prize Distribution
on
Friday, 26th November, 1965

PRESENTATION OF PRIZES
by
A. J. CORK, ESQ., D.F.M., F.L.S,
Headmaster, Blackminster Secondary Modern School

CHAIRMAN, MRS. D. CARTER, J.P.

make it a better school and the responsibility to do so. It is what goes on within the school, its day-to-day life, that sets the standards. Fine buildings do not necessarily mean a fine school. I am sure it will be the aim of staff and children to make full use of the additional facility and improved working conditions." Mr Binyon, the Chairman, said that he had grown up with the school and, having worked with the last four Headmasters, he was sure that Badsey School had been fortunate in their

Above left: Bronze statue of the Roman god, Mercury, donated to the school in 1952 as a House trophy by Mr C E Miller, Headmaster of Prince Henry's Grammar School, whose sons, Martin and John, attended Badsey School. The House system was discontinued in 1981 and the trophy only came to light over 20 years later when the school attic was being extended.

Above right: Annual Prize-Giving, 1958, the first public function in the new School Hall. For the first time, it was possible to accommodate the whole school (265 on roll). Note the serving hatch where school dinners were served from the kitchen which is now a classroom. Note also the House trophy on the right. Teachers at back are: Mrs Gorin, Mrs Williams, Mrs Peet and Mr Hunt.

Below: Prize-winners at the Annual Prize-Giving, 1961. Back row: Carol Stewart, -, Linda Baron, Susan Lake, John Lake, Maureen Lewis, David Partridge, Christopher Harwood, Ian Major, Nigel Hurman, Clifford Hartwell, Francis Keen. Middle row: Margaret Bent, David Stewart, Mary Braby, Allan Clements, Timothy Harrison, Irene Thompson, Penelope Betteridge, Rosemary Tucker, Mark Norledge, -, Alan Reeves, -. Front row: Jean Taylor, Timothy Bell, Rosalind Grinnell, Elizabeth Hall, Susan Hewlett, Jacqueline Hardwick, Margaret Tyszkow, Stephen Churchley, Valerie Davies, Clara Tucker, Rosalind Bannister.

selection. He was struck by the pride and interest shown by old scholars in their old school, a spirit that still continued and was a healthy sign of school life.

Mr Binyon died in 1963 and a prize was awarded each year in his memory. But prize-giving was not to continue for much longer, and the last ceremony was held in 1968.

School Hours and Holidays

In 1959, the school hours were changed to 9.15 – 12.15 and 1.35 – 4.05 (Infants 3.50), because of problems with the lateness of the Wickhamford bus. Mr Harvey felt this was a great improvement as the Wickhamford children were then in time for morning assembly. The hours were further revised in 1968 to reduce the Infant day to 5 hours, leaving the Junior day at 5½ hours.

The school holidays were more or less as we know them today, with extra holidays on special occasions such as the Silver Wedding of King George VI in April 1948, the Coronation of Queen Elizabeth II in June 1953, the wedding of Princess Margaret in May 1960, the wedding of Princess Anne in 1973. For most of its existence, the school had closed for one day on Ascension Day, but 1951 was the last year that it happened.

Before the war, it had been rare for people to go away on holiday, but this became more common in the 1950s. In September 1953, Mr Harvey reported that quite a number of children were absent on holiday with their parents as this was the chief summer month for gardeners to have the opportunity to leave their crops.

Closures

Despite the severe winters of 1962 and 1963, the school remained open, thanks to the dedication of the Caretaker, Mr Hall. However, heavy snowfall in February 1969 caused flooding in three classrooms from melting snow. As the heating was not working in the two new classrooms and these classes had had to relocate to the main building, it was necessary to send all the children home.

The industrial disputes of the early 1970s had an impact on the school. The coal-miners' national strike of February 1972 caused the school to be closed on one or two days because of power cuts. Each area of the country was given a designated "high risk day" for power cuts. For Badsey it was Tuesday and Friday and, on those days, children travelling to school by bus from Wickhamford and Blackminster areas were told to stay at home.

The School Health Service

The school health service continued to expand in the post-war years. In 1961, a mobile dental unit, which had all the latest equipment including an X-ray unit, visited the school for the first time. It was located at the school and was there for the greater part of the Easter holidays treating the children who had been examined during the previous term.

The school nurse continued to visit. Karen Woodcock, who was a pupil at the school from 1961-1968, recalls that the nurse was stationed in the cloakroom (separated from the corridor by a tall, wooden partition, painted dark red) where she undertook the health checks. Karen has vivid memories of the children lining up, holding out their hands, then having their hair inspected, looking for nits.

Vaccination for the more serious diseases meant that the school was no longer closed for long periods of time because of epidemics. But vaccinations were not as yet available for measles, mumps and rubella, and there were outbreaks from time to time, causing many absences. An influenza epidemic hit the school in January 1951, when only 159 out of 214 children were present. In October 1957 Mr Harvey was ill with gastric influenza and, on returning to school, found that over half the school was absent, apparently from the same cause.

Mr Harvey noted in the Log Book in February 1966: "Attendance very poor during this last week or two. The usual situation at this time of the year, for many many years, in spite of the local and national press publicity given to such outbreaks, treating each one as an item of news instead of the same old yearly routine of coughs, colds, sore throats, diarrhoea, measles, etc, etc."

Meal-Times

When school meals began in 1946, meals were delivered from the central kitchen at Blackminster School and a Meals Supervisor visited the surrounding schools. Two classrooms had to be vacated from 11 o'clock onwards in order for them to be prepared for the dinner-time session. With the building of the extension in 1958, the school had its own kitchen and dining facilities. The school was thus able to appoint its first Cook-in-Charge and six General Assistants.

All the teachers ate in the Hall with the children, and each of the staff took turns to do dinner duty. The meals were excellent. One member of staff, "Mac" McGowan, really enjoyed his food, and always positioned himself at the end of the table ready for any extras. A particularly enjoyable occasion was the Christmas meal which was always well received.

Alterations were made to the kitchen in 1970. The work was not completed by the start of term, so for the first few days, the children were provided with sandwiches.

On 15th February 1971, Great Britain adopted decimal currency. Three days later, school dinner money was collected, using the new coinage, without any undue problems.

Outings

After the restrictions of the war-time years, the school was once more able to participate in outings. During Mr Harvey's time, the whole school was closed for the day each year whilst the two top classes were taken on a major outing. The trip was often far afield, not arriving back in Badsey until late in the evening. The trip in June 1953 was a special one to London to enable the children to see the Coronation decorations. 69 children and staff visited London by rail and were taken by coach along the Coronation route to see the decorations; a river trip was also made from Westminster Bridge to Greenwich.

David Ellison, aged 10 at the time and in

Kitchen staff and caretaker, 1964. Back row: Mrs Vera Martin, Mr Roy Hall (caretaker), Mrs Joan Hartwell, Mrs Kathy Churchley, Mrs Joan Enstone. Front row: Mrs Hilda Byrd, Miss Grace Churchill (Cook-in-charge), Mrs Margaret Hemming.

Mrs Peet's class, recalls the outing of 1954 to Cheddar Gorge and Caves and a boat trip from Weston to Cardiff and Penarth: "It was a windy day and there was some doubt as to whether the boat trip would actually take place. It did, however, and the Channel was particularly rough. The boat rose and fell as it rode the waves and many of the children were physically sea-sick – fortunately it didn't affect me and I really enjoyed the experience whilst getting thoroughly drenched!"

The school journey in 1961 was to Whipsnade Zoo. One of the most interesting features for the children was the fact that the route chosen brought in a large part of the new M1 motorway. During the 1960s, a holiday was sometimes given in June so the children could visit the Three Counties Agricultural Show at Malvern. Many parents in previous years had requested that their children might accompany them on such a visit.

A special trip took place during the May half-term holiday 1967 when Mr David Miller took a group of six boys camping in North Wales. During the Easter holiday 1975, Mrs Ryder took a party of 27 children on a week's adventure holiday in Minehead.

Extra-Curricular Activities

The annual village Flower Show was revived

Above: Group of top class Juniors at Weston-super-Mare on the Annual School Trip, July 1954.
Photo on left: -, Sheila Bonehill, -, Dorothy Mitchell, Ann Stewart, Patsy Stewart, Rosalie Addis, David Ellison, -, Jannette Roberts, Mary Churchill.
Photo on right: -, Tony Rose, -, Michael Taylor, Peter Hall, Michael Wells, Martin Gooddall, Brian Smith.

Left: Swimming group at Clevedon on a school outing, about 1954. Back row: Rosalie Addis, Jannette Roberts, -, Mary Churchill, Kathleen Bond, Michael Wells, Christopher Welch, Jimmy Roberts, Norman Sadler. Front row: Mrs Beryl Osborne, Christine Sadler, Miss Pat Barnard, Pat Nisbett, Sue Beesley.
Below: At the May half-term holiday 1967 Mr

David Miller took a party of six top class boys camping at Rhiw, near Pwhelli, North Wales. They hired a minibus and borrowed a tent from the Gottfried family; but the tent somehow got forgotten and they slept the first night in the dormobile! Moray Porter's parents drove with the tent to Wales the following day. Boys on beach, back row: Raymond Harris, Moray Porter, Robert Hemming. Front row: Robert Bennett, Robert Lord, Clifford Gottfried.

after the war and Mr Harvey was instrumental in ensuring that the schoolchildren had a major role in the event, as they had done in pre-war years. Although the Show was now held on a Saturday, the children continued to prepare work for the exhibitions and competitions, and Mr Harvey donated a cup to encourage children to take part. The school became less involved in the Flower Show after Mr Harvey left, provoking criticism from some areas. But times were changing and, because the Show was held during the school holidays, it was no longer possible for staff to organise the display of children's work. From then on, children were encouraged to submit entries in their own names, rather than as a school-led contribution.

Continuing the tradition started by Mr West in 1945, the school celebrated Harvest Festival each year, attended by Managers and former members of staff. The produce was usually sent to places such as Avonside County Hospital, the Children's Hospital, Birmingham, or Dr Barnardo's homes, near Worcester. From 1954-1961, the produce was sold and put in a fund for providing Christmas presents for the Infants Christmas parties, but from 1962, the produce sold was allocated to charities.

Christmas festivities played an important part in the post-war years. Parties for all age-groups were held at the end of term, which included tea, games and puppet shows. Sometimes a Carol Service was held or the production of a Nativity Play. These became so popular that, by 1966, the Carol Concert had to be given in duplicate to avoid the overcrowding of the previous year. From 1946-1971, a music festival was held each July at Blackminster School, in which an Infant Choir and a Junior Choir attended. Each year the school received very creditable reports.

To mark the Coronation of Queen Elizabeth II, a special programme of activities was given on 22nd May 1953, prior to breaking-up for the Whitsun holidays. Class 1 gave a puppet play and also acted an excerpt from the life of King Alfred. Models of the Coronation regalia, made by the staff, were used in a short service which explained the symbolism of certain

Front cover of Badsey School Magazine (artist unknown). There were 11 issues between 1971-1981.

Coronation rites. Badges of the Empire countries were introduced by the children before being placed in front of the school as part of the school decorations. A flag-pole was provided by the Coronation Committee of the village and a Union Jack by Mrs D Stewart. An extra three days was added on to the Whitsun holidays in order to celebrate the Coronation and, on the actual day, all children had the opportunity of taking part in sports and a tea party held on the Recreation Ground. A few weeks later, the last of the Coronation functions was held when 118 Juniors and three staff visited the Regal Cinema, Evesham, to see the Coronation Technicolour Film, "A Queen is Crowned".

During the County Primary School years, two publishing ventures took place. The first was a school newspaper, introduced in 1960. The newspaper, priced one penny, came out monthly, and consisted of a four-page duplicated sheet. The first edition, edited by Norbert Tucker, had a crossword, correspondence, illustrated jokes, a serial, verse, a quiz and recipes for raspberry toffee. There were also advertisements:

Fifteen toy soldiers. For 1/3. GOOD CONDITION. Apply N Tucker.

For Super Geraniums, contact Robert Hale, in Class 1. They are within pocket money range. 1/9 each or 18/- a dozen.

The advertising rates were calculated with professional deliberation: "Front page – large, 1s; small, 6d. Any other page – large, 6d; small, 3d."

Some years after the newspaper had folded, Mr Chaplin introduced a school magazine in 1971. The School Magazine of Summer 1975 contained the following verse by Diane Burford, who left in July 1974 to go to Blackminster.

My School Days

I wandered in to school at five,
To find a teacher good and kind.
At six I went into Miss Smith's,
To find that she would stand no tricks.

To Mrs Gorin's I went at seven,
I did lots of drawing (I thought mine was
heaven),
But as I look back, I must confess,
They must have been an awful mess.

I realised that when I was eight,
Much harder work I had to face.

When I was nine, I learnt to swim,
My first few strokes were very grim,
Then Mr Treharne with powerful voice,
Soon came along and I quickened my pace.

When I was ten and in Mrs James,
My favourite lesson was the games,
At netball I could handle the ball
Because you see I am very tall.

Now my eleventh birthday gone,
I find I must be moving on.
So thank you all for being so kind,
My year as Head Girl has been just fine.

Amongst the ideas that Mr Chaplin introduced was the celebration of the school birthday. From 1972, for about 12 years, it was the custom to observe 21st June as the school's birthday, being the anniversary of the opening of the building on School Lane in 1895. The children, staff and Managers assembled for a birthday Act of Worship, wearing blue and yellow buttonholes to mark the occasion and then enjoyed a celebration lunch. The following year, Mr Chaplin was in hospital on the occasion of the school's birthday, after suffering a heart attack. The children sent carnations which were dyed blue and yellow. At the birthday celebration in 1974, a dramatic 'rock' presentation of *Joseph and His Coat of Many Colours* was performed by the older children. The Toast "Badsey School" was proposed by the Chairman of Managers, Mr Ron Churchill, who was leaving the district on his appointment to the Methodist Church Ministry.

As part of the Royal Silver Wedding celebrations in November 1972, the Managers and children bought two trees to be planted near the Village Hall. In March 1973, 32 pupils were engaged in a tree-planting ceremony outside the village Remembrance Hall. They planted eight trees, one bought by themselves, as a part of the National "Plant a Tree in 73" campaign. They were distressed to learn that two of the trees planted had been wantonly damaged – by adults at a wedding party!

Getting to School and Road Safety

In the post-war period, the village was growing rapidly and road transport was increasing. The Minister of Transport and Civil Aviation launched a "Mind that Child" campaign in 1956 to reduce casualties to children on the roads, and a campaign was started in Badsey to try to improve safety on the main Evesham Road between Synehurst Crescent and Horsebridge Avenue. The Road Safety Sub-Committee would not agree to a zebra crossing but a "Children Crossing" school sign was erected in April 1957. The safety issue was again debated over ten years later when there was a series of letters between officers of the PTA, West Mercia Constabulary and Worcestershire County Council. The request for a pedestrian crossing came to naught, but a School Crossing

Patrol was authorised in September 1971. The deaths of two children in the 1970s caused a further campaign to be mounted, but the campaigners had to wait a further 30 years before a crossing was at last authorised.

By the late 1960s, there was concern about the increasing amount of traffic into School Lane at peak periods. The first Crossing Patrol was established in September 1969, when Mr Roy Hall, the school caretaker, undertook this extra duty, at the junction of School Lane and Willersey Road.

From 1960 onwards, pupils at Badsey County Primary School had the opportunity to participate in the National Cycling Proficiency Test. The first test took place on 31st May 1960 in school and village streets. The examiners consisted of four members of the County Police Force under the organiser, Mr G Roy of the Worcestershire County Council Road Safety Committee. 29 children took the exam and 23 passed. The awards were presented at the end of June by Mrs Carter, Chairman of Managers. From 1960 until 1992, the cycling proficiency test was a regular annual feature of school life.

In the post-war period, increasing numbers of staff used cars to get to school. In the absence of a school car park, an arrangement was made with the landlord of The Bell Inn on School Lane. From 1969 this was no longer convenient as the pub was closing down and converting to residential accommodation; for a short period, staff used the car park at The Wheatsheaf or parked on the road. By January 1974, a car park was established on the school field with an entrance from Willersey Road, but staff were experiencing some difficulties with access, particularly with the fact that a footpath had not been constructed between the car park and the school. The issue of car parking was not resolved until several years later, and many of the staff continued to park in School Lane until matters improved.

Non-Teaching Staff

The Caretaker at the beginning of the County Primary School years was Mr Cecil Keen, who retired at the end of March 1959 after almost 30 years' service. For many years, it was a joint post shared with his wife. In view of the recent extensions carried out at the school, it was possible to advertise for a full-time caretaker. Mr Roy Hall, a former pupil of Badsey Council School, was appointed. An Assistant Cleaner, Mrs A M Holley, was appointed at the same time, as the school was entitled to 11 hours' cleaning assistance. In November 1962, at the Annual Prize-Giving, it was not just the children who received an award. Mr Hall had the honour of being presented with an award for the "Best Kept School Surround" awarded by the Council for Preservation of Rural England.

The winter of 1962 was an extremely severe one, but Managers were pleased to note that, owing to the Caretaker's vigilance during the spell of severe weather, no serious damage had occurred to the school's heating installation and plumbing. The winter of 1963 was also severe. The temperature remained well below freezing by day and night and only the extra care taken by Mr Hall enabled the school to remain open as all the outside toilets were frozen and had to be flushed by buckets and the pans emptied of water each evening. Mr Hall retired in 1974 after 15 years' service, and was succeeded by Mr Pike.

School Sports Day, about 1968. School Manager and parent, Frank Goldstraw, with participants in the sack race. Mrs Churchill, Mrs James and Miss Smith are at the table. Note the old barns in the corner of the field which were later pulled down for new housing on School Lane.

Secretarial assistance during this period was provided by the wife of the Headteacher, Mrs Harvey undertaking the role until 1967 and Mrs Chaplin from 1972. In the intervening period, Mrs Cooke held the post. During the industrial disputes of 1974, which affected the whole country, Mrs Chaplin had to work under difficult circumstances. Whilst the fuel crisis lasted, no electric fire was allowed in non-teaching areas of the school and no electric lighting in the same areas on Thursdays and Fridays. Essential work was carried out by candlelight and paraffin heater.

Children's Superintendents were employed to supervise the children during the lunchtime break, and ancillary assistance in the classroom was employed from the mid-1960s.

Parents

From 1958, the system of an introductory school visit for new children with their parents was instigated, which was much appreciated. In the following decade, a parents' evening was first held in November 1967, when the parents were invited into the school to see members of staff. There was a great response, with practically every child having one parent and a number having two present.

The 1960s saw a rise in parents becoming more vocal and wishing to take a greater part in the life of the school. One of the first things introduced by Mr Chaplin was a Parent Teacher Association. In February 1968, a General Meeting was held and over 100 parents attended with Reverend Braby, Chairman of Managers, presiding. He introduced the new Headmaster who outlined the aims and objects of a Parent Teacher Association. A committee of five parents and five teachers, with the Headmaster as Chairman, was elected by ballot. A constitution was drawn up and the committee began organising fund-raising events.

The first main event was the school fête held on the playing-field in July 1968. Sideshows and competitions were organised and special items included a Fancy Dress Competition (over 60 entries), a display by the Badsey Brownies and another by the BBC

Evesham Judo Club. About 500 people attended and approximately £120 was made for PTA funds. A children's Disco was held in the School Hall in 1973, a new venture for the PTA. This turned out to be a great success and made a handsome profit. PTA activities during the latter part of the winter of 1974 were severely curtailed by the fuel crisis which prevented them using the school for meetings. At one time it looked as if the New Year's Party would have to be cancelled. The party was finally held in the Remembrance Hall on 7th February. They had oil stoves for heating and candles on the table in case of power cuts.

Managers

As it had been since 1903, the Managing Body of the school was made up of six Managers. Mr Binyon, who first became a Manager of the old Board School in 1902 and had been Chairman since 1929, stepped down as Chairman in 1959 when failing health made it impossible for him to continue. The school had benefited greatly from his wise counsel over a very long period of time spanning four Headteachers and three name changes. Mrs D Carter, who had first become a Manager in 1934 and thus had very great knowledge and experience of the school, was elected to take over. Mr Binyon's resignation as a Manager in 1961 after 59 years' service was received with great regret.

In 1974, the county of Worcestershire ceased to exist when it became part of the new county of Hereford & Worcester. LEA appointments were made for three years and were due for renewal in 1973, but in view of the county boundary changes, existing Managers continued in office for an extra year. However, in September 1974, a pre-arranged Managers' Meeting had to be cancelled because no Managing Body had been reconstituted under new County of Hereford & Worcester regulations. The first newly-formed Management Body met in January 1975 and was double the size of the previous group. It comprised 12 members (8 LEA and 4 Minor Authority representatives) and included a member of the teaching staff, a parent representative and the Headmaster. Mrs Beryl Osborne, a parent and a former teacher at the school, was elected Chairman, a position she held until 1988.

Becoming a First School

The Plowden Report of 1967, which drew heavily on the work of psychologists such as Jean Piaget, who identified certain stages of child development, was significant in influencing some counties, including Worcestershire, to alter the structure of their schools. It was suggested that 12 or 13, rather than 11, was a better age for transfer to secondary school. As early as October 1968, Mr Chaplin was absent from school in order to attend a conference in Worcester on "The Middle School".

By 1972, the reorganisation plans for the area had become firmer. Two secondary schools, Blackminster and Bredon Hill, were to become Middle Schools. The other two secondary schools, Prince Henry's Grammar and Evesham Secondary Modern, were to become High Schools with no selected intake. Children were to transfer at age ten to Middle School and at age 13 to High School. There was undoubtedly some concern amongst parents and, in March 1972, Mr Chaplin chaired a lively meeting attended by 120 staff and parents, which was addressed by the County Education Officer and the Vice-Chairman of the County Education Committee.

The end of the summer term 1975 was a sad occasion. Not only did it see the retirement of Miss Smith, who had served the school so well since 1938, but it also saw the departure of some 90 children. "Not only do we lose our traditional "top class" but also the third-year juniors," wrote Mr Chaplin in the School Magazine. The wheel had come full circle. In 1854, the National School was aimed at the 5-10 age-group. Now the new Badsey First School, as it was to be called, was to be for the same age-group – the major difference, of course, being that, as the name implied, the school was just the first stage of a child's education.

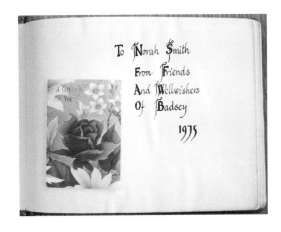

Miss Norah Smith retired in July 1975 after teaching in the school for over 37 years. A presentation of a garden swing and a special book of memories was made to her at the school's annual fête. Miss Smith is pictured below with Mrs Beryl Osborne, Chairman of Managers.

Above: Aerial view of the school from a helicopter which flew over as a special attraction on the day of the school building's 100th birthday, June 1995. The children stood on the school field in the shape of "100". The Recreation Ground can be seen at the top of the picture (with the old pavilion burnt down in the late 1990s) where, for many years (until the school acquired its own playing-field), the children went for their games lessons, walking along Sands Lane to get there.

Below: Close-up of the school site. Top left, the School House for the Headteacher, sold in 1991; next-door is "Avenell" built in the former garden of the School House; top right, houses built in the 1960s on the site of Glebe Farm. Bottom left, new housing on School Lane built on the site of old cottages demolished in the 1970s; bottom right, a portakabin on a site leased to School Lane Nursery School.

The school buildings have been extended enormously over the years, and the land for the playing-field was acquired in 1961. For a plan showing when the extensions were built, turn to Appendix F.

The school logo, in use from 1982.

8

BADSEY FIRST SCHOOL 1975-2001

In September 1975, Badsey became a school for children up to the age of ten and hence it changed its name to Badsey First School. It was important that close links were established with other schools in the area and so the schools were formed into "pyramids". Badsey was one of seven Vale First Schools which fed into Blackminster Middle School, which in turn fed into Evesham High School. The Headteachers of all the schools in the pyramid met on a regular basis. By hearing the issues that affected the High School, the First and Middle School Heads had a clearer picture of their role in the system. It also meant that they were able to band together to provide facilities on a shared basis.

The links also meant it was easier to smooth the transition from one school to the next. From the very outset, staff from Blackminster Middle School visited Badsey to talk to the children who would be going there in the autumn term and the First School children also had the opportunity to visit their new school. In 1992, a trial teacher exchange scheme began with the Middle School which continues to this day.

The Headteacher

Mr Hugh Chaplin retired at the end of the summer term 1981 after 13 years at Badsey, taking advantage of the LEA scheme for early retirement.

Trevor Clark who succeeded as Headteacher was, in the words of one of his colleagues, "a charismatic showman, a Londoner, who was very much in touch with children". Members of staff who taught under him described him as a new broom who brought colour into the life of the school. In many ways he was not a traditionalist, quickly abolishing the House system and the institution of Head Boy and Girl, but it was he who introduced the school uniform, recognising that that was what parents wanted. The wearing of school uniform was voluntary at first but quickly proved very popular, with many parents buying the school sweatshirt with embroidered design. Mr Clark also introduced the school prospectus and a system of rewards shared at Friday assembly, with badges or stickers being given. Mr Clark left at the end of December 1987. His final entry in the Log Book said: "I have gained so much from my time here. I have enjoyed the support of a loyal and hardworking staff. They have added greatly to my life and understanding of other people. If one adds to this the children, the parents, the Governors and those too numerous to mention, the result is a true *team*. A team that I'm sure can now bear the loss of one of its members. I shall *never* forget Badsey nor shall I want to."

The Deputy Head, Mrs Fiona Gardner, stood in for a term, until Mr Gerard Hughes was available to take up the post in April 1988. Mr Hughes, who had previously been Deputy Head at The Windmill School, was another very child-centred Headteacher, who very quickly won a reputation for knowing the name of every child and parent in the school. His assemblies acquired popular approval with parents and younger children being invited to a Friday assembly presented by each class in turn. Under Mr Hughes' headship, which lasted until 2001, the school flourished under the challenges brought about by far-reaching changes in educational policies. During his 13 years at the school, major building projects took place and the Victorian building was transformed into a suitable working-place for meeting the demands of the late 20th century.

The Teaching Staff

During the early years of the First School there were always huge uncertainties as to the number of staff that could be employed as the number of staff depended on the number on roll. In 1975, with 280 children on roll, the staff consisted of Head plus nine teachers. By 1980, however, the number on roll had declined to 234, so the school's teacher establishment was now eight plus Head. Discussions began about early retirement and redeployment but in the event, it was unnecessary for a teacher to be redeployed.

By September 1985, there were 197 on roll. Uncertainties always remained as to how many staff the school was allowed. Mr Clark wrote in the Log Book in April 1986: "Despite the fact that our projected numbers indicate that we should be Head plus eight next September, we must wait until the FIRST DAY OF TERM and count the number of bodies entering our portals! Mrs Pearce is standing by to continue teaching at this school if numbers allow. I am ready for my holiday this year."

This situation continued until the introduction of Local Management of Schools in 1990 which made it easier for Headteachers to take control of the staffing situation and to employ the number of teachers that best suited the school, rather than being beholden to a formula devised by the LEA. Thus, with the school expanding, it was possible to take on a new teacher, Miss Rebecca Didlick, to take part of the Reception Class in 1995. From the mid 1990s, Teaching Assistants were employed on a larger scale.

The 1981 Education Act, which came into force in April 1983, made provision for children with special educational needs; but the LEA was slow to respond, and it was not until the summer term of 1984 that a teacher was appointed on a one-term contract to teach small groups of remedial children. It was not until 1987 that the school was able to employ a part-time Special Needs teacher. For children who were provided with a statement of special needs, centrally-funded support assistants were employed, specifically for that child.

A TRIO OF HEADS WITH STAFF

Top: September 1975, the staff during the school's first year as a First School, situated in the playground outside the Main Hall. Back row: Mrs Rosalie Pratt, Mr David Dodridge, Mr Mike Stout, Mrs Sylvia Cross, Mrs Jean James. Front row: Mrs Joyce Watkin, Mrs Pat Gorin, Mr Hugh Chaplin (Headteacher), Mrs Wendy Ryder, Mrs Yvonne Bowring.

Middle: School staff, about 1984. Back row: Mrs Ruby Pickering (Secretary), Mrs Yvonne Bowring, Mr David Dodridge, Mrs Marion McGowan, Mrs Bet Benfield (Teaching Assistant). Front row: Mrs Pat Gorin, Mrs Esther Digby, Mr Trevor Clark (Headteacher), Mrs Jean James, Mrs Joyce Watkin.

Bottom: School Staff, 1990. The photo shows the old entrance to the school, before the entrance hall was extended and computer suite built. Back row: Mrs Bet Benfield (Teaching Assistant), Mrs Pat Gorin, Mrs Judy Sparrow (Secretary), Mrs Jean James, Mrs Helen Ormerod, Mrs Christine Cross, Mrs Wendy Proctor. Front row: Miss Kay Thomas, Mrs Lesley Faulkner (Deputy), Mr Gerard Hughes (Headteacher), Mrs Jackie Dudley (temporary staff), Mrs Louise Albon.

In July 2001 at one of Mr Hughes' famous assemblies, the children sang a special song for Mrs James on her final day at Badsey School.

The school was fortunate during this period to have a succession of Deputy Heads who then went on to take up Headships elsewhere: Mr Mike Stout at Wolverley Sebright, Mrs Esther Digby at Hindlip, Mrs Fiona Gardner at Inkberrow, Mrs Lesley Faulkner at Pinvin and Mrs Helen Brambani (née Leedham) at The Littletons. In July 2001, the school said goodbye to Mrs Jean James after 34 years' teaching at Badsey.

Admissions and Class Size

The highest number on roll at any time during the First School history was reached in the summer term 1977 when there were 293 pupils. The numbers were always greatest in the summer term because of the policy of a termly intake. At that stage, it was extremely difficult to assess future intake numbers because of the large amount of houses being built in Badsey and Aldington. By January 1981, most of the classes were overcrowded, with numbers varying from 31-36 in the top four classes and slightly lower numbers in the younger classes.

In 1977, because of bulging schools, it became necessary for the LEA to exclude all "rising fives" throughout the county; children were therefore unable to enter school until the term after they became five. This had a knock-on effect at Mrs Goldstraw's Nursery, causing her great problems. As a stopgap measure, children were admitted individually throughout the term on the Monday following their fifth birthday. The issue of "the rising fives" remained a problem throughout the

1980s. Mr Hughes, the new Head in April 1988, was faced with the problem that the school could not, after all, admit that term's expected intake of "rising fives" as they lacked the numbers to employ an extra teacher. The matter was resolved by September 1989, as "rising fives" were admitted as resourced pupils under new LEA policy.

The nursery which had served the children of Badsey so well since 1965, closed at the end of the summer term 1987 on Mrs Goldstraw's retirement. Mrs Fiona Laidlaw and Mrs Heather Gibbons agreed to take on the nursery but an alternative site was required. As the LEA had advised that it would be desirable for the school to take steps to bring the nursery within the school, Mr Clark offered part of the school field for the unit. A mobile classroom was installed and the nursery opened for business in September 1987. On Mrs Laidlaw's departure from the village, Mrs Gibbons took sole charge; in 1994, she renewed the lease of the nursery school for a period of 15 years.

In 1987, there were concerns that the upper age of the school would yet again be reduced. In March 1987, a special meeting was held at the school to discuss the Wychavon Review of Education. The most contentious issue raised within the document was that the age range at the school would change from 5-10 years to 5-9 years, with the loss of about 35 to 40 children. The meeting was well attended by about 50 parents and all the Governors. The unanimous view of the parents was that they did not want a transfer to Middle School

1991, Mrs Gorin's class in one of the "temporary" classrooms. Note the old-fashioned desks with flip-top lids still in use. Through the windows, the nursery can be seen to the left and children playing in the playground.

at nine. The outcome of the review was not known until July 1988, by which time Mr Hughes was Head. He wrote in the Log Book on 22nd July: "Last day of term. This was lightened by the great news that the Secretary of State has overturned the proposed plans for age-range changes in the Wychavon review so we will stay as we are for the immediate future."

To begin with, the classes were simply called Class 1, Class 2, etc, with Class 1 being the top class, but from 1982, the classes were known by the initial of the teacher's surname, eg Class J for Mrs James. With the introduction of the National Curriculum, the naming of classes by their teacher's initial remained but, throughout the country, a standard system of year-groups was adopted, with children beginning in Reception, then progressing to Year 1 (5-6 year-olds) and finishing in Year 13 (17-18 year-olds). Four key stages of education were identified: 5-7, 7-11, 11-14, 14-16. Years 1 and 2 were Key Stage 1, at the end of which Standard Attainment Tests (SATs) were taken,

and Years 3-6 were Key Stage 2, when further SATs were taken. With the First Schools in the Evesham area ending at Year 5 in the middle of Key Stage 2, it meant that it was more than ever necessary for strong links with the Middle School.

From 1991, the Government introduced the system of setting the standard intake number for schools. For Badsey the recommended number was 40 per year, 240 for the school. It became compulsory that the school could not offer places to out-of-area children until the LEA had approved the place. The Government intended a more open enrolment by compelling schools to admit up to their physical capacity. In 1993, an extension comprising two new classrooms was added, and in 1995, the former kitchen, which for the previous 12 years had been used as a resources area, was converted into a Reception classroom. The increased accommodation permitted a capacity of 270, so from 1996 the LEA increased the intake from 40 to 45 a year.

In 1997, the Government introduced nursery

Above: Mrs James' class, Class 1, June 1982. School uniform had been introduced in January 1982 on a voluntary basis. As these children were in their final year at the school, only a few were wearing uniform. Back row: Ian Robbins, Guy Cassey, Paul Clark, Matthew Taylor, Darren Court, Richard Ballard, Francis Meadows, Stephen Major. Second row: David Smith, Jeffrey Bird, Ian Stratton, Katy Sadler, Helen Aberdein, Russell Evans, Jamie Lamb, Philip Goddard. Third row: Ian James, Martin Foster, Justin Welsh, Sharon Wayland, Rachel Anderson, Colin Young, Scott Witheford, Ryan Thomas. Front row: Sonya Andrews, Fiona Ball, Esther Monk, Emma Bezant, Mrs James, Rachel Ford, Jenny Elliott, Claire Anderson, Sarah Fray.

Below: Leavers, July 1986, including Philip Moore (back row, fourth from right), who went on to study at Chetham's School of Music, Manchester, and the Royal Academy of Music, and is now an acknowledged concert pianist. Back row: Philippa Bullen, Richard Sams, Matthew Overd, Ross Jones, Daniel Smith, Andrew Smith, Neil Allen, Maxine Ritchie, Sharon Marshall, Sarah Gorin, Joanna White, Philip Moore, Debbie Willies, Andrew Aston, Alun Hemming. Middle row: Lee Suthern, Richard Evans, Matthew Harris, Christopher Salisbury, Thomas Maskew, Adam Ealey, Dean Smith, John Charlton, Daniel Byrd, Robin Fisher, Matthew Thom, Duncan Hemming, Anthony Nastasi, Graham Bullock. Front row: Nicholas Taylor, Ryan Jelfs, Richard Locke, Rachel Caswell, Caroline Maden, Lisa Collett, Mrs Gorin, Mr Clark, Mrs James, Louise Sadler, Helen Lamb, Helen Thomas, Sarah Hawker, Hannah Monk, Lisa Hawton, Philip Smith.

Summer 2001, Miss Anderson's class, Year 3. Back row: James Leak, William Pask, Tom Owens, Matthew Osborne, Ben Bird, Jonathan Spinks, Christopher Curtis. Second row: Jacob Hall, Louise Sparrow, Samantha Newman, Karys Bolland, Charlotte Stanley, Isabelle Watton, Gina Phillips, David Waters. Third row: Connor Trotman, Dan Humpston, Dion Mayhew, Philippa Halling, Eleanor Hardwick, Charlotte Cook, Daniel Webb, Thomas Round, Joe Evans. Front row: George Mountney, Jamie Layton, Rupert Owens, Joshar Andac, Richard Byron, Max Brambani, Daniel Taylor.

vouchers whereby the parents of four-year-olds were entitled to vouchers to cover five half days per week. Vouchers were accepted for "rising fives" from April 1997 and from September 1997 the school decided to accept all four-year-olds in one yearly intake, instead of a termly intake of "rising fives". Thus, for the first time in 60 years, children were admitted to the school soon after their fourth birthday.

By 1998, the physical capacity of the school was reached and some places had to be refused. In addition, it became law that Key Stage 1 classes were limited to 30 maximum. That was already Badsey's policy, but it had repercussions on school structure. The number of Key Stage 2 pupils meant that some classes were over optimum, but the situation resolved itself naturally over the next two to three years as the bulge years passed.

The School House

Mr Chaplin was the last Headteacher to reside in the School House. Mr Clark, who started in 1981, had his own house at Inkberrow so the property was let.

In September 1984, the County Property Office notified the school that it intended to sell the School House. The sale began to proceed, but then the Property Department

September 1997, Connor Trotman and Jonathan Spinks, two of the youngest children to be admitted for 60 years. Connor was just 4 years and 1 week old on the first day of term.

Above: The School House (right) was no longer required for use by the Headteacher and was sold in 1991; part of the garden was sold for building land. The red-brick boundary wall was demolished, thus revealing the school buildings more clearly. On the left was a resources room, now a classroom and formerly the kitchen.

Below: Summer 1991, Mrs James' class studied the progress of the building of "Avenell" in the garden of the original School House.

hit a problem which turned out to be excellent news for the school. The conveyance of 1894 to the original Badsey School Board was under the Elementary Education Act and the Charity Commissioners had ruled that Badsey School and the School House were held on trust for charitable purposes. A scheme therefore had to be framed to authorise the sale of the School House and to make provision for the application of the proceeds of sale. Five Trustees were appointed, including Mrs Beryl Osborne and Mrs Pat Goldstraw, who still remain as Trustees to this day; the Clerk was Peter Cooke who still retains the post. The inaugural meeting of Badsey School Charity Trust took place on 17th April 1989.

The southern end of the School House garden was on land purchased by the LEA in 1920. It was decided to sell the School House in conjunction with this land after obtaining planning permission. Planning permission was obtained by September 1989, but the sale could not go ahead until access arrangements were completed. As part of the conditions relating to the house sale, it had been agreed to close the access between the School House and the car park (which at that stage was on the Infant playground).

Once the LEA knew that planning permission for further development had been obtained, they reassessed their position and wanted a bigger share of revenue which angered the Governors and Trustees. The Trustees stood their ground in negotiations with the LEA. The matter was eventually resolved in April 1990 when it was agreed that the School Trust would receive two-thirds and the LEA one-third of money realised from the sale of the School House and garden. The LEA also undertook to provide a new car park at the rear of the school with access from Willersey Road and to seal off the present front access. The Trustees were congratulated for standing their ground through negotiations with the County Council.

The house was placed on the market in May 1990. By the following May, it had been sold for £67,500 and the building land had been sold for £32,000. After the deduction of expenses, two-thirds of the money was paid to the School Trust and proceeds were then invested with the interest to be used for school and other educational purposes.

Premises

School Headteachers in the 1970s and 1980s were hindered by their lack of any real say in the maintenance of the school building of which they were in charge, and were frustrated by the lack of authority to act in an emergency. Throughout 1979 and 1980, there were numerous problems with heating. By January 1981, a new boiler had been installed in the main boiler-house, but it did not immediately solve the heating problems, as low temperatures were still experienced in most

Left top and middle: 1992, preparations for a classroom extension begin. The portakabin arrives amidst much excitement from the watching children and is erected on the playing-field.

Left bottom: 1993, the new extension takes shape. On the left-hand side at the back are the new toilets built in 1990. In the centre back is the Main Hall.

Above: The new extension was opened at the school fête on 4th July 1993 by Mr Russ Clayton, Chairman of the County Education Committee.

of the classrooms. Heating remained a problem until a change was made from oil-fired to gas heating in March 1982, and the ceilings in the classrooms were lowered to conserve heat.

Mr Clark, who became Headteacher in September 1981, soon found out about the problems of inheriting a Victorian school building which had been much added to over the years. On his first meeting with Mrs Osborne, Chairman of Governors, in the midst of discussions about a "nominee" for redeployment, they were interrupted by a sudden torrent of rainwater flooding in through the ceiling of the Head's study! On 21st June 1984 Mr Clark wrote in the Log Book: "This school is 89 years old today. In many places it looks as if it hasn't been decorated since!!"

Throughout the 1980s, the poor state of the school building and its fixed resources remained a problem, but budgetary constraints meant that little was done. Mr Clark's complaints were many but the most serious were the very poor decorative order, draughtiness of the school along all the corridors, and lastly the fact that there were still outside toilets. Ideally, he felt that the toilets should be rebuilt and incorporated into the main school. As a compromise solution, wash-basins were installed in the outside toilets. Severe wind and rain in November 1987 highlighted the many leaks and inadequate drainage in the school. When Dyno-Rod came to clear the drains around the boiler house, they discovered blockages going back many years.

When Mr Clark left at the end of 1987, most of the problems concerning the buildings were unresolved and it was left to Mr Hughes to take up the cause. Staff from the LEA visited in October 1988 to discuss proposals for a covered way to the outside toilet block. The consensus was that merely joining them to buildings would not be cost effective, and money was made available for a new toilet block. Work on the new toilets began in November 1989. At last, by May 1990, the outside toilets were finally gone, nearly 100 years after they were first built.

Having sorted out the toilets, Mr Hughes then began a campaign for redecoration of the school by sending photos of the poor décor to the County Surveyor, Chief Education Officer and County Councillors. The immediate plans

The new adventure playground, 1997.

were approved. Carpets were placed in corridors and improvements made to staff accommodation. The process of improving the school environment was moving at a far faster pace than in previous decades. Two factors assisted Mr Hughes in his drive to modernise the buildings: the introduction of LMS (Local Management of Schools) in 1990 gave schools more control over the way the money was spent and the sale of the School House generated a valuable source of income. Whilst other schools had to embark on major fund-raising campaigns, Badsey was in the enviable position of having a pot of money to call upon for building projects.

In 1990, the subject was raised by the LEA of replacing the two mobile classrooms which had been in position since 1968. This work was to be completely funded by the LEA, but because of financial strictures, the work did not begin until 1992. By March 1993, the new extension of two classrooms and an activity area was complete. At the same time, the School Trustees undertook a parallel project to extend the small easterly classroom. They agreed to donate £5,000 to the school as their part of a 50/50 building project with the LEA to modernise and extend the classroom and cloakroom area. Modifications were made at Easter 1993.

Despite the 1993 extension, with a rise in the number of children the school site was still not large enough. School meals had been phased out in 1982 and it was decided to convert the old kitchen into a new Reception classroom with funding from the LEA and the School Trust. By January 1996 the work was complete, comprising classroom, resources area and Special Educational Needs room. A new adjoining entrance and cloakroom area was built at Easter.

The main entrance to the school from the younger children's playground was uninviting and insecure, so in 1999, again funded by the LEA and the School Trust, the entrance was improved. The building line was extended and a new computer area was created to the right of the entrance. The presence in Evesham of a nationally-known computer company set up by former pupil, Richard Austin, meant that computing expertise was close at hand. The school's unusually-shaped building, added to much over the years, with minimal space for cabling, presented particular challenges in installing a computer network. With the aid of a government grant, the school opted for a pioneering wireless network which offered enormous potential, the benefits of which should soon be fully realised with recent improvements to network security and the purchase of further laptop computers.

Playgrounds and Playing-fields

From September 1981, the front playground on the eastern side of the school by the old School House was used as a car park, so all the children used the western playground. This was made easier by the removal of the fixed playground apparatus which had become obsolete. "This is a momentous occasion as this equipment had been scheduled for removal for a long time!" wrote the new Headteacher, Mr Clark.

The car park reverted back to its original purpose as a playground in 1990 once the School House had been sold. In 1994, the PTA paid for a weather station and remarking of the playground and an adventure playground, also paid for by the PTA, was completed by the end of 1997.

The problem of the school front garden was raised from time to time. The matter was resolved when the PTA decided to create a Millennium Garden and the Parish Council donated a commemorative milepost. It was erected on the spot where, nearly 80 years earlier, a First World War shell had stood for some 20 years.

Curriculum

During the 1970s and 1980s, a high degree of autonomy was granted to teachers, aided by the abolition of the "11+" which freed the curriculum for more creative learning. Mr Chaplin tended to keep to more traditional methods but Mr Clark introduced innovative ideas. Mr Clark was keen to embrace new technology and, in January 1982, he gave a lecture to a group of Deputy Heads entitled "Computers in First Schools". The school's first computer was installed in the autumn term 1982. Technology continued to move at a fast pace and, in the 1990s, the internet increasingly became part of the curriculum.

The National Curriculum was introduced in September 1989 which led to major changes. After the freedoms of the previous two decades, teachers, who had had virtually no say in the National Curriculum's design or

Chris Woodhead, Chief Inspector of Schools, on a visit to Badsey in 2000. The pupils pictured are Harley Pike, Grant Habitts, Ben Jones, Thomas Round, Dahra Pike, Sophie Grinnell, Samantha Newman and Max Brambani. Picture courtesy the Journal Series, Evesham. A Newsquest publication.

Chris Helm of Badsey Parish Council unveiling the milepost in the Millennium Garden, 2001.

construction, were required to work to a very prescribed set of aims. It divided the curriculum into discrete subjects, making integrated "Topic" work more difficult, and turned teachers from being curriculum innovators into curriculum deliverers. Constant revisions to the National Curriculum in the early years caused teachers huge amounts of work. In Badsey, Lady Harford, County Councillor, visited to check on any problems because a number of schools had complained of overload. The first National Curriculum was too vast in its aims with little chance of working and was soon drastically reduced.

The main purpose of the National Curriculum was to establish standards and to promote continuity and coherence. For each key stage there were attainment targets and level descriptions which set out standards expected. The first Standard Attainment Tests (SATs) were administered in 1991 when Key Stage 1 pupils underwent assessment in English and Mathematics. Workloads for Year 2 teachers increased markedly and rotas and timetables were redrawn to provide them with the time needed to complete all the paperwork, which consequently meant more work and less non-contact time for everybody else. It was a particularly onerous task for the teachers concerned and the school had to be reorganised to allow Mrs Bees and Mr Hughes to take the rest of the class while the teacher was working with small groups. Mr Hughes vented his dissatisfaction on the County Inspector for assessment at a meeting in April 1991, when he told him in no uncertain words that SATs were expensive and time-consuming. Test results were published in newspapers, which quickly led to the production of "league" tables.

As far as Key Stage 2 assessment was concerned, First Schools found themselves in the strange position of doing the bulk of the preparation for the work but not entering the children for the tests as these were undertaken in their first year at Middle School.

Whilst the content of the National Curriculum was refined and reduced, constant changes and enormous amounts of paperwork took their toll on staff morale. The Literacy Hour was launched in January 1999, followed by the Numeracy Hour the year after. The Labour Government which had come to power in 1997 continued the policy of increasing state control by spelling out content and teaching methods in great detail. A new generation of teachers was being trained which had never been given freedoms in teaching.

School reports which for many years had been just a single sheet of paper, had become an A4 ring-bound booklet for each child.

Whilst the political arguments were being fought at a national level, Badsey meanwhile continued to produce excellent work. An Ofsted (Office for Standards in Education) report of 1996, which ran to 28 pages, found that standards of achievement were above average in relation to national expectations in the core subjects of English, Mathematics and Science and in the foundation subjects of Information Technology, Geography, Art and Music. The report concluded by saying: "The school uses its links with local businesses and the community purposefully to enhance curriculum provision and recognises the value of the village as a resource for learning. The positive nature of the school's links with parents and the community make a significant contribution to its success in attaining high standards of achievement and good quality of learning for its children."

Physical Exercise

The School Sports Day continued to be an important event in the school calendar. The last year that House trophies were awarded was 1981. In the following year, with each child taking part for his or her own enjoyment, every child received a reward for taking part and certificates for the first four in all events were awarded. The parents were involved to a much greater extent, taking part as judges, marshalls and recorders.

Football matches were played against local schools. The first Evesham First Schools' five-a-side football competition was held at Badsey in 1988, organised by Mrs James and Mr Hughes. This continues to be an important fixture in the sporting calendar to this day. With the departure of the final year children to Blackminster, it was uncertain whether hockey would be able to continue with the problem of finding enough to play 11-a-side games. It continued for a few years and House matches were played nine-a-side.

Despite economies, Evesham area teachers were keen to maintain a Schools' Swimming programme. In 1978, the children were able to start using the new Evesham Baths but, from 1980, because of economy cuts, the LEA no longer financed transport for swimming instruction. This caused a few problems, but swimming lessons recommenced in January 1981. The first "Evesham First Schools" swimming gala took place in 1983. In 1984, Badsey came first in the section for schools of 100 children or more, a title which they held on to for nine successive years. A review of swimming allocations in 1994 led to Badsey's sessions being cut from three to one. Four years later, the LEA withdrew central funding for swimming, but the Governors agreed to continue swimming tuition for Year 4 and Year 5 pupils funded out of the school budget. In 1999, swimming was reduced to one year only

with the target of each child being able to swim 25 metres.

School Hours and Holidays

In 1977, a new First School day of 5¼ hours was introduced, as previously the school had been divided into 5½ hours for Juniors and 5 hours for Infants. The school day became 9.10-12.15 and 1.30-3.40. In 1984 the hours changed to 9.15-3.15, which they remain to this day.

From 1987, teachers' in-service days (five days over and above those worked by children) were begun, commonly known then as "Baker Days", after Kenneth Baker, the author of the act. The in-service days were usually taken up with pre-year preparation and planning and training sessions in conjunction with other First Schools in the pyramid.

Closures

Industrial action by tanker-drivers took place on several occasions in the late 1970s and many schools had to close because of lack of fuel. In spite of the strike action and severe wintry weather, Badsey School stayed open. On one occasion in April 1979, Mr Chaplin reported that the school had no fuel oil but the children wore warm clothing during the cold snap. During this period, various economy measures were taken, such as lengthening the Christmas holiday by one week in order to save on fuel and lighting.

The school was closed in January 1982 because of bad snow making the roads impassable. Messages about school closure were broadcast to parents via local radio, a new means of notification, which worked well. The children returned a few days later, but severe weather conditions meant very poor and cold conditions in school, frozen outside toilets, and no water to the outside classrooms. The school was closed again the next day as the extreme temperatures had frozen the heating oil and the inside toilets were then out of use.

There were several snowy winters in the 1980s. On one occasion in January 1987, Mr Clark wrote in the Log Book: "There are still huge drifts around the outside toilet block –

Above: Sports Day, 1979, with the "temporary" classrooms in the background belonging to Mr Dodridge and Mrs James. The cars in the background show where the car park was originally situated on the eastern perimeter. Back row: Claire Jelfs, Paula Young, James Baker, Michael Hawker, Daniel O Smith, -, Mark Fisher, Richard Perry, Adrian White, Rory Grinnell, Kylie Webb, Tracey Marshall, Tina New. Front row: Sarah Hall, Sally Ann Hughes, Mark Jelfs, Anthony Davies, Gary Bradshaw, Andrew Major, Lee Smith, Mark Cole, Mark Payne, Hayley Clark, Heather Andrews, Donna Sullivan, Emma Jordan, Suzie Smith.

Below: Sports Day, July 1980, Mr Stout's class. The children are holding bears as mascots for the School Houses. Back row: Mark Scarrott, Gareth James, Jeanette Nisbett, Laura Willett, Sharon Ford, Sarah Simms, Simon Clements, William Dudfield, Tim Cother, Darren Careless, Stephen Potter, James Goldstraw, Jonathan Granger, Richard Helm, Zoe Roadnight. Front row: Cindy Taylor, Alan Smith, Karen Dennick, Sarah Hemming, Sharon Dennick, Lisa Edwards, Christine Handy, Rosalyn Merrett, Karen Granacki, Jane Thompson, Jenny Kedward, Robert Smith, Sally Ann Fray.

yes, still outside toilets and it's now 1987!!!" The last time that the school was closed for snow was in February 1991.

Since the late 19th century, the school had always closed for elections. In 1976, Parish Council Chairmen from all over the county made their objections known to the County Authority. General Election Day 1979 was the first time the school was able to carry on its usual work as the Village Remembrance Hall had become the official Polling Station in Badsey.

Meal-Times

The death-knell was sounding for the School Meals Service. In 1975 Mr Chaplin had cause to complain in the Log Book: "Recently, a considerable amount of food is being wasted, especially by the younger children. The children would appear to be accustomed to only certain foodstuffs at home and are loathe to try anything slightly different." By 1980, reduced numbers were taking school dinners, the number having halved since the price was raised to 45p for one course. 58 children had a school meal on 14th September 1981, which represented just a quarter of the children.

In 1982, the LEA took the decision to cease school meals in the primary sector. Mrs Osborne, Chairman of the Governors, made a presentation to the kitchen ladies who were made redundant. Trevor Clark wrote in the Log Book on 28th May 1982: "Today marks the end of the school meals service for Primary Schools in the county. This is a very regrettable situation, not only for the ladies who lose their jobs, but also as it marks the largest manifestation yet of the erosion of the service as we know it." From then on, unless they went home to dinner, all children took sandwiches.

The kitchen equipment was not removed from school until the following May. "We now have a cold, dirty, dusty, cavernous gap," wrote Mr Clark. The room was then utilised as a resource room.

In 1985, a new EEC-subsidised milk scheme was introduced, administered by parents who collected the money each Friday. From 1997,

when the school began admitting younger children, free milk was available to children until their fifth birthday. In the 21st century, Key Stage 1 children began to receive an item of fruit each day.

Outings

School outings were a regular feature of the school calendar. They were taken on a year-group basis, to places such as Slimbridge, Cotswold Rare Breeds Park, Avoncroft, Black Country Museum, Severn Valley Railway.

In May 1992, a party of 40 Year 4 and Year 5 children with four teachers and Parent Governor, David Osborne, left for a long weekend visit to York staying at a Youth Hostel. "A first for the school," wrote Mr Hughes in the Log Book. Little did he know that long before his time (some 46 years earlier), a previous Headteacher had taken a group of children for five days to a youth hostel in Shropshire.

In 1995 the school first went to Osmington Bay on the Dorset coast for an activity weekend. This provided an excellent opportunity for the children to undertake physical challenges not normally provided at school, such as climbing, abseiling, fencing and archery. Every year since then, Year 5 pupils have attended the course.

Extra-Curricular Activities

The school year continued to feature the normal annual events, beginning with the Harvest Thanksgiving Service. In October 1985, Badsey School took part in the "Schools for Africa" appeal which involved filling 26 kg sacks full of sugar, wholewheat flour or pulses. The school managed 12 full sacks and, at the Harvest Thanksgiving Service, the service took the form of a talk by Mr Clark, music, poems and prose and a video recording from the "Live Aid" concert showing the desperate plight of the people of Ethiopia and Sudan.

Christmas parties, Carol Services and latterly a Christmas Concert were held during Mr Chaplin's time, which many parents attended. Christmas concerts became more ambitious during the 1980s, enhanced by new stage lights

Above: June 1995, Victorian tea-party to commemorate the 100th birthday of the school building. All the staff and children dressed up in Victorian costume for the day.

Left: Famous old boy, Alistair McGowan (TV star and impressionist, pupil 1969-1972) opens the 100th birthday celebrations.

Below: Mrs James and class with the helicopter which flew over the school on the 100th birthday celebrations.

Opposite: Headteacher, Mr Gerard Hughes, setting a fine example for the birthday celebrations, June 1995.

Perhaps the most successful production during this period was Mr Hughes' swan-song in December 2001, a stunning production of *Joseph and the Amazing Technicolor Dreamcoat* using the school's new stage and lighting for the first time.

A Spring Concert of Music and Literature was a regular feature under Mr Chaplin's headship. The School Birthday continued to be celebrated on 21st June for a few years after Mr Chaplin's departure, but then the custom declined.

In October 1983 Badsey schoolchildren took part in a BBC Radio 2 programme. It was the pilot of a new series which looked at village life and people around the country. It was recorded in front of a village audience of some 200 people. The school recorder group played two pieces.

School Clubs were begun in the 1980s. The children had the opportunity to do football, short tennis, country dancing, art and craft, running or recorder after school.

A First School Music Festival was held at Badsey in March 1978, attended by eight schools. This was the revival of a festival which had ceased in 1971. A few children began receiving violin tuition. Gradually, more instruments were added to the range of instruments being taught, until it was possible, a few years later, to set up a pyramid orchestra.

In June 1995, the school celebrated the 100th anniversary of the school building, which also coincided with the 700th anniversary of

and stage blocks provided by the PTA. With the introduction of the National Curriculum, there was less time for rehearsals so, for a time in the 1990s, the Christmas event took the form of a traditional concert with more singing and poems, rather than an actual play. By the end of the 1990s, the plays were becoming more ambitious again, with performances such as *Charlie and the Chocolate Factory*.

2001 production of Joseph and the Amazing Technicolor Dreamcoat; Alex Sandham as the Pharaoh. Design © 1991 The Really Useful Group Ltd.

St James' Church. A week of celebrations was held in June, commencing with the summer fête. Former pupil, Alistair McGowan, by then a famous impressionist well-known to the children via television, opened the fête. Later in the week, a Victorian Day was held, with everyone dressed in Victorian costume. A helicopter flew over the school and took photographs. The children were placed on the field to make 100, photos were taken, then the helicopter landed, and the children were able to talk to the pilot and have their photos taken beside the helicopter.

Getting to School and Road Safety

Car parking was an issue in the early days of the First School. A car park had been built at the rear in 1974, but there was no path leading to the school. In 1977, work started on constructing a path which partly alleviated the problem. But the car park was only large enough for four cars, its approach route was difficult and a broken gate hindered access, so the staff tended to park in the road. The problem was resolved by turning the front infants' playground into a car park from January 1982. However, when the School House was sold in 1990, the right of way into the playground was sold so staff had to revert to parking elsewhere. Another car park at the rear was built on the southern boundary, with space for 16 cars, but the work was not completed until 1993 when the extension was built.

Cycling Proficiency Test, about 1980, with Mrs Jean James and PC Trevor Earle. The old toilet block can be seen on the right-hand side.

Cycling Proficiency Tests continued, although from 1976 the police were no longer involved with administering the test. The organisation of the test thus was primarily the responsibility of Mrs James, but from the mid 1980s, the LEA sent a Road Safety Organiser to assist. Cycling Proficiency Tests were held for the last time at Badsey in 1992. After that, the decision was taken for children to take the test in their first year at Middle School. Very few children cycled to school and the cycle sheds were demolished at the same time as the outside toilets in 1990. Children either walked to school, mostly escorted by parents, dropped off by car or came on the Wickhamford bus.

Non-Teaching Staff

The Caretaker until September 1978 was Mr Pike, and was replaced by Mrs Mary Knight, who took on the post of Cleaner-in-Charge; Mrs Daphne Cleaver was offered the post of cleaner. The change from the job title of "Caretaker" to "Cleaner-in-Charge" was a step taken by the LEA on economic grounds. Mr Chaplin felt that the high cost of getting very minor repairs done was counter-balancing any saving from the changeover. In 1988, cleaning services were contracted out, but Mrs Knight and Mrs Cleaver were prepared to carry on under the new terms. They remained in post for over 20 years, in latter years often assisted by their husbands.

The School Secretaries during this period were Mary Chaplin, Ruby Pickering, Judy Sparrow and Su Trinder. In the early days, additional administrative support for the school and teaching staff was provided by an ancillary helper. Mrs Davies, who had fulfilled this role for 13½ years, left in 1979 and was replaced by Mrs Benfield. With the economy measures of the late 1970s, the combined hours of the Secretary and Ancillary Helper were reduced from 43 to 34, and then again to 28. Teaching Assistants began to be used more extensively from the mid-1990s.

Managers, Governors and LMS

The early years of the First School were

depressing times money-wise and there was little the Managers could do to assist. Much of Mr Chaplin's time was taken up with meetings about economy measures. Nationwide teachers' strikes were a feature of this period and occasionally Badsey staff who were members of the National Union of Teachers were absent to take part in demonstrations against proposed economies. Until the 1990s, financial stringencies placed burdens on cash-strapped schools.

The body of people who supported the Headteacher in the management of the school had always been known as Managers, but in 1980 the term changed from Manager to Governor. The numbers on the Governing Body also increased to 12, their ranks swelled by the Headteacher and staff and parent representatives who were allowed more say in the running of the school. Margaret Thatcher's Conservative Government which came to power in 1979 began to introduce a series of Education Acts aimed at weakening the powers of the LEAs and increasing the rights of parents. The 1980 Act permitted more parents on governing bodies, the parental right to choose schools, appeals procedures and the publication of exam results. Further Acts, particularly those of 1986 and 1988, were far-reaching, diminishing the importance of LEAs, with the focus now on the Department for Education & Science and schools.

The 1988 Education Act was the most significant piece of educational legislation since 1944, effectively taking power from the LEAs and giving it to the Secretary of State. It brought about a number of changes, paving the way for "Local Management of Schools" (LMS). Since 1903, when schools had first come under LEA control, the only financial control that they had was in the budget relating to books and materials. The teachers were employed and the buildings maintained by the LEA. The introduction of LMS in April 1990 brought immense changes and schools were given far greater control, managing most of the budget. The role of the Headteacher changed dramatically. He now had to learn about managing a budget, recruitment and selection procedures, employment law and buildings maintenance. At the same time, the role of the Governing Body changed. For the first time, Governors had legal responsibilities in relation to control of the budget and implementation of the National Curriculum. LMS also introduced a market-place economy. School budgets were based largely on pupil numbers placing an onus on schools to attract as many pupils as possible.

There was scepticism among a number of Headteachers in Worcestershire, but initial reactions from Mr Hughes and Mrs Pike, Chairman of Governors, were favourable because higher pupil numbers that year meant more money. Soon after implementation, the sharp end of LMS was seen when a water leak under the school led to a bill more than five times the usual amount. Over time, however, Headteachers began to adjust to their new role, and Mr Hughes was able to maximise the benefits of LMS to the school's advantage, revitalising the school to be the highly-respected First School that it is today.

Parents

Open Evenings for parents, which had started in 1967, continued on a termly basis, and were well attended. Under Mr Clark, the practice of having additional parents' evenings where he spoke about a particular topic, was introduced. Parents were also encouraged to help in school. By October 1988, over 30 parents were helping on a regular basis.

The Parent Teacher Association, which had been established in 1968, continued to thrive. The fête was held each summer and children's discos became regular features. A PTA Party was held each winter and from 1981 an Autumn or Christmas Fayre was held. Each November, there was a Firework Party. The first one, held in 1982, despite rain, was a great success with approximately 500 people in attendance. By 1984, the event had become well established. "This is becoming a traditional annual event in the community. It is very gratifying to see the school at the centre of a regular village event," wrote Mr Clark in the Log Book. By 1989, the numbers were up to approximately a thousand in attendance. However, by the mid-1990s, the event was less well attended, and competition from a similar event at Badsey Recreation Club meant that the PTA decided to discontinue the school event.

In 1999, the PTA paid for the 40-year-old curtains in the Main Hall to be replaced. These were kindly made for free by Mrs Corinne Formanuik whose children were just completing their time at the school.

The summer fête in 2000 was incorporated into the village Millennium celebrations and the fête culminated in an act of worship on the school playing-field conducted by the Reverend Dr Adrian Hough, Vicar of Badsey and also parent of a child at the school.

Out-of-School Club

In June 1992, Mr Hughes began discussions with Mrs Gibbons, Manager of the Nursery, about a joint project to set up an after-school club every night for children of parents at work, to be a self-supporting venture with termly fees. A club was started in November 1994 but, after two false starts, it closed in October 1995, due to lack of support.

The plan finally came to fruition in September 1997 when Mrs Shirley Tutton, already employed at the school as a Teaching Assistant, took on the role of providing out of school provision, supported by the School Trust. The Club was patronised not

only by Badsey schoolchildren, but also former Badsey pupils in attendance at Blackminster. During the holidays, a number of children from other schools in the region without such facilities, used the facility. For the first time in the school's history, the buildings were in use 12 hours a day, 50 weeks a year.

The Turn of the Century

The school ended the 20th century in good shape, highly respected in the local community and the county. Mr Hughes left at the end of 2001 to become Headteacher at the largest First School in the county and it was now the turn of a former pupil to take up the reins.

As part of the village's Millennium celebrations, Badsey School participated in the carnival and held a special fête. Left to right: Governor, Alan Tutton, organising the barbecue at the fête; Governor, Clive Richards, taking part in the procession; schoolchildren holding the Badsey First School banner.

Mrs Elizabeth Spencer, Headteacher since 2002.

9

BADSEY FIRST SCHOOL TODAY

Badsey First School in 2004 is a thriving school and has strong links with the community. It provides an enriched curriculum, promotes life-long learning, admissions figures are healthy and, most importantly, the children appear to enjoy their schooldays.

The Headteacher

On the departure of Mr Hughes, Mrs Helen Brambani, the Deputy Head, assumed the role of Acting Head for a term until Mr Hughes' successor was able to take up her appointment.

The person chosen to lead Badsey First School in the 21st century was Mrs Elizabeth Spencer who, at the age of 28, had become Hereford & Worcester's youngest Headteacher when she was appointed to the headship of Cleeve Prior CE First School in 1981. Unknown to the Badsey Governors who appointed her, the headship of Badsey First School was a most fitting post for Mrs Spencer. As Elizabeth Wheatley, she had spent six years at the school as a pupil and has strong family roots in the area.

Mrs Spencer is well respected in the county and is one of nine Headteachers who meet regularly with Julien Kramer, Director of Education, and the Education Management Group of the Authority. Their remit is to plan the vision for Worcestershire.

The Teaching Staff

In the academic year 2003-2004, the school has ten teachers: Mrs Collins in Year 5, Mrs Stirling in Year 4/5, Mrs Lee in Year 3/4, Mrs Avery in Year 3, Mrs Bevington in Year 2, Mrs Cross in Year 1/2, Mrs Jones/Mrs Evans in Year 1, and Mrs Proctor and Miss Saunders in the Foundation years, formerly called Reception. Mrs Jones and Mrs Evans are the first teachers in the history of the school to undertake a Job Share. Mrs Proctor retires in July 2004 and is to be replaced by Mr David Holley, the first male teacher to be appointed since the 1980s; he will take a Year 3/4 class.

At the end of 2002, the school bade farewell to Mrs Brambani who, having had the opportunity to experience headship for a term, was successful in being appointed as Headteacher of The Littletons CE First School. She was replaced by Mrs Dorothy Bevington.

In 2002, the old system of statementing and taking children with Special Needs out of classes for extra tuition gave way to a new Code of Practice. Mrs Bees, the Special Needs teacher, retired in 2002, and Mrs Tara Collins took on the role of SENCO (Special Educational Needs Co-ordinator). This function is now more of an advisory role, as the classroom teacher has responsibility for the special needs of any child in the class.

Admissions

Badsey First School is permitted to take up to

May 2004, Mr Julien Kramer, Director of Education for Worcestershire, with a group of children on the occasion of the official opening of the Learning and Teaching Area.

45 children per year-group. The catchment area continues to be the three parishes of Badsey, Aldington and Wickhamford, but there are insufficient numbers of children from within the catchment area to make up this number so many children come from outside the area. Admissions are buoyant, however, and the school is over-subscribed for September 2004 entry. In the academic year 2003-2004, a third of the children at the school live outside the catchment area, the numbers made up as follows: 53% from Badsey, 3% from Aldington, 10% from Wickhamford, 20%

May 2004, the teachers in the new staffroom. Back row: Mrs Wendy Proctor, Mrs Julie Jones, Mrs Kathryn Evans, Mrs Christine Cross. Front row: Mrs Tara Collins, Miss Hannah Saunders, Mrs Alison Stirling, Mrs Lucy Lee, Mrs Dorothy Bevington. (Not pictured: Mrs Emma Avery.)

Top and bottom: May 2004, the new Learning and Teaching Area, created in a room which began life in 1895 as "the Babies' room" for 3-4 year-old children, then part became a scullery in 1946 and then a staffroom and storeroom. The room is divided into a book area and computer area.

from Evesham and 14% from neighbouring villages.

Premises

Since the school was built in 1895, it has been extended many times and now covers an area roughly twice the size of the original buildings. All previous extensions had been outwards, but the most recent project extended upwards making the most of the Victorian building's high ceilings. By the summer of 2003 the work was almost complete. The former library was converted into a staffroom, and the former staffroom became a Learning and Teaching Resource Area housing the library and a computer suite. Use was made of the loft space which was converted into a work area for Teaching Assistants and houses the computer server. The extension was made possible by using £15,000 from the Trustees, £20,000 from the LEA and the remainder, just over £12,000 from the school's Devolved Capital Grant. The finishing touches were completed in 2004 and the new area was opened officially by Julien Kramer, Director of Education, on Friday 7th May 2004.

Improvement of the school's surroundings continues and the next major project is the refurbishment of the boys' and girls' toilets, including a disabled toilet.

Playgrounds and Playing-fields

In 2002, preparations began for the reclamation of the pond area and the slabbed courtyard outside the nearby classroom area. An Eco Club, under the direction of Mrs Proctor, was formed to encourage children to take an interest in the environment, and each class has two Eco Club representatives.

The school has a grounds development

January 2004, the school and playing-fields from the south on a snowy day, showing the nursery and 1993 extension.

plan, an ambitious project which will evolve over the next few years. Staff and pupils have all had an input and the children provided ideas and designs. The grounds development will include table-top games, a Stephenson's screen (to house weather-station equipment), story area, sandpit, wigwam, den-building area, willow sculptures and high mounds to run over.

Curriculum

The National Curriculum is still in place but is no longer as prescriptive as it was in the 1990s. The Literacy and Numeracy strategies have become incorporated into the National Primary strategy and teachers are being encouraged to be more creative again. This has meant that certain subject areas, which had seemed in danger of being sidelined, can now come to

July 2003, Mrs Collins, Year 5 teacher, with Artist-in-Residence, Glenn Hinton, and some of the children who worked on an African mask project. Back row: Chloe Causier, Sophie Grinnell, Alice Hall, Katie Barnes, Joshar Andac, George Mountney, Charlotte Stanley. Front row: Glenn Hinton, Christopher Curtis, Max Brambani.

Sam Phillips, aged 4, working on a pottery wolf.

the fore again. Emphasis is also placed on good handwriting for all children and joined-up handwriting is taught from the Foundation year. At a county workshop in March 2004, Badsey was selected as a case study as it was felt that the school was providing a broad and rich curriculum.

For the last two years the school has taken part in an exciting "Lads and Dads" project aimed at improving boys' literacy skills and enthusiasm for learning. The project aims to link reading and sport, whilst fostering the bond between the adult and the child.

Art plays an important part in the life of the school with termly visits from an Artist-in-Residence. In January 2004, the youngest two classes in the school joined forces with School Lane Nursery for a Foundation Stage Artist-in-Residence Project. The project focused on nursery rhymes and all the pupils produced their very own three little pigs, big bad wolf or straw house. For the last two years, artwork from pupils has been selected for display in the cloisters of Worcester Cathedral as part of the county's "Voices and Vision" Festival.

A House system was introduced in September 2003 for Key Stage 2 pupils: Bredon (blue), Cleeve (yellow), Malvern (red) and Cotswold (green). House points are awarded for good work and behaviour, counted each week and the house with the most points has their colour ribbon tied to the house trophy. It was felt that stickers for good work had lost their appeal for the older children and, with the influence of the "Harry Potter" books, the children were very receptive to the idea of Houses and so the House system was reintroduced 23 years after it had been abolished.

In order to assist in classroom teaching, inter-active whiteboards have been purchased for each classroom and were installed in July 2004. Information & Communication Technology (ICT) is an integral part of the curriculum. There are three computers in each classroom and computers in the lobby, science area and Learning and Teaching Area. There are 16 children's laptop computers, with a trolley, giving a ratio of one computer to every six pupils.

Sports

The school continues to prove successful in inter-school football matches and for the last three years have been the winners of the Terry Overthrow Memorial Shield.

The school is participating in an Evesham Area School Sport Co-Ordinator Partnership, which is part of the Government's Physical Education strategy where families of schools come together to enhance sports opportunities for all. The Evesham High School Specialist Sports College partnership is due to start in September 2004 and the DfES will provide funding for three years.

Testing

Standard Attainment Tests (SATs) continue to be held every May for Year 2, whilst Year 3, 4 and 5 pupils also take part in tests. In order to provide continuity between the First and Middle School, Mrs Collins acts as a liaison with the Key Stage 2 Co-ordinator at Blackminster. This helps the school to plan more effectively, ensures there is no repetition in the curriculum and eases the transition of pupils from Badsey to Blackminster.

The school is to have an Ofsted inspection in September 2004, which will give staff and Governors the opportunity to celebrate the school's successes with the inspectors.

Extra-Curricular

The pyramid orchestra meets regularly with a

March 2004, the school football team in their new kit provided by the Football Foundation with Football Manager Mr Andy Bolland (a parent and former pupil) and Assistant Mr Tom Hill, Parent Governor. Back row: Jordan Hughes, Harvey Monk, James Roberts, Dan Andrew, Tom Evans, George Gallot, Jacob Meadows. Front row: Tom Attwood, Joshua Gibbons, Alex Trotman, Sam Ford (Captain), Matt Andrew, Niall Wilson.

concert being held at Evesham Arts Centre at the end of the summer term featuring musicians and choirs from the seven First Schools in the Blackminster Pyramid. Mrs Spencer has compered the concert for ten out of the 15 years it has been held.

In July 2003 the School Choir, accompanied by Mrs Jones, had the opportunity to rehearse with Lillian Boutte (the official Music Ambassador for New Orleans and successor to Louis Armstrong), an internationally renowned jazz, blues and gospel singer. Lillian sang alongside the children who learnt a repertoire of gospel and jazz songs in two days. Her genuine love for the music and charismatic personality engendered an enthusiasm and drive that ensured an unforgettable experience. The event represented an exciting new development for Worcestershire's "Voices and Visions" Festival of Visual and Performing Arts. At the Forum Theatre, Malvern, Badsey pupils joined with a choir and band of over 200 children for what proved to be an outstanding finale to "Voices and Visions" 2003.

In the summer term 2004, the school produced its own compact disc, which features every child in the school singing, and special items by different classes.

Outings

The annual visit to Osmington Bay Outdoor Centre continues to be a popular weekend for Year 5 pupils. On the trip in 2004, the children had the opportunity to participate in archery, abseiling, rock climbing, mountain biking, a night hike, fencing, problem solving, a blindfolded sensory trail and a disco.

Each class goes on one outing a term to places such as Pershore Abbey or Chedworth Roman villa.

School Hours & Holidays

The school day begins at 9.15 and ends at 3.15, with a 45-minute lunch-break for Key Stage 2 and a one-hour lunch-break for Key Stage 1, making a total of 5¼ hours per day for Key Stage 2 and 5 hours for Key Stage 1.

The school is in session for 190 days a year in contrast to 200 days in the first half of the 20th century. The neighbouring county of

Gloucestershire, in line with a few other counties, has recently switched to the six-term year, but Worcestershire has deferred taking a decision on this for the moment.

Closures

On two occasions early in 2004, snowfall caused the closure of some schools in the vicinity, but for Badsey it was work as normal. The only time the school has had an enforced closure in this period was when there were serious problems with the roof. As early as 1997, the LEA had agreed that the school needed a new roof but that for the foreseeable future it would only be patched up when necessary. Just a short time into Mrs Brambani's Acting headship, a number of tiles fell off the roof in three separate incidents within as many days. The school was closed for two days whilst a local firm undertook emergency repair work. Further work was undertaken during the Easter holidays and the roof was completely retiled during the summer vacation.

School Health Service

It is now nearly a hundred years since the school health service was inaugurated and children's health in the nation as a whole has improved dramatically. But some things don't change. Whilst "the nit nurse" no longer visits to inspect children's heads, there are cases of head lice from time to time.

The old illnesses of scarlet fever, measles, mumps, and the like are a thing of the past but chicken-pox still exists as does the regular cold. Asthma is on the increase, with a number of children bringing inhalers to school. The average attendance over the last three years has varied between 93.1% and 95.2%, comparable to the figures of a hundred years ago.

Transport and Road Safety

These days, children either walk to school, come by bus, or are taken by car. Road safety in School Lane still remains an issue. Currently, 34% of children at the school live outside the catchment area, so it seems inevitable that they will be brought to school by car.

Pupils, staff and Governors are currently devising a travel plan. Congestion near the school at the beginning and end of the day is being monitored by pupils who are carrying out traffic surveys and preparing leaflets encouraging those who live within walking distance to walk to school. Once completed, the travel plan may enable the school to access a capital grant.

Nearly 50 years after the issue was first raised and 34 years after five-year-old Graham Salter, son of John and Betty Salter, was killed, traffic lights have at last been installed on the Bretforton Road. The official opening was held on 15th July 2004 with Mrs Spencer and Mrs Salter in attendance.

Parents

In March 2004, the PTA said goodbye to its energetic Chairman of three years, Kathryn Hough, who left the village to take up a one-year appointment as a doctor in the Shetland Isles. Under Kathryn's chairmanship, the PTA

February 2004, mountain-biking at Osmington Bay Outdoor Centre, Dorset.

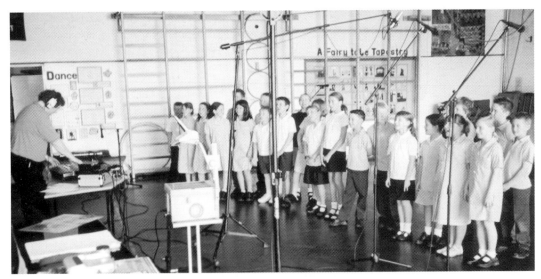

May 2004, Mrs Stirling's class recording a song for the school's first CD.

had an active programme of Quiz Nights, Fashion Shows, Beetle Drives, Discos and the annual Christmas Fayre and summer fête. Kathryn did not, however, secure her ambition to get the Queen to open the fête in her Golden Jubilee year. Instead she had to settle for another Elizabeth: the new Headteacher, Mrs Spencer. On that day, all the children were presented with a special Jubilee medal as a gift from the PTA.

Governors

The Governors of Badsey First School meet termly for full Governing Body meetings and on other occasions for sub-committee meetings. Dr Peter Phillips, Managing Director of a medical implant company, has been Chairman since 1998. His daughter, Gina, was

Dr Peter Phillips, Chairman of Governors.

a pupil at the school from 1997 to 2003 and his son, Sam, is in Year 1.

The World Wide Web

In 2002, the school developed its own website, www.badseyfirst.ik.org, giving up-to-date news on school events. There is a guestbook with comments from former pupils.

Over 170 former pupils have registered with www.friendsreunited.co.uk, the website which enables pupils who attended the same school to keep in touch with one another.

150th Anniversary Celebrations

On 27th April 2004, Badsey schoolchildren went into the playground to hear a special peal of bells at St James' Church to commemorate 150 years of formal education in Badsey. "Badsey Surprise Major", a full peal of 5056 changes, was rung in 2 hours 43 minutes by members of the Worcestershire & District Association. The peal was dedicated to Eve Bent, a former School Governor, local Councillor and choir member, who died in February 2004.

As part of the 150th celebrations, every child in the school, with the assistance of the Artist-in-Residence, has made a clay tile which has been fired. The tile features either a self-portrait or something to do with education. The tiles are on display in all the corridors in the school.

On 25th September 2004, subscribers to this book will assemble for the launch of the book at the school, at which there will be an exhibition of photographs and documents, guided tours, and a commemorative painting by former pupil, Michael Barnard, will be unveiled. Further anniversary events are planned for later in the term.

Leaving Badsey First School

The Leavers' Assembly, started during Mr Hughes' time at the school, has become something of a tradition. On the last day of the summer term the parents of the Year 5 leavers are invited to a special assembly where the children produce an entertainment. In 2003, for the first time since Prize-Giving stopped in 1967, all the leavers were presented with a book and a pen as a memento of their time at Badsey School.

In the summer term 2003, the Year 5 leavers were asked to record their memories of their time at Badsey First School. Many remembered the trips they had been on – to the Butterfly Farm at Stratford, the Teddy Bears' Picnic at Bishopswood Environmental Centre – and also visitors to the school, for example the man who brought a tarantula and a hissing cockroach. The weekend trip to Osmington Bay featured highly, as did school concerts.

Art was overwhelmingly the favourite lesson, but PE was also a favourite, particularly

July 2003, Jonathan Spinks and Connor Trotman in shirts signed by their schoolmates. Since the mid 1990s, it has been the tradition to sign each other's shirt on the last day of term.

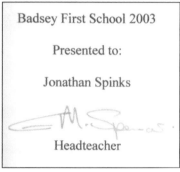

> Badsey First School 2003
>
> Presented to:
>
> Jonathan Spinks
>
> Headteacher

July 2003, Mrs Spencer presenting books to leavers at the final assembly.

with the boys who enjoyed the school team matches. Many of the children made reference to the two Headteachers they had had during their time at Badsey. Mr Hughes was particularly remembered for his funny stories in assemblies. Not surprisingly, as it was Mrs Collins' class who wrote the memories, the teacher who was described the most was Mrs Collins.

"She's funky and groovy and she makes things fun!" (Kathryn Barnes)

"Mrs Collins is a very stylish teacher, she wears all the top fashion. She is firm and fair but can get upset if you are naughty." (Jessica Jefford)

In 70-80 years' time, what will these children remember of their time at Badsey School? The overall tone of the memories is one of great enjoyment in a friendly, secure environment. Perhaps we shall leave it to Alice Hall to finish with her comment, quite simply: "BADSEY IS THE BEST!!"

Above: A family of Sparrows. Nine-year-old Adam Sparrow's forebears have had connections with the school since 1888. Front row: Adam Sparrow (pupil 2000-present day), sister Louise (pupil 1997-2003), grandmother Judy (School Secretary 1988-1999). Back row: great-uncle Terry (pupil 1939-1944), parents Paula (née Tandy, pupil 1971-1976) and John (pupil 1972-1977), grandfather Patrick (pupil 1941-1946). Great-grandfather Alfred William Sparrow (pupil 1906-1914) and Great-great-grandfather Alfred Cecil Sparrow (1888) also attended, the latter just for a year when the family first moved to Badsey.

Below: The Barnard clan. Pat Goldstraw (née Barnard) and just some of her many family members, who all attended Badsey School. Back: Kate Williams, Pat Gorin, Mark Barnard, Michael Barnard, Sarah Rickey, Pat Goldstraw, Susan Goldstraw, Stephen McMeikan, Jennifer Dennis, Cathy McMeikan, Thomas Hardwick, Pat Westmacott, Ian Hardwick. Seated: Jane Rickey, Liz Hardwick. On grass: Olivia Marshall, Eleanor Hardwick, Chloe Westmacott.

Silver birch planted by Mrs Norah Smith, 1995.

10

CONCLUSION

From small beginnings in 1854 catering for 78 children in the age-range 5-10, Badsey School has expanded and adapted over the years to meet the changing educational issues of the day. From once having an age-range up to 14 and peaking at a high of just over 300 pupils, the school is back to the age-range with which it started but it can now cater for 270 children. 150 years ago, it would have been unthinkable for the Vicar and other School Managers to send their children to the local village school. Even in more recent times, the Vicar and Headteacher sometimes opted for private education, but it is encouraging that our most recent Vicar sent his daughter to the school. Badsey is a thriving community school, still serving the needs of the parishes of Badsey, Aldington and Wickhamford, and is a celebration of all that is good in the state system of education.

We are fortunate to live in a time when everyone, no matter what his or her station in life, has access to a good education. By the 1920s, Badsey was a showcase school for the county and it has continued to live up to that reputation. Evan Llewelyn Harry, the young graduate who surveyed the village in 1929, concluded the school chapter by saying: "More remarkable than anything else is the corporate feeling set up in this school. Teacher and pupil develop a bond of affection which lasts through the adolescent period. Insufficient time has elapsed to say how much longer it will last but it seems that a life-long bond is the only natural culmination that can be reasonably forecasted. Boys and girls alike are proud to be old pupils of this school." Over 70 years later that sentiment is still true.

Economic life in the Vale has changed and market gardening has largely been replaced by haulage companies and light industries. Very few Market Gardeners are left and nowadays the parents are more likely to be accountants, prison officers, computer engineers. The changing patterns of work mean that many parents commute long distances to their jobs and Badsey is, for many families, just a pleasant village in which to live. Whilst many children at Badsey School today come from families which have only recently moved to the village, there are still a fair number whose parents, aunts, uncles, grandparents, great-grandparents were educated at the village school. For these people, it is still very much a family affair. When my son started at the school in 1997, around a third of his class came from families with more than one generation who had attended the school.

Nearly 80 years after she left, Molly Corbett (née Evans, pupil 1916-1925) stands in front of a brightly-coloured fire made by the children of Mrs Cross' class. In Molly's schooldays, a coal fire was the only means of heating. She remembers Miss Bird sitting on the iron guard in front of the fire and blocking the heat from the rest of the class!

Knight, Hartwell, Bird, Roberts, Jelfs, Harwood, Crisp, Keen, Hall, Mason, Collett, Ballard, Barnard, Sparrow – over the years, these families have sent many children to Badsey School. Nowadays, these names on the school roll are not so common, but one family that can boast of five generations with the same name attending the school is that of nine-year old Adam Sparrow.

Another local family with an equally impressive record is the Barnard family. There are no longer any children by the name of Barnard at the school but the descendants of the Barnards are many. School Trustee, Mrs Pat Goldstraw (née Barnard), is a former pupil, teacher and Governor of Badsey School. Pat's Great-great-great-grandfather was William Barnard who taught at the Sunday School before the National School opened. Pat's mother and several aunts were Student Teachers at the school and another aunt, Evelyn, taught at the school for a time in the 1930s, going on to marry Bill McKanan-Jones, who was later awarded the MBE for his work in education. Evelyn's great-great-niece, Cathy McMeikan, wrote a poem in 2001 on the occasion of leaving Badsey First School.

I've been at Badsey for five years now,
Times have just flown, I don't know how,
It seems only yesterday I was in Year One,
But as I'm ten and leaving, my time's nearly done.

Badsey was great, happy and small,
I have many good memories of you all,
It is sad to be moving but I have to go,
But bear in mind I'll miss you all so.

Thank you, teachers, for helping me learn,
Thank you, Mr Hughes, for being kind, not stern,
Thank you, Mrs Bees, for teaching me to sing,
Thank you, supply teachers for just coming in!

As I travel to my future, I will not forget my past,
I'll make sure all my happy memories really do last.

My son, too, was happy at this school. Like many parents, I feel fortunate that there are many schools such as Badsey that give children a good start in life. I hope that all Badsey pupils, whenever they were at the school, will remember their schooldays with fondness.

APPENDIX A
THE HEADTEACHERS OF BADSEY SCHOOL

Miss Sarah Bradley, National School, 1854-1860s
Miss Ann Meredith, National School, 1870s[1]
Miss Colbourn, National School, c mid 1870s
Miss Ruth Silvester, National School, c 1879-1880[2]
Miss Antoinette Marsden, National School, 1881-1883
Miss Letitia Stone, National School, 1883-1885
Miss Elizabeth Wagstaff, National School, 1885-1888[3]
Miss Alice Kelland, National School, 1889-1893[4]
Miss Mary Edgerton, Board School, 1893-1894
Mr John McDonald, Board and Council School, 1894-1913[5]
Mr Frank Amos, 1913-1944, Council School[6]
Mr Ronald West, 1945-1946, Council School[7]
Mr Maurice Harvey, Council and County Primary School, 1946-1967[8]
Mr Hugh Chaplin, County Primary and First School, 1968-1981[9]
Mr Trevor Clark, First School, 1981-1987[10]
Mr Gerard Hughes, First School, 1988-2001[11]
Mrs Elizabeth Spencer, First School, 2002-present day

The Infant Department

From 1896-1937, the Infant Department was run as a separate Department with its own Head.

Mrs Elizabeth Mason, 1896-1922[3]
Mrs E D Thompson, 1922-1923
Mrs Martha Catherine Morris, 1923-1926[12]
Mrs Frances Kissack, 1926-1928
Mrs Martha Catherine Morris, 1928-1937[12]

Further notes about the Headteachers

[1] Became Mistress of Little Marcle School, Herefordshire.
[2] Taught at Coventry until her marriage to John Cull, 1883; lived at Cull's Bakery, Badsey High Street; died 1939, buried at Badsey.
[3] Married John Mason, later returned as Head of the Infant Department; died 1955.
[4] Married Geoffrey Jones, lived at Norfolk House, Badsey Fields Lane; died 1939, buried at Badsey.
[5] Died 1913, shortly after retirement, buried at Badsey.
[6] Retired to Laverton; died 1970, buried at Badsey.
[7] Seconded to staff of Cooper's Hill Training College, Surrey, later became Head of a school in Bristol.
[8] Retired to a bungalow in Badsey; died 1971, buried at Badsey.
[9] Retired to Shakespeare Trust House at Stratford; died 1991.
[10] Became Head of Ravens Bank First School, Redditch; now retired and lives in Spain.
[11] Now Head of Chawson First School, Droitwich.
[12] As Martha ("Patsy") Mustoe, trained as a Pupil Teacher at Badsey; married A Morris, widowed in the First World War; died 1960, buried at Badsey.

APPENDIX B
THE TEACHERS OF BADSEY SCHOOL

The teaching staff today at Badsey First School comprises one Headteacher, ten qualified teachers and nine Teaching Assistants with an average of 30 children per class but, in the past, the staff/pupil ratio was far lower. A hundred years ago, 75% of teachers were female, but male and female teachers were not paid equally. Today, the teaching profession at primary level is still predominantly female, but now there is equal pay for equal work.

The following is a list of the staff who have taught at the school during its entire history (where female staff have married during their teaching career at the school, they are listed under both names):

Mrs Louise ALBON (also Carne), First School, 1989-1993

Miss Elsie ALDINGTON, Council School, 1920-1922

Mr Frank Edmund AMOS, Council School, 1907-1910

Mrs Jean McDonald AMOS (also McDonald), Council School, 1912-1923 & 1930-1944*

Miss Emma ANDERSON (also Avery), First School, 1994-present day

Mrs Emma AVERY (also Anderson), First School, 1994-present day

Miss E Patricia BARNARD (also Goldstraw), County Primary School, 1952-1956*

Miss Edith BARNARD, Council School, 1921-1922*

Miss Evelyn BARNARD, Council School, 1930-1934*

Miss Alison BARNSLEY (also Stirling), First School, 1995-present day

Miss Dorothy BATTY, Council School, 1919-1920

Mrs Barbara BEES, First School, 1990-2002

Mr Anthony BARRY, County Primary, 1968-1970

Mrs Dorothy BEVINGTON, First School, 2003-present day

Miss Lilian Maud BIRD (also Woodward), Council and County Primary School, 1908-1942

Mrs Yvonne BOWRING, County Primary, 1974-1985

Mrs Helen BRAMBANI (also Leedham), First School, 1992-2001

Mrs Sarah BROOKES, Council School, 1921-1924

Mrs Dorothy BULLOCK, Council School, 1923-1924

Miss Louise CARNE, First School, 1989-1993

Miss Agnes CARR, Council School, 1912-1912

Mrs Evelyn CASTLE, Council School, 1942-1943

Mrs Phyllis CHURCHILL, County Primary, 1956-1971

Miss Olivia CLIFFORD (also Robinson), First School, 1990-1992

Mrs Tara COLLINS, First School, 2001-present day

Mrs Carol CRIBB, First School, 1988-1989

Miss Alice Ellen CRISP, Board & Council School, 1894-1915

Miss E Helena CRISP, Council School, 1916-1921*

Mrs Christine CROSS, First School, 1990-present day

Miss Lilian CULL, Council School, 1907-1915*

Miss Rebecca DIDLICK, First School, 1995-2003

Mrs Esther DIGBY, First School, 1983-1985

Mr David DODRIDGE, County Primary School, 1971-1988

Miss Florence DOWDESWELL, Council School, 1906-1907

Mrs Jackie DUDLEY, First School, 1990-1990

Mrs Susan ESSEX, First School, 1994-2001

Mrs Kathryn EVANS, First School, 1998-present day

Mrs Lesley FAULKNER, First School, 1989-1991

Mrs Christine FELTON, County Primary School, 1972-1974

Miss Kate FOWLER, National School, c 1890-c 1892

Mrs P FRANCIS, County Primary School, 1965-1967

Mrs Fiona GARDNER, First School, 1985-1988

Mrs H M GARFIELD, County Primary School, 1970-1972

Miss Julie GATFIELD (also Jones), First School, 1992-present day

Mrs E Patricia GOLDSTRAW (also Barnard), County Primary School, 1952-1956*

Mrs Pat GORIN, County Primary School, 1967-1994

Mrs Sylvia GORIN, County Primary School, 1954-1972*

Miss Dorothy GRAHAM, Council School, 1928-1934

Miss Lluella HALLETT, Council School, 1922-1923

Miss Catherine HARKER, Board School, 1893-1894

Miss Emily HARTWELL, Council & County Primary School, 1907-1951*

Mrs Kitty HARTWELL, National School, 1854-c 1860s

Miss Kathleen Lacey HATTON, Council School, 1942-1948

Mr A W D HAYES, County Primary School, 1964-1965

Miss Joan HEATH, Council School, 1943-1944

Mrs Winifred HODGETTS, Council & County Primary School, 1945-1954

Mrs A Beatrice HOWELLS, Council & County Primary School, 1939-1951

Miss Constance I HUGHES (also Quaye), County Primary School, 1950-1953

Miss Amy HUNT, Council School, 1912-1930

Mr W J HUNT, County Primary School, 1953-1964

Mrs Sue IRELAND, First School, 1978-1982

Miss Ethel JACKSON, Council School, 1923-1923

Mr Harry Hilton JACKSON, County Primary School, 1948-1953

Mrs E Jean JAMES (also Jones), County Primary School, 1967-2001

Miss E Jean JONES (also James), County Primary School, 1967-2001

Mrs Julie JONES (also Gatfield), First School, 1992-present day

Mrs J M LAKEY, First School, 1979-1980

Mr M LEDBURY, First School, 1982-1983

Mrs Lucy LEE, First School, 2001-present day

Miss Helen LEEDHAM (also Brambani), First School, 1992-2001

Mr Robert LEWIS, Council School, 1914-1918

Mr Ian LLOYD-OSWELL, First School, 1988-1992

Miss Ethel MASON, Council School, 1924-1928

Miss Jean McDonald McDONALD (also Amos), Council School, 1912-1923 & 1930-1944*

Miss Margaret Anne McDONALD, Board & Council School, 1894-1939

Mr George McGOWAN, County Primary School, 1967-1970

Mrs Marion McGOWAN, County Primary & First School, 1975-1990

Mr William McKANAN-JONES, Council School, 1932-1939

Miss Jemima MEREDITH, National School, c 1860s-c 1870s

Mr David MILLER, County Primary School, 1964-1967*

Mrs Martha MORRIS, Council School, 1918-1919*

Mr A J MORTON, County Primary School, 1957-1964

Mrs Helen ORMEROD, First School, 1989-1990

Mrs Beryl OSBORNE, County Primary School, 1954-1956

Mr Norman OWENS, County Primary School, 1954-1957

Mr William PAGE, Council School, 1932-1939

Mrs P PALMER, County Primary School, 1971-1972

Miss Ada PEARMAN, National School, 1887-1888

Mrs Eileen PEET, County Primary School, 1951-1967

Mrs Rosalie PRATT, County Primary & First School, 1972-1977

Miss Marion PREECE, Council School, 1920-1921

Miss Cheryl PRICE, County Primary School, 1968-1970

Mrs Wendy PROCTOR, First School, 1988-2004

Mrs Constance QUAYE (also Hughes), County Primary School, 1950-1953

Mrs Olivia ROBINSON (also Clifford), First School, 1990-1992

Mrs Wendy RYDER, County Primary & First School, 1973-1978

Miss Hannah SAUNDERS, First School, 2003-present day

Mrs E SCOTT, First School, 1988-1993

Mr Victor SEALEY, Council School, 1923-1932

Mr William SHAW, County Primary School, 1956-1956

Mrs D E SMITH, County Primary School, 1958-1959

Miss Elizabeth SMITH, National School, 1888-1889

Miss Norah SMITH, Council & County Primary School, 1938-1975

Miss Rose SPARROW, Council School, 1910-1911*

Mr Herbert STALEY, Council School, 1910-1913

Mrs Alison STIRLING (also Barnsley), First School, 1995-present day

Mr Michael STOUT, First School, 1975-1982

Mr Harold TATE, County Primary School, 1952-1954

Miss Jane TEBBY, First School, 1992-1995

Miss Kay THOMAS, First School, 1985-1992

Mr Doug TREHARNE, County Primary School, 1970-1975

Mr Malcolm TURTLE, County Primary School, 1951-1952

Mrs A Ruth TYRELL, First School, 1987-1988

Mrs Betty WALKER, County Primary School, 1951-1952

Mr Frank WALKER, Council School, 1910-1910

Mr A R WARD, County Primary School, 1966-1968

Miss Helena WARMINGTON, National School, 1885-1887*

Mrs Joyce WATKIN, County Primary School, 1966-1989

Mrs R WESTON, County Primary School, 1972-1973

Miss Constance WILLIAMS, Council School, 1924-1928

Mrs Julia WILLIAMS, County Primary School, 1957-1967

Mr Walter WILLIAMS, Council School, 1911-1912

Mrs Lilian Maud WOODWARD (also Bird), Council & County Primary School, 1944-1951

Miss N E YOUNG, County Primary School, 1959-1961

* Also a pupil at the school

Pupil Teachers

From 1846, for over 60 years, the main method of teacher training was via the Pupil Teacher system. Able children were able to carry on for five extra years at school as Monitors or Pupil Teachers and received modest salaries. At 18, they could compete for Queen's Scholarships, taken up at a training college. Under a new scheme adopted in 1904, all pupil teachers apprenticed from 1904 had to attend a Pupil Teacher Centre for instruction at least five half days each week during the school year. By 1907 a new system of bursaries and student teacherships was in operation but for a few years Worcestershire elementary teachers clung to the old system. The last two Pupil Teachers to be apprenticed were Prudence Warmington and Edith Knight who began their indentures in 1907. The following is a list of all the Monitresses and Pupil Teachers who trained at Badsey and, where known, their future careers:

Fanny ADDIS (1867-1944), pupil at Badsey 1870s, Monitress c1881 at National School, did not remain in teaching, married Thomas Marshall in 1885 and ran The Wheatsheaf; buried at Badsey

Clara Jane ADDIS (1874-1964), pupil at Badsey c1879-1888, Monitress 1888 at National School, did not remain in teaching, married Walter Harwood in 1900; buried at Badsey

Fanny Elizabeth BENNETT (1879-1956), pupil at Badsey c1884-1892, Monitress 1893-1896, PT 1896-1900 in Mixed Department at Board School, gained Queen's Scholarship 3rd Class, married Thomas Knight; buried at Badsey

Hilda Julia Ann BUTLER (1884-1977), pupil at Badsey c1889-1898, Monitress 1898-1900, PT 1900-1904, gained King's Scholarship 3rd Class, taught at Badsey for a few months then went to St George's School, Worthing, married George Hart; buried at Badsey

Elsie COCKERTON (1877-?), Monitress 1893-1894

Lilian Ruth CULL (1888-?), pupil at Badsey 1891-1901, Monitress 1902-1904, PT 1904-1907 in Infant Department at Council School, gained King's Scholarship, taught at Badsey 1907-1915, married Herbert Drew in 1915 and taught in London

Maud Naomi CULL (1889-1948), pupil at Badsey 1892-1902, Monitress 1906-1907, PT at Hampton 1907, did not remain in teaching, joined Women's Land Army in WW1 and worked in family bakery, married Arthur Harrison in 1915, 4 children attended Badsey School; buried at Badsey

May Sylvester CULL (1885-?), pupil at Badsey 1890-1898, Monitress 1899-1900, PT 1901-1903 in Infant Department, gained King's Scholarship 3rd Class Division I in 1904, went to teach at Worthing, Sussex, married Mr Allen

Annie Maria ENSTONE (1885-?), pupil at Badsey 1890-1898, Monitress 1899-1900, PT 1901-1903 in Infant

Fanny Bennett (1879-1956), one of the first Pupil Teachers trained at Badsey.

Emily Hartwell (1888-1960), who spent 58 years of her life at Badsey School, first as pupil and Pupil Teacher and then as a member of staff. This photo was taken after she had retired.

Department, gained King's Scholarship 3rd Class Division I in 1904, went to teach at Newchurch, near Warrington

Florence Jane HARRIS (1889-?), pupil at Badsey 1893-1902, Monitress 1903-1904, PT 1904-1907, did not remain in teaching, married Norris Haines in 1910

Emily Bertha HARTWELL (1888-1960), pupil at Badsey 1893-1903, Monitress 1903-1904, PT 1904-1907 in Infant Department, taught at Badsey until retirement 1904-1951; buried at Badsey

Clara KNIGHT (1869-?), pupil at Badsey 1870s, Monitress 1883-1885 at National School, married William Hiden in 1892 and left the village

Edith Beatrice KNIGHT, not educated at Badsey, PT 1907-1910 in Mixed Department, Passed Part II of King's Scholarship in 1910

Douglas Scott McDONALD (1886-?), pupil at Farnborough c1890-1894 and at Badsey 1894-1900, Monitor 1900-1901, PT 1902-1902 in Mixed Department, did not pursue a career in teaching though helped out when father ill

Constance MOUNTFORD (c1889), not educated at Badsey, Monitress 1903-1903 in Mixed Department, left without notice when parents moved to Birmingham

Martha Catherine MUSTOE (1881-1960), pupil at Frampton Mansell 1880s and at Badsey c1889-1893, Monitress 1893-1897, PT 1897-1901 in Infant Department, gained Queen's Scholarship 3rd Class in 1901, married A J H Morris, taught at Badsey 1918-

1937, Head of Infant Department 1923-1926 and 1928-1937; buried at Badsey

Millicent Gertrude PETHARD (1887-?), pupil at Badsey 1894-1900, Monitress 1900-1902, PT 1903-1905 in Mixed Department, gained King's Scholarship in 1906, taught at Badsey for a few months then at Bramley National School, Surrey

Ellen Ann SEARS (1883-1923), pupil at Badsey c1888-1897, Monitress 1897-1899 in Infant Department, passed exam to train as PT but left on medical advice, married Ernest Stanley in 1903; buried at Badsey

Myra SHERWOOD (c1868-1922), pupil at Bretforton, Monitress 1883-1885 at National School, did not pursue a career in teaching; buried at Badsey

Millicent Mary SIMMONDS (c1892-?), from Paxford, PT 1906-1909 in Mixed Department, proceeded to Bristol Training College

James D SLIMMING (c 1891-?), son of a schoolmaster, pupil at school in Essex, began PT training at Poole in Dorset, PT at Badsey 1906-1908 in Mixed Department, failed Part I and left

Rose Emma SPARROW (1889-1923), pupil at Badsey 1892-1901, Monitress 1902-1904, PT 1904-1907 in Mixed Department, passed Preliminary Certificate, teacher at Pershore Council 1907-1910, teacher at Badsey 1910-1911, married Frederick Bond 1911; buried at Badsey

Prudence Jecolia WARMINGTON (1891-?), pupil at Badsey 1896-1905, Monitress 1905, PT 1907-1910 in Mixed Department

Student Teachers

As the new system of secondary education spread, entrance to the profession was soon through the secondary schools, and aspiring teachers undertook a year's preliminary training at a local school. The following is a list of the Student Teachers who trained at Badsey, prior to entering a training college:

Helen Edith BARNARD (1903-?), pupil at Badsey 1907-1916 and PHGS 1916-1921, ST 1921-1922

Gladys Julia BREWER (1906-?), pupil at Badsey 1912-1918 and PHGS 1918-1924, ST 1924-1925

Constance Juliet CRISP (1908-?), pupil at Badsey 1913-1920 and PHGS 1920-1925, ST 1925-1926,

went to St Catherine's College, Tottenham, taught in Warwick and Worcester

Elizabeth Helena CRISP (1894-1952), pupil at Badsey 1897-1907 and PHGS 1907-1911, ST 1912-1914, teacher at Badsey 1916-1921; married Harold Idiens, buried at Badsey

26 . 4 . 88 .

ENGLAND AND WALES.

1. Names, &c., in full of a quorum of the managers.

MEMORANDUM OF AGREEMENT between¹ *The Venerable Charles William Holbech Vicar of Farnborough and Revd Wm J. W. Tharrow Curate of Farnborough*

hereinafter called *the Managers*, on behalf of the Managers of the *Farnborough National*

2. Names, &c., in full, of father or other surety of the pupil-teacher.

School and² *John Henry Mc Donald* _____ hereinafter called *the surety*,

3. Father, or as the case may be.

the³ *Father*

4. Name in full of the pupil-teacher.

of⁴ *Margaret A. Mc Donald*

hereinafter called the *pupil-teacher.*

Pupil Teacher papers for Miss Margaret McDonald who taught at Badsey from 1894-1939. Miss McDonald undertook her apprenticeship at Farnborough National School where her father was Headteacher. The Memorandum of Agreement is a standard one for all Pupil Teachers. At the age of 16, having passed the qualifying exam and been accepted, the Pupil Teacher and her parent had to attend a Managers' meeting whereupon the document was signed by the Chairman, the Pupil Teacher and the parent.

Rose Marion CRISP (1901-1979), pupil at Badsey 1904-1914 and PHGS 1914-1919, ST 1919-1920; married Frederick Barnard, buried at Badsey

Stella Mary CRISP (1906-?), pupil at Badsey 1911-1918 and PHGS 1918-1923, ST 1923-1924, taught at Offenham and a girls' private school in Kenilworth

Ivy May GREENING (1909-?), pupil at Church Lench c1914-1919 and Badsey 1919-1922 and PHGS 1922-1926, ST 1926-1927; married Mr Wells and moved to South Littleton but son Brian attended Badsey School

Lucy Florence HILL (1897-?), pupil at Elmley Castle c1902-1908 and Badsey 1908-1909 and PHGS 1909-1914, ST 1914-1915

Lilian Rose KEEN (1907-1998), pupil at Badsey 1910-1920 and PHGS 1920-1925, ST 1925-1926, taught in a number of Vale schools; married George Crawford and moved to Scotland

Teacher Training Today

The Student Teacher scheme ended in the late 1920s. Students from then on went straight to teacher training college. In 1944, three-year courses at training colleges were introduced rather than two. Students at Worcester Training College (now University College, Worcester) undertook periods of teaching practice at the school. The 1970s saw progress in the professional training and status of the teacher and by the end of the decade teaching had become an all-graduate profession, with students either undertaking a Bachelor of Education degree or a Bachelor of Arts or Bachelor of Science degree followed by a Postgraduate Certificate in Education. In-service training also became important.

APPENDIX C
NON-TEACHING STAFF

A school will not function properly without the support staff who do a valuable job. The role of Caretaker is one that has been around for many years (indeed, in the last 113 years, the care of the school has been entrusted to just six people), but some of the other jobs are of a more recent creation.

Caretakers

Mrs Emma Wilson, 1891-1929
Mr A Cecil Keen, 1929-1959
Mr R A Roy Hall, 1959-1974
Mr Jack S Pike, 1974-1978
Mrs Mary Knight, 1978-2001
Mrs Pat Lake, 2001-present day
Pat Lake is assisted in the cleaning by Mrs Carol Mumford and Mrs Karen Jefford (née Pike, pupil 1969-1975), whose parents both worked at the school.

Duties of a Caretaker 1900
• Light the fires by 7.30 am
• Dust classrooms and corridors
• Clean the toilets and wash-basins
• Clean and empty the toilet closet pans twice a week
• Change the lavatory towels twice a week
• Empty the wastepaper bins in the playground
• Keep the coal stored properly in the Coal House
• Scrub floors
• Be in attendance when the school let for evening meetings
• Clean windows

Secretary

Prior to the Second World War, the post of School Secretary did not exist. It was Mr West, who became Head in 1945, who first asked for clerical assistance. It is not known who the first person in the post was, but from 1946 to 1981 the task was largely undertaken by the Headmaster's wife, firstly Mrs Harvey and then Mrs Chaplin. Until a separate office was formed in the 1980s, the Secretary worked in the Headteacher's office. Items of office equipment such as a telephone and typewriter, which we would regard as standard today, were not acquired until the 1940s. The school did buy a duplicator in 1934, but items such as a photocopier and computer were acquired in the 1980s.

Mrs Marjorie Harvey, 1946-1967
Mrs F Cooke, 1968-1972
Mrs Mary Chaplin, 1972-1981
Mrs Ruby Pickering, 1981-1988
Mrs Judy Sparrow, 1989-1999
Mrs Su Trinder, 1999-present day
Mrs Nichol Brown, 2003-present day

Teaching Assistants

Teaching assistance has been used in the classroom since the mid-1960s, but the role of the Teaching Assistant has become stronger in the last decade. There are currently nine Teaching Assistants: Mrs Norma Begley, Mrs Elizabeth Clark, Mrs Pauline Ella, Mrs Elaine Hill, Mrs Sylvia Jones, Mrs Karen Mason, Mr James Morris, Mrs Anne Poulter, Mrs Shirley Tutton.

Left below: May 2004, Mrs Nichol Brown at work at the photocopier. It is only since the 1980s that copiers have been in general use in schools.

Below: May 2004, Mrs Su Trinder at work in the school office. Note the standard office equipment of today: printer, computer, telephone and fax. What will the office of the future be like?

Top: Cecil (pupil 1897-1907) and Alice Keen, appointed Caretakers of the school in 1929.

Above: Mrs Mary Knight (right) with her Assistant, Mrs Daphne Cleaver. Mary first joined the school staff as a general assistant in the school kitchen in 1964; she was appointed Caretaker in 1978.

Below: Mrs Pat Lake (née Grinnell, pupil 1965-1971), the present day Caretaker, commenced duties in 2001. Her husband, Robert (pupil 1961-1968), is the school's handyman.

Cooks

From 1946 to 1981 a School Meals Service was provided but it was not until 1958, when the kitchen was built, that the first Cook was employed (previously, meals had been supplied by Blackminster Central Kitchen). The following people fulfilled the role of Cook-in-Charge:
Miss Jeanette de Ville, 1958-1961
Mrs Gladys (Sue) Long, 1961-1962
Miss Grace Churchill, 1962-1964
Mrs A White, 1964-1966
Mrs J Watkins, 1966-1967
Mrs Little, 1967-1968
Mrs J Causer, 1968-1969
Mrs Edna Jones, 1969-1981

Midday Supervisors

Since the School Meal service started, and after its demise, staff have been employed to supervise the children during the midday break. Initially they were called Children's Superintendents but now they are called Midday Supervisors.

Crossing Patrol

The first Crossing Patrol was appointed in 1969 with Mr Roy Hall, the Caretaker, initially fulfilling the role at School Lane; a further Crossing Patrol was appointed for Bretforton Road, a job held by Mrs W Fray for some time. Mrs Bet Benfield undertook the role at School Lane from 1979 and was succeeded by Mrs Fiona Roden who has done the job since the late 1980s. Mrs Sheila Mee acts as Crossing Patrol on Bretforton Road.

Above: May 2004, Midday Supervisors. Back row: Helen Welch, Elaine Hill, Sarah Pask, Norma Begley, Karen Wheatley, Sarah Riddick. Front row: Iris Perry, Fiona Roden, Jackie Newman, Karen Coldicott.

Right: June 2004, some of the Teaching Assistants. Back: Norma Begley, Pauline Ella, Karen Mason, Elaine Hill, Sylvia Jones. Front: James Morris, Shirley Tutton.

Below: Mrs Fiona Roden, the school's "Lollipop Lady" sees children safely across School Lane. Note the barrier on the right-hand side erected in 1935 after a child was killed; this was long before the job of Crossing Patrol was created.

MANAGERS AND GOVERNORS

The body of people which supports the Headteacher in the management of the school had always been known as Managers but from 1980 the term changed from Manager to Governor. The current role of the Governing Body is to act as a "critical friend" to the school involved in monitoring and advising.

Chairmen of Managers/Governors

Rev Thomas Hunt, National School, 1854-1887
Rev Charles Gepp, National School, 1887-1893
Mr Arthur H Savory, Board School, 1893-1899
Mr Leonard White, Board School, 1899-1902
Mr Alfred Butler, Board School, 1902-1903
Sir Julius Sladden, Council School, 1903-1928
Mr Charles Binyon, Council & County Primary School, 1929-1959
Mrs Doris Carter, County Primary School, 1959-1966
Rev Peter Braby, County Primary School, 1966-1969
Mr Ronald Churchill, County Primary School, 1969-1974
Mrs Beryl Osborne, County Primary & First School, 1975-1988
Mrs Sue Pike, First School, 1988-1991
Mrs Sheenah Beaven, First School, 1991-1993
Mrs Simone Hancox, First School, 1993-1996
Mr Clive Richards, First School, 1996-1998
Dr Peter Phillips, First School, 1998-present day

Chronology

1854-1893. National School. The Managers were the Minister and at least three other persons, who had to be members of the Church of England and subscribers of at least 20 shillings a year, and were elected by subscribers of at least 10 shillings a year.

1893-1903. Board School. Triennial elections held to elect seven Managers to the School Board; meetings held monthly.

1903-1974. Council School and County Primary School. Six Managers appointed every three years, four by the LEA and two by the Minor Local Authority (one by Badsey Parish Council and one by either the Aldington or Wickhamford Parish Meeting).

1975-present day. First School. Many changes have occurred in the last 29 years with a number of Education Acts redefining the constitution. From 1975 there were 12 Managers (including for the first time the Headteacher, and a specific post for a parent). In 1980, the term "Manager" was changed to "Governor". Further Acts increased the number of Parent Governors and made an Annual Parents' Meeting compulsory from 1986. The introduction of "Local Management of Schools" in 1990 placed greater responsibilities on Governors. The number of Governors was increased to 13 in 1999. The current Governing Body is required to reconstitute at some time during the next 2 years.

Many individuals or families have served the school for many years. The longest-serving Manager was Charles Binyon, OBE, a Manager for 59 years, 29 of which as Chairman. The oldest Manager was William Mustoe, a Manager for 36 years, who died in post aged 102. Father and son, John and Frank Knight, were both Managers for many years and the Butler family of Aldington Manor represented Aldington for nearly 40 years. The longest-serving Governor on the current Governing Body is Derek Harwood who was co-opted in 1989 and is a former pupil and Head Boy of the school. The following is a complete list of people who have served as Manager/Governor at some point during the school's history.

Mr George AGG, Council School, 1910-1921
Miss Emma ANDERSON, First School, 1999-2003
Mr Thomas APPELBEE, National School, 1854-1879
Mr Richard ASHWIN, National School, 1854-c1868
Mr J ATKINSON, First School, 1975-1975
Mr Edwin BALLARD, Council/County Primary,
    1947-1960
Mrs Sheenah BEAVEN, First School, 1989-1994
Mr George BELL, Board/Council School, 1901-1906
Mrs Eve BENT, First School, 1975-1984
Mr Charles BINYON, Board/Council/County Primary
    School, 1902-1961
Mr Walter BLAKE, Board/Council, 1899-1902 &
    1907-1933
Mr Thomas BLYTHE, National School, c1868-c1873
Mrs Vivienne BOWLER, First School, 1975-1988
Mrs Yvonne BOWRING, First, 1977-1981 & 1983-1985
Rev Peter BRABY, County Primary School, 1958-1973
Mrs Helen BRAMBANI, First School, 1995-1999
Mr R BREWER, First School, 1983-1987
Mr Frederick BULLOCK, National School, 1888-1889
Mr Alfred BUTLER, Board/Council, 1896-1903 &
    1906-1912
Mr Percy BUTLER, Council School, 1904-1905
Mr Wilson BUTLER, Council School, 1912-1933
Mr John BYRD, National School, 1888-1888 & 1893-1893
Mr Thomas BYRD, National/Board, 1881-1884 &
    1889-1893
Mr William BYRD, National School, c1869-c1875
Mr Benjamin CARTER, National School, 1889-c1893
Mrs Doris CARTER, Council/County Primary,
    1934-c1974
Mr Hugh CHAPLIN, First School, 1977-1981
Rev Wilfred CHAPMAN, County Primary, 1956-1957
Mr Edward CHURCHILL, County Primary, c1950-1956
Mr Ronald CHURCHILL, County Primary, 1961-1974
Mr Trevor CLARK, First School, 1981-1987
Mrs M A COLE, First School, 1977-1981
Miss Georgina CORBETT, National School, 1884-1885
Mrs J CORBETT, First School, 1975-1977
Mr L DACOMBE, First School, 1988-c1990
Mr David DODRIDGE, First School, 1975-1977
Mrs Sonya EALEY, First School, 1996-present day
Mrs Christine FELTON, First School, 1981-1983
Mrs Fiona GARDNER, First School, 1986-1988
Rev Charles GEPP, National School, 1887-1893
Mr Frank GOLDSTRAW, County Primary/First,
    c1973-1985
Mrs Pat GOLDSTRAW, First School, 1987-1992
Mrs Marcia GRANGER, First School, 2003-present day
Mr R C HALE, First School, 1983-1985
Mrs Simone HANCOX, First School, 1992-1997
Lady Caroline HARFORD, First School, 1985-1992
Mrs V HARMAN, First School, 1976-1981
Mr Derek HARWOOD, First School, 1989-present day
Mr Harry HATCHER, First School, 1975-1977
Mr Tom HILL, First School, 2004-present day
Mr Frederick HOOPER, National/Board, c1881-c1886 &
    1893-1894
Mrs Kathryn HOUGH, First School, 2002-2004
Mr Gerard HUGHES, First School, 1988-2001
Mrs Gwen HUGHES, First School, 1992-present day
Rev Thomas HUNT, National School, 1854-1887
Mr J IDIENS, Board/Council School, 1902-1904
Mr J F T INGLEDEW, Council School, 1903-1906

Mrs Jean IVES, First School, 1977-1993
Mrs Jean JAMES, First School, 1989-1992
Mrs C JELFS, First School, 1975-1977
Mr Samuel JOHNS, Council School, 1945-c1949
Mr Arthur JONES, Board/Council, 1899-1901 &
    1934-1947
Mr Francis JONES, County Primary School, 1955-1956
Mr Joseph JONES, National School, c1881-c1886
Mrs Julie JONES, First School, 2003-present day
Mr George KING, Council/County Primary, 1947-1960
Mr Charles KNIGHT, Board School, 1901-1902
Mr Frank KNIGHT, County Primary/First, c1974-1983
Mr John KNIGHT, Council/County Primary, 1929-1955
Mr Joseph KNIGHT, Board School, 1896-1902
Mr Gordon LASHFORD, First School, 1994-2002
Rev Adrian LEAK, First School, c1975-1980
Mrs P LOCKE, First School, 1983-c1992
Mr Thomas MARSHALL, Board School, 1893-1896
Mr John MASON, Board School, 1893-1903
Rev Peter MITCHELL, First School, 1983-1994
Mr William MUSTOE, Council School, 1908-1944
Mr William MYATT, National School, 1888-1889
Mr David NOYES, First School, 1980-1982
Ms Elizabeth NOYES, First School, 2003-present day
Mrs Beryl OSBORNE, County Primary/First, 1960-1996
Mr David OSBORNE, First School, 1990-present day
Mr P PARFITT, First School, 1985-1987
Mr P PARR , First School, 1994-1995
Mr Tony PASK, First School, 1999-2003
Mr David PATTEN, First School, 1994-2000
Mr George PETHARD, National School, c1881-1893
Mr William PETHARD, Board/Council School, 1902-1908
Dr Peter PHILLIPS, First School, 1998-present day
Mrs Sue PIKE, First School, 1986-2003
Mr John POOLE, National/Board School, 1889-1896
Mr Clive RICHARDS, First School, 1992-present day
Mr H L RICHARDS, Council School, 1907-1909
Mr Arthur SAVORY, National/Board, 1873-89 &
    1893-1897
Mr Robert SEAMAN, First, 1980-1981 & 1983-1985
Mrs A E SHARP, First School, 1975-1976
Mr Jerry SHARP, Board School, 1894-1896
Mr Thomas SHEAF, National School, 1854-c1859
Sir Julius SLADDEN, National/Board School, c1881-1928
Mr A SMALL, First School, 1983-1992
Mrs F SMITH, First School, 1986-1990
Mrs Iris SMITH, First School, 1982-1983
Mr Terry SPARROW, First School, 1988-1989
Mrs Elizabeth SPENCER, First School, 2002-present day
Mr George STEWART, County Primary, 1956-1959
Mrs B C STRATTON, First School, 1977-1981
Mr Benjamin SWIFT, Council School, 1921-1947
Mr Francis TAYLOR, National School, c1859-c1879
Mr Samuel TAYLOR, National School, 1854-1859
Miss Jane TEBBY, First School, 1994-1995
Mr Douglas TREHARNE, First School, 1975-1975
Mr Alan TUTTON, First, 1995-1999 & 2001-present day
Mr Charles TUTTON, County Primary School, 1960-1967
Mrs Shirley TUTTON, First School, 1999-present day
Mr W John WARMINGTON, Board School, 1893-1899
Mr E T WARNE, First School, 1987-1990
Mr Leonard WHITE, Board School, 1896-1903
Mr Edward WILSON, National School, c1881-1893
Mr J G WOOD , Board School, 1899-1900
Mr J K WOODWARD, National School, 1889-c1893

APPENDIX E
NAMES ON THE HONOURS BOARD

From the early years of the 20th century, County Council scholarships were awarded for a free place at Grammar School. The Honours Board, provided by the LEA, with the names of the successful scholars, was not erected until 1936. Some of the earliest award-winners appear to have been omitted, so this error has been rectified here. A second Board was added in the 1940s. The final names added were those who gained a scholarship in 1944, the last cohort to go to the Grammar School under the "free place" scheme, before the 1944 Education Act made all secondary places free. The list below gives the names of all those awarded scholarships, date awarded, and the name of the school to which the pupil transferred.

Margaret AMOS (1931), MGC**

D Ian W ANDERSON (1932), PHGS

Eric G ANDERSON (1926), PHGS

Ronald BALLARD (1932), PHGS

E Helen BARNARD (1916), PHGS

Evelyn BARNARD (1923), PHGS

Gladys A BARNARD (1918), PHGS

E Patricia BARNARD (1943), PHGS

Sylvia M BARNARD (1925), PHGS

Derek J BARRAND (1944), PHGS

Lorna M BAYLISS (1936), PHGS

J Henry BIRD (1917), PHGS

Donald W BLAKE (1938), PHGS

Anthony J BRAZIER (1939), PHGS

David H BRAZIER (1942), PHGS

Arthur E BREWER (1916), PHGS

Dorothy L BREWER (1917), PHGS

Gladys J BREWER (1918), PHGS

Irene BROOKS (1930), PHGS

Winifred BROOKS (1925), PHGS

V Phyllis BUTLER (1917), PHGS

Edward CHURCHILL (1920), SQBS§

George E CHURCHILL (1919), KSW*

Joan W COCKERTON (1929), PHGS

Anthony J COLLETT (1937), PHGS

Norman W COLLETT (1942), PHGS

Peter H S COLLETT (1932), PHGS

Mary COOK (1942), PHGS

Alice M COX (1942), PHGS

James W COX (1939), PHGS

Ruth M COX (1918), PHGS**

Evelyn M CRANE (1923), PHGS

O Zena CRANE (1925), PHGS

Constance J CRISP (1920), PHGS

E Helena CRISP (1907), PHGS¶

Philip E CRISP (1916), PHGS

Rose M CRISP (1914), PHGS

Stella CRISP (1918), PHGS

Stephen CRISP (1923), PHGS

Laura CULL (1906), PHGS¶

Diana M DAFFURN (1944), PHGS

D Ramona R DAFFURN (1942), PHGS

Gordon R DARBY (1940), IGS

Valerie J DAVIES (1944), PHGS

Norris W DAYS (1936), PHGS

I D Barbara DORE (1919), PHGS

Helen A ECKLES (1944), PHGS

David J EDWARDS (1943), KSW

Doris M ENSTONE (1929), PHGS

Edmund P ENSTONE (1936), PHGS

Joan A ENSTONE (1928), PHGS

William B FIELD (1911), Left

Daisy G FORD (1934), PHGS

Norman C GIBSON (1942), BSS

Dorothy M GREEN (1926), PHGS

J Stanley GREEN (1917), PHGS

Edith A GREENING (1923), BCS**

G Nancy GREENING (1926), PHGS

Ivy M GREENING (1922), PHGS

Dorothy GRIFFIN (1942), PHGS

Muriel F HAINES (1934), PHGS

Colin HALL (1938), PHGS

George E HALL (1922), PHGS

Kathleen HALL (1929), PHGS

Ronald W HALL (1937), PHGS

George S HALSE (1935), PHGS

Frances B HANCOX (1911), PHGS

Celia HARRISON (1942), PHGS

Shirley HARRISON (1944), PHGS

Deryck HARTWELL (1940), PHGS

Donald HARTWELL (1943), PHGS

Mavis HARTWELL (1938), PHGS

Norman R HARTWELL (1928), PHGS

Pamela A HARVEY (1944), PHGS

Bertie S HATCH (1915), PHGS

Percy D HATCH (1924), PHGS

Stanley HATCH (1933), PHGS

Harry HATCHER (1922), BCS**

Edward HEMMING (1940), PHGS

Charles HERITAGE (1924), PHGS

Derrick HILL (1937), PHGS

Lucy F HILL (1909), PHGS

Alma M HOLBROOK (1936), PHGS

John P HOLBROOK (1930), PHGS

Iris D HUBBARD (1937), PHGS

Douglas A JELFS (1923), PHGS

George W JELFS (1925), PHGS

Mary JELFS (1940), PHGS

G Brian JENNINGS (1944), PHGS

Christopher J K JONES (1944), CGS

Frank E JONES (1913), PHGS

Patrick G D JONES (1939), PHGS

Elsie KEEN (1939), PHGS

Eva M KEEN (1922), PHGS

Josephine M KEEN (1944), PHGS

June I KEEN (1941), PHGS

Lilian R KEEN (1920), PHGS

Margaret KEEN (1933), PHGS

Nancy (A L) KEEN (1932), PHGS

Frank E KNIGHT (1925), PHGS

Joan M KNIGHT (1922), PHGS

P Edna KNIGHT (1926), PHGS

Ruth KNIGHT (1923), PHGS

Hazel L LONGMORE (1941), PHGS

Kenneth C LONGMORE (1939), PHGS

Jack MALIN (1923), BCS*

Mary K MARSHALL (1929), PHGS

Thomas W MARSHALL (1933),
    OSHS§

Marjorie MARTIN (1943), PHGS

Frederick C MASON (1922), BCS*

Thomas MASON (1906), PHGS¶

Ruth E MORRIS (1921), PHGS

E Lucy MUSTOE (1919), PHGS

Patricia MUSTOE (1931), PHGS

Ivor K NAYLOR (1938), PHGS

Dennis E OAKLEY (1933), PHGS

Mary OCKWELL (1944), PHGS

Mavis OSBORNE (1937), PHGS

Elsie E PERKINS (1918), SQBS**

J Douglas PETHARD (1925), PHGS

Doris I PHILLIPS (1941), IGS

Arthur R A PLANT (1938), PHGS

Maurice V PORTER (1938), PHGS

Holloway H REED (1927), PHGS

Ronald J REED (1931), PHGS

Ivy B SADLER (1918), PHGS

Thomas J SADLER (1927), PHGS

Nellie SALTER (1927), PHGS

Douglas L SANDFORD (1924), PHGS

Jean W SANDFORD (1942), PHGS

R Roger SAVORY (1941), PHGS

Philip H SMITH (1940), PHGS

David L SOUTHERN (1943), PHGS

Samuel J SOUTHWELL (1940), PHGS

Esme M SPARROW (1925), PHGS

Terrence C SPARROW (1944), PHGS

Margaret STANTON (1935), BCS**

Hazel I STEWART (1937), PHGS

James W STEWART (1929), SQBS§

Mary STEWART (1944), WGS

E May SUMMERS (1943), PHGS

Sylvia D SUMMERS (1941), PHGS

Janet M SUTTON (1943), PHGS

T Derek TATE (1944), Home

W Muriel L TAYLOR (1931), PHGS

M Anne TULLETT (1944), PHGS

Maywen B TUTTON (1942), PHGS

C Ralph TUTTON (1939), PHGS

Gwendoline WARMINGTON (1907),
    PHGS¶

Thomas WARMINGTON (1906),
    PHGS¶

Anne M WATSON (1941), PHGS

Frances E C WHEELER (1924), BCS*

Margaret WILSON (1942), PHGS

Lilian M WOODWARD (1926), PHGS

* In the early years of scholarships, there was a shortage of free places. These children passed the County Council scholarship exam but were not awarded a scholarship.

** Awarded County Council scholarship but place not accepted.

¶ Gained a County Council scholarship in the first years of the examination, but omitted from Honours Board.

§ Not on Honours Board as did not gain a County Council scholarship, but gained scholarship to boarding school.

BCS – Badsey Council School

BSS – Birmingham Secondary School

CGS – Campden Grammar School

Home – Returned home

IGS – Ilford Grammar School

KSW – King's School, Worcester

Left – Left the neighbourhood

MGC – Malvern Girls' College

OSHS – Old Swinford Hospital School

PHGS – Prince Henry's Grammar
    School, Evesham

SQBS – Sibford Quaker Boarding
    School

WGS – Worcester Grammar School

APPENDIX F
THE SCHOOL BUILDING

The current school building on School Lane (or Bakers Lane as it was known before the school was built) was built in 1895. Stratford-on-Avon bricks were used in the construction supplied by Messrs Espley & Co at a cost of 28s 6d per 1000, delivered to Littleton & Badsey Station. The architect was Edward Lingen Barker of Hereford and the builder was Frederick Gardner of Bengeworth. The school has been much added to over the years, but the original building of 1895 was as follows:

Badsey Mixed and Infant Board School

		Square Feet		Children
East room	20'0" x 22'0"	440		44
Mixed schoolroom	31'6" x 22'0"	693		68
Two classrooms	20'0" x 22'0"	440		44
Infants' schoolroom	30'0" x 20'0"	600	}	
	18'0" x 20'0"	360	}	118
Total		**2533**		**274**

Expenditure	£	
Cost of site	90	
Cost of buildings	1190	
Estimate of furniture (see below)	90	
Architect's commission	57	10s
Other (law costs, compensation for tenants)	72	10s
Total	**1500**	

Breakdown of Furniture Estimate	£	
65 boys and 65 girls' desks @ 7s per child	45	10s
18 infants desks @ 5s per child	4	10s
2 tables @ £4 each	8	
5 chairs @ 6s each	1	10s
3 pupil teachers' desks @ £2 each	6	
2 galleries for infants	20	
2 cupboards @ £2 5s 0d	4	10s
Total	**90**	

A further £288 was spent on playgrounds, walls and fences.

Since 1895, the school buildings have more than doubled in size, but the number of children that can be accommodated is almost identical. In 1895, 8 square feet was allowed per child allowing a total of 274 children. Nowadays, the number permitted is 270 with a complex formula being used for assessing net capacity. The first extension was built just five years after the school opened. Ten more extensions have followed, the main period of building activity being in the 1920s and 1990s. The latest extension – the Learning and Teaching area, completed in 2004 – has gone upwards rather than outwards, making use of the high roof of the Victorian building to create a resource area and workspace. "It never ceases to amaze me how this school keeps expanding like elastic," said School Trustee, Pat Goldstraw, in 2003.

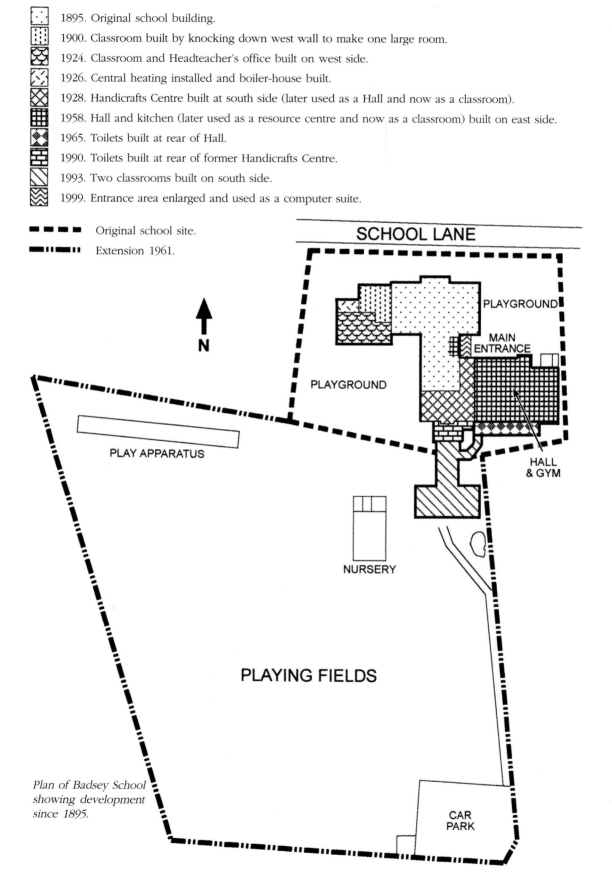

1895. Original school building.

1900. Classroom built by knocking down west wall to make one large room.

1924. Classroom and Headteacher's office built on west side.

1926. Central heating installed and boiler-house built.

1928. Handicrafts Centre built at south side (later used as a Hall and now as a classroom).

1958. Hall and kitchen (later used as a resource centre and now as a classroom) built on east side.

1965. Toilets built at rear of Hall.

1990. Toilets built at rear of former Handicrafts Centre.

1993. Two classrooms built on south side.

1999. Entrance area enlarged and used as a computer suite.

Original school site.

Extension 1961.

SCHOOL LANE

N

PLAYGROUND

MAIN
ENTRANCE

PLAYGROUND

HALL
& GYM

PLAY APPARATUS

NURSERY

PLAYING FIELDS

CAR
PARK

*Plan of Badsey School
showing development
since 1895.*

ELIZABETH SEWARD'S CHARITY

250 years ago, an educational charity was set up in Badsey by Elizabeth Seward, which still exists to this day.

Chronology

- 2nd June 1753. Elizabeth Seward, widow of Benjamin Seward, made a will bequeathing the interest or dividends of £400 South Sea annuities for teaching poor children to read in Badsey, Evesham and Bengeworth. The Badsey school was to receive six shillings a month and the other schools four shillings each a month, the money to be administered by successive Ministers of the congregation of Particular Baptists.
- 6th February 1754. Will proved in the Prerogative Court of Canterbury by Elizabeth's step-sons-in-law, William Snook and Richard Hall (husbands of Benjamin's daughters, Frances and Eleanor).
- 1836. A report of the Charity Commissioners indicated that the money was still regularly received and employed for the purposes expressed in the will.
- 1853. Reverend Thomas Hunt, seeking to establish a National School in the village, indicated to his patrons, Christ Church, Oxford, that the charity Baptist school was still in existence.
- 1872-1881. Directories describe Miss Edith Jones and later Miss Mary Eliza Jones as being in charge of the Baptist School.

BOARD OF EDUCATION.

In the Matter of ELIZABETH SEWARD'S EDUCATIONAL FOUNDATION for BADSEY, EVESHAM, and BENGEWORTH, founded by Will proved 6 February 1754 and comprised in an Order of the Charity Commissioners of 30 October 1903, under the Board of Education Act, 1899, so far as it is applicable to BADSEY (near Evesham), in the County of WORCESTER;

- About 1882. The Baptist School ceased to exist as the Misses Jones were not qualified teachers and so the school was not recognised by the Education Department. The Seward Trustees were not prepared to give the money to an unrecognised school.
- 1880s. Money given to four boys from Aldington to attend the British School in Evesham.
- 1882. Edith and Mary's father, Joseph Jones, began a correspondence with the Charity Commissioners in London, and with Reverend Todd, Secretary of the Seward Trustees, to try and find out what had happened to the Seward bequest. He felt the money had been given wrongly to Aldington children when it should have gone to Badsey children.
- 1893. Badsey National School, under the auspices of the Church of England, ceased to exist. Badsey Board School (non-denominational) came into being, thus the Trustees felt able to apply the money to this school.
- 1895-1896. Correspondence between Reverend Charles Gepp and the Trustees of the Seward bequest, and the Charity Commissioners, concerning non-payment of the money to Badsey children in the 1870s and 1880s. The dispute hinged on a technicality as to whether Aldington was separate from Badsey and therefore the money wrongly given to Aldington children. The argument went nowhere, but opened up discussions on distribution of the money in future.
- 1896. Reverend Todd, Secretary of the Trustees, consulted the Charity Commissioners; the Trustees were in favour of a scholarship.
- 1897. Charity Commissioners endeavoured to find out more about the terms of the will and the disposal of the South Sea stock, especially after the stocks were converted in 1854.
- 1903. County Council took over from the School Board and wrote to find out when the last payment had been received.
- 1904. Managers of Badsey Council School resolved: "that an application of the Elizabeth Seward Charity for the purposes of secondary education for poor boys at Prince Henry's Grammar School, Evesham, would be the best means of dealing with this charity so far as regards the portion belonging to Badsey parish."
- 7th November 1906. "Elizabeth Seward's Educational Foundation for Badsey" established (No 398), at the same time as one for Evesham and

Bengeworth (No 397). Julius Sladden was appointed as the County Council representative for both charities.

- 1907-1998. Trustees met once a year in March or April in Evesham to organise the distribution of the money, in liaison with the Headteacher.
- 1960. Charities Act made it compulsory for charities such as the Seward Foundation to be registered with the Charity Commissioners.
- 1962. Badsey Charity registered with the Central Register of Charities in 1962 (Charity Number 527427), separately from the Evesham and Bengeworth Charity (Charity Number 527451).
- 1977. Responsibility for the recommendation of a Badsey child for an award transferred from the Headteacher of Badsey School to the Headteacher of Blackminster Middle School (as Badsey had become a First School, with children leaving at the age of ten).
- 24th September 1998. Local Trustees of the two charities made a resolution that they wished to devolve responsibility to the Trustees of the Elizabeth Seward Charity, ie going back to the terms of the original will, to successive ministers of the congregation of Baptists.
- 1998-present day. Trustees meet every November at Baptist House, Didcot, Oxfordshire.
- 1st November 2001. Trustees of the two charities made a resolution to transfer the Elizabeth Seward's Educational Foundation for Evesham and Bengeworth into the Trust for Badsey, "to simplify administration and reduce costs of two very similar educational charities operating in the same geographical area and having both been founded under the will of Elizabeth Seward proved in 1754."
- 2002. Evesham and Bengeworth foundation removed from the Central Register of Charities, having combined with the Badsey charity.

Distribution of the Money

From 1754 to 1881, the money was used for "for teaching poor children to read". In the 1880s it was used to pay the fees of four boys at the British School in Evesham and in the 1890s it was applied to the Board School.

In the 20th century, with compulsory education for all, the terms of the original bequest were no longer appropriate and instead the money was used to assist children to progress with their studies. Initially, it was used to fund a scholarship to Prince Henry's Grammar School. In 1907, three girls entered for the Seward Scholarship exam which took place over two days. The scholarship was awarded to 12-year-old Gwendoline Warmington, daughter of Walter R Warmington, the innkeeper at The Bell Inn.

The scholarship was for £4 per year for three years. Other recipients of the Seward scholarship were May Ballard (1911), Bertie Hatch (1915) and Henry Bird (1917).

As more free places became available at the Grammar School under the County Council scholarship scheme there was no longer the same need and the emphasis then switched to the funding of prizes. The first evidence of this is in July 1915 when the prize-winners of a General Knowledge paper, Joseph Illsley, Arthur Brewer and Lily Roberts, received prizes courtesy of the Trust. In the inter-war year period, at the annual prize-giving, whilst Mr Binyon provided the money for class prizes, the Seward Trust frequently gave a sum of £2 towards prizes for special subjects, as funds permitted. In 1927, it was reported that practically all the Seward prize-winners obtained 90% or more in a very exhaustive test. When the prize-winners lived outside the parish and were not eligible under the Trust Deeds, the prizes were provided by Mr Binyon. The last record of money for prizes being provided by the Seward Trust was in November 1939.

Charles Fowler, the Secretary of the charity, writing in 1961, gives an indication of how the money was spent in the post-war period: "Before the days of free education, we used to pay the fees (or part of them) for a pupil to attend the Grammar School. Now there are no fees, we pay the bills for such things as school blazers, flannels, etc, purchased by the Headmaster for pupils recommended to us by the Headmaster. We also sometimes help pupils to purchase books when they go to a university."

Nowadays, the Headteacher of Blackminster Middle School nominates a Year 6 pupil (aged 10-11) resident in Badsey, based on need and circumstances. The most recent recipient received a grant of £30.

APPENDIX H
PARENT TEACHER ASSOCIATION

The Parent Teacher Association (PTA) was formed in February 1968, the aims being to strengthen the links between home and school and to raise money. The Headteacher became Chairman and a committee of five parents and five teachers was elected. Mrs Magowan (mother to Elizabeth and Joanne) was the first Secretary and Mr Portman (father to Laurence, Jayne and Richard) was the first Treasurer). They and Mr Stan Goldstraw, Mr Harrison and Mr Ives made up the first five parent representatives. In 1984, the constitution was changed to enable someone other than the Headteacher to be Chairman, thereby allowing a greater degree of independence in decision making. Mrs Pam Locke of Wickhamford was the first parent to hold this position. The following is a list of Chairmen of the PTA since its formation:

Mr Hugh Chaplin, 1968-1981
Mr Trevor Clark, 1981-1984
Mrs Pam Locke, 1984-1985
Mr Trevor Clark, 1985-1986
Mrs Fiona Laidlaw, 1986-1987
Mr Julian Ridgers, 1987-1988
Mr Gerard Hughes, 1988-1989
Mr Steve Aldren, 1989-1991
Mr Charles Marshall, 1991-1992
Mrs Corinne Formanuik/Mrs Helen Stanbra, 1992-1994
Mr Alan Tutton, 1994-1997
Mrs Suzanne McSwiney/Mrs Ruth Hunt, 1997-1998
Mrs Suzanne McSwiney, 1998-2000
Mrs Kathryn Hough, 2000-2004

Kathryn Hough, Chairman 2000-2004

**BADSEY SCHOOL PTA
SUMMER FETE**
28th June 2003
To be opened at 2p.m.
by Mike George Radio Presenter
BBC Hereford and Worcester
Entry £1 - lucky programme
Accompanied children free

Celebration Reed and Brass Band
Arena displays by pupils
Pupils' art exhibition

Attractions include bouncy castles, local history display,
skittles, barbecue, bar, teas and more!

Left: Bronze token presented to all Badsey pupils at the PTA summer fête 2002, to commemorate 50 years' reign of Queen Elizabeth II.
Above: Mrs Spencer with "Dennis the Menace" (aka John Jenkinson of The Evesham Hotel) who provided much merriment at the opening of the 2004 PTA fête. Kathryn Hough's poster for the 2003 PTA fête.

APPENDIX I
HEAD BOYS AND GIRLS

Mr Amos introduced the post of Head Boy and Head Girl in the 1920s and gave these pupils the responsibility of a number of administrative duties. The Head Boy was responsible for ringing the bell, and had to go to the back door of the School House at 8.30 each morning in order to collect the key. He then opened up the school and rang the bell. Until 1930, this involved pulling the rope of the original bell in the bell-tower, but when this was removed because it was too dangerous, a hand-bell was used, which was placed on a ledge in the corridor, close to the original rope. When the original bell was still in use, there were two bells to summon children to school. "First bell" as it was known was rung at 8.45 am and sounded through the village and was a reminder to children that they should be getting to school. "Second bell" was rung just a few minutes before school was due to start at 9 am. The Head Girl's duties included going to each class and writing down the numbers present.

The post of Head Boy and Girl lasted until 1981. In the post-war period, the post of Deputy was also created. No list of Head Boys and Girls survives, but the following (incomplete) list has been compiled from information obtained from past students. Apologies are given for any omissions or errors.

	HEAD BOY	HEAD GIRL
1930-31	Frank FIELD	–
1933-34	Kenneth ELLISON	Jean KNIGHT
1935-36	Walter WARMINGTON	–
1936-37	–	Dorothy COX
1938-39	Bernard REDGEWELL	Jean SMITH
1940-41	Roger SAVORY	Hazel LONGMORE
1941-42	David BRAZIER	Celia HARRISON
1942-43	David SOUTHERN	Pat BARNARD
1943-44	Brian JENNINGS	–
1945-46	–	Shirley EVANS
1947-48	David ROUSE	–
1950-51	David CASWELL	–
1951-52	Martin MILLER	–
1952-53	Michael STEPHENS	Josie SMITH
1953-54	Billie CHURCHILL/Derek HARWOOD	Margaret BROTHERTON
1954-55	Michael WELLS	Mary CHURCHILL
1955-56	William CROSBY	Susan HARTWELL
1956-57	John NEWBURY	Maureen GREGORY
1958-59	John HARWOOD	Diane HARTWELL
1959-60	Norbert TUCKER	Katie GORIN
1960-61	Clifford HARTWELL	Maureen LEWIS
1961-62	Christopher TUCKER	Rosemary TUCKER
1962-63	David STEWART	Mary BRABY
1963-64	Paul HARVEY	Margaret TYSZKOW
1964-65	Stephen TUCKER	Sara KITCHER
1965-66	Trevor SOUTHERN	Julia WILLIAMS
1967-68	Ian HARDWICK	Jane GOLDSTRAW
1973-74	Stephen EVANS	Diane BURFORD
1975-76	Nigel CARELESS	Caroline BYRD
1978-79	Richard SMITH	Joanna BOWRING
1979-80	Stephen POTTER	Sarah SIMMS
1980-81	Sean WITHEFORD	Sally STRATTON

APPENDIX J
"WE WILL REMEMBER THEM" –
THE NAMES ON THE WAR MEMORIAL

One teacher and 23 former pupils died in the First World War, "the war to end all wars". Their names are commemorated on the War Memorial which still hangs on the wall of the Main Hall. The Board is headed by the former emblem of Worcestershire County Council and contains an extract from the famous poem, "For the Fallen" by Laurence Binyon (1869-1943) who visited Badsey School on a number of occasions as his brother, Charles, was a School Manager.

William Henry BARNARD, pupil 1899-1910, Lance Corporal, Lincolnshire Regiment 2nd Battalion, died 1 Jul 1916, France, aged 20.

Francis Henry BLAKE, pupil 1898-c1902, Rifleman, Rifle Brigade, died 30 Jul 1915, Belgium, aged 22.

Cecil Henry BYRD, pupil 1906-1909, Lance Corporal, Machine Gun Corps (Infantry), died 11 Aug 1918, England, aged 22.

William Edward CLEVELEY, pupil 1902-1912, Lance Corporal, Rifle Brigade 6th Reserve Battalion, died 31 Dec 1917, England, aged 18.

Vincent COLLEY, pupil 1903-1906, Private, Canadian Infantry (Eastern Ontario Regiment) 2nd Battalion, died 12 Jun 1916, Belgium, aged 22.

Frank COX, pupil 1901-1911, Gunner, Royal Field Artillery, died 13 Jul 1916, Salonika, aged 17.

Cecil Harry CRANE, pupil 1895-1904, Private, Worcestershire Regiment 4th Battalion, died 6 Aug 1915, Turkey, aged 23.

Walter CRANE, pupil 1899-1910, Private, Worcestershire Regiment 10th Battalion, died 2 Jul 1916, France, aged 19.

John Sidney CULL, pupil 1893-1903, Lance Corporal, Machine Gun Corps (Cavalry), died 25 Oct 1918, Iran, aged 27.

Harold GASKIN, pupil 1892-c1901, Sapper, Royal Engineers SX Cable Section, died 2 Dec 1915, Turkey, aged 28.

Horace A HALFORD, pupil 1894-1899, Lance Corporal, Worcestershire Regiment 2nd Battalion, died 21 May 1917, France, aged 30.

Frederick Thomas HARTWELL, pupil 1896-1906, Lance Sergeant, Worcestershire Regiment 3rd Battalion, died 9 Oct 1916, France, aged 23.

Charles HARWOOD, pupil 1902-1912, Pioneer, Hampshire Regiment 11th Battalion, died 22 Apr 1918, France, aged 19.

Alfred Henry HISCOCK, pupil 1904-1905, reported missing.

Albert HUXLEY, pupil 1898-c1909, Lance Corporal, Worcestershire Regiment 2nd/8th Battalion, died 21 Nov 1917, France, aged 22.

Thomas KNIGHT, pupil c1887-c1896, Private, Worcestershire Regiment 2nd/8th Battalion, died 6 Nov 1918, France, aged 36.

Robert LEWIS, teacher 1913-1918, Corporal, Gloucestershire Regiment 12th Battalion, died 25 Apr 1918, Belgium.

Arthur Henry Logan McDONALD, pupil 1904-1911, Private, Machine Gun Corps (Infantry) 48th Company, died 16 Aug 1917, Belgium, aged 19.

Ernest William Knight MARSHALL, pupil 1896-c1908, Private, Worcestershire Regiment 3rd Battalion, died 16 Mar 1915, France, aged 21.

George MASON, pupil 1894-1904, Second Lieutenant, Worcestershire Regiment 8th Battalion, attached 2nd Battalion, died 20 May 1917, France, aged 26.

Charles Henry ROBBINS, pupil c 1890-c1898, Col-Sergeant (Acting Quartermaster-Sergeant), Worcestershire Regiment 3rd Battalion, died 7 Nov 1914, Belgium, aged 30.

Louis Henry SPARROW, pupil c 1887-1897, Corporal, Worcestershire Regiment 1st Battalion, died 22 Oct 1916, France, aged 33.

Edward Francis WAKEFIELD, pupil 1896-c1907, Sergeant, Rifle Brigade 10th Battalion, died 22 Feb 1916, Belgium, aged 23.

Thomas WILLOUGHBY, pupil c 1890-c1899, Private, Worcestershire Regiment 1st/8th Battalion, died 24 Apr 1917, France, aged 32 (omitted from the school War Memorial Board but is included on the Wickhamford Memorial; as a former pupil, this error has been rectified here).

For the Fallen (September 1914)

With proud thanksgiving, a mother for her children,
England mourns for her dead across the sea.
Flesh of her flesh they were, spirit of her spirit,
Fallen in the cause of the free.

Solemn the drums thrill: Death august and royal
Sings sorrow up into immortal spheres.
There is music in the midst of desolation
And a glory that shines upon our tears.

They went with songs to the battle, they were young,
Straight of limb, true of eye, steady and aglow.
They were staunch to the end against odds uncounted,
They fell with their faces to the foe.

They shall not grow old, as we that are left grow old:
Age shall not weary them, nor the years condemn.
At the going down of the sun and in the morning
We will remember them.

They mingle not with their laughing comrades again;
They sit no more at familiar tables of home;
They have no lot in our labour of the day-time;
They sleep beyond England's foam.

But where our desires are and our hopes profound,
Felt as a well-spring that is hidden from sight,
To the innermost heart of their own land they are
known
As the stars are known to the Night.

As the stars that shall be bright when we are dust,
Moving in marches upon the heavenly plain,.
As the stars that are starry in the time of our darkness,
To the end, to the end, they remain.

Laurence Binyon
(1869-1943)

PATTERN OF COMMUNITY AND CHURCH SCHOOLS THROUGHOUT WORCESTERSHIRE

Throughout the country, there are three types of first and primary schools: Community, Voluntary Controlled and Voluntary Aided. In the vast majority of cases, the reason why a school is Community or Voluntary has its roots in the 19th century. Badsey started life as a voluntary church school but is now under LEA control; the reasons why this came about can be read in Chapters 2 and 3. Today, the main difference between the types of school is the way in which they are governed. Briefly:

- A Community School is funded and maintained by the Local Education Authority; religious education is provided in accordance with the LEA's agreed syllabus.
- A Voluntary Controlled School is funded and maintained by the Local Education Authority; religious education is provided in accordance with the LEA's agreed syllabus, together with some opportunity for denominational instruction; the Church appoints Governors, but there is no Church majority on the governing body.
- A Voluntary Aided School is funded and maintained by the Local Education Authority; the provision of religious education, control of admissions and employment of teachers is in the control of the Governors (the majority of Governors being appointed by the church) and 15% of the cost of repairs and capital projects is raised by the Governing Body.

In 1900, nearly 53% of all elementary schools in England were provided by the Church of England, just over 34% by School Boards or local councils, and a further 6% being Roman Catholic. By 1984, the proportion of state schools had nearly doubled to 65% while that of the Church of England had fallen to 25%, although the proportion of Roman Catholic schools had also risen, to 10%.

Worcestershire has a mixture of first schools (age 5-9 or 5-10) and primary schools (age 5-11). Of the 188 first and middle schools in the county, 89 are Community and 99 are Voluntary Aided or Voluntary Controlled which is typical for more rural parts of the country where the church held sway for longer and did not relinquish control to a Board. In the Evesham area, Badsey was not typical. Today, just 30% of the Evesham area schools are Community. The following list shows the schools in the Evesham area by "pyramid" grouping, ie the Middle School which they feed into:

BLACKMINSTER PYRAMID

	Type	Pupils
Badsey	Community	248
Bretforton	Community	54
Cleeve Prior CE	Voluntary Controlled	60
Honeybourne	Community	136
The Littletons CE	Voluntary Controlled	156
Offenham CE	Voluntary Controlled	97
Pebworth	Community	61

BREDON HILL PYRAMID

Ashton-under-Hill	Community	64
Bredon Hancock's Endowed	Voluntary Aided	140
Broadway	Community	92
Cropthorne w. Charlton CE	Voluntary Controlled	83
Eckington CE	Voluntary Controlled	85
Elmley Castle CE	Voluntary Controlled	73
Overbury CE	Voluntary Controlled	74
Sedgeberrow CE	Voluntary Controlled	174

SIMON DE MONTFORT PYRAMID

Bengeworth CE	Voluntary Controlled	340
St Richard's CE	Voluntary Controlled	515

ST EGWIN'S CE PYRAMID

Church Lench CE	Voluntary Controlled	59
Harvington CE	Voluntary Controlled	144
Swan Lane	Community	305
St Andrew's CE	Voluntary Controlled	190

There are also two Voluntary Aided Roman Catholic schools in the Evesham area.

Information taken from "Information for Parents 2004-2005, Admissions and Transfers to Schools", Worcestershire County Council Educational Services. The numbers of pupils are based on 2003 figures.

BIBLIOGRAPHY

PRIMARY SOURCES
Worcestershire Record Office

Vestry Minutes, 1833-1902, BA 8474, Ref 850, Parcel 2.

Managers' Minutes, 1893-1903, BA 695, Ref 250.6, Parcels 5 & 6; 1903-1923, BA 7466, Ref 705:739, Parcels 2, 6 & 7; 1924-1955, BA 5038, Ref 250.6, Parcel 2; 1955-1974, BA 9037/22, Ref 468.

Governors' Minutes, 1974-1999, BA 13849.

School Log Books, 1893-1993, BA 13849.

Elizabeth Seward Foundation, BA 11858.

Educational Trusts in County of Hereford & Worcester, BA 9476, Ref 429:001.

Worcestershire County Development Plan, 1951, BA 10841, Ref 468, Parcel 29.

Maps and Plans, BA 4473, Ref 004.4, Parcel 1.

Papers relating to Schoolmasters, 1602-1696, BA 2729, Ref 744, Parcel 1.

Census Returns, 1841-1901.

Parish Registers.

Public Record Office, Kew

Elizabeth Seward Charity, ED49/8491.

Parish File, 1872-1905, ED2/469.

Parish File, 1893-1915, ED21/18670.

Enlargements 1920s, ED21/42497.

Handicrafts Centre, 1927-1929, ED70/2597.

Sale of Old School, ED49/8321.

Merger of Departments, ED21/63484.

Christ Church Library, Oxford

Badsey Parish File.

Church of England Record Centre

Badsey National School File.

Other Primary Sources

Charity Commission for England and Wales.

Evesham Journal (at Evesham Library and Worcestershire Record Office).

Parish Magazine (in the care of the Vicar).

Lawes Agricultural Trust (photocopies of market gardening letters also at Worcestershire Record Office).

SECONDARY SOURCES

Chapman, Colin R, *The Growth of British Education and Its Records,* Lochin Publishing, 2nd ed, 1992.

Curtis, S J, *History of Education in Great Britain,* Greenwood Press, 1953.

Goldstrom, J M, *Education: Elementary Education, 1780-1900,* David & Charles, 1972.

Harry, Evan Llewelyn, *An economic and social survey of the parish of Badsey, Worcestershire,* MSc Dissertation, The University of Aberystwyth, 1931.

Horn, Pamela, *The Victorian and Edwardian Schoolchild,* Alan Sutton, 1989.

Inglis, Ruth, *The Children's War, Evacuation 1939-1945,* Collins, 1989.

Martin, Christopher, *A Short History of English Schools, 1750-1965,* Wayland Publishers, 1979.

Morton, Ann, *Education and the State from 1833,* Public Record Office Readers' Guide No 18, PRO Publication, 1997.

Ryder, Vincent, *All Bull and Black Pears, A Celebration of 100 Years of Hereford & Worcester County Council,* Malvern Publishing Co Ltd, 1989.

Savory, Arthur, *Grain and Chaff from an English Manor,* 1920.

Education in Worcestershire, Handbook prepared for the Education weekend held in Malvern, 14th-15th May 1926.

Information to Parents 2004-2005, Admissions and Transfers to Schools, Worcestershire County Council Educational Services, 2003.

Various trade directories (eg, *Topographical Directory of England,* 1840, Samuel Lewis; *Bentley's Directory,* 1840; *Kelly's Directory,* 1880) available at Evesham Library and Worcestershire Record Office.

SUBSCRIBERS TO THE BOOK

G A Aldrich
Mrs I E Allen
Fiona Allen
Jessica Allen
Margaret Amos
Joshar Andac
Deric Anderson
Julie Andrew
Paula Andrews (née Ealey)
Jo Attwood (née Anderson)
Mrs Muriel Austin
Velma Bailey (née Baker)
Mr & Mrs Michael J Barnard
Mr Mark J Barnard
Mr & Mrs R Barnes
Mrs G Barrand
Chris Bayliss
Mary Beadle (née O'Brion)
Joan Bearman
The Beasley Family (née
        Tomkins)
Robert Bennett
A C & R S Bennington
Mrs Rachel Betteridge (née
        Hartwell)
Jane Binyon
John Bird
Blackminster Middle School
Ralph & Elizabeth Bolland
T L & J S Brotherton
Bob & Betty Butler
Mrs Peg Byrd
Suzanne Byrd
Andrew & Sue Campbell
Nicola Campbell
Sally Carter
P & M Castle
Mary Chaplin
Mrs S M Clarke
Dulcie Cleaver (née Jelfs)
N L & D Cleaver
The Coldicott Family
Mrs Susan Cole
Norman Collett
Tara Collins-Bullock
Graham Corbett
Linda Core

Margaret Crawford
Richard Cudd
Christopher Curtis
John & Will Dallimore
The Dance Family (née
        Barrand)
Sue Daniels
Roger & Maureen Davies
Rosalind Davies
Ross Davis
Barry Day
Esmé (née Jelfs) & Don Dennick
Gladys Dodd (née Cave)
Elizabeth Dyer (née Cleaver)
Sonya Ealey
John Ealey
James Ealey
Adam Ealey
Ollie Ecmanis
Lilli Victoria Ecmanis
E & A Edwards
David Ellison
Amy & Nathan Evans
Karen Evans (née Woodcock)
Ann Evans
Les, Sharon, Kirsty & Thomas
        Evans
D F Field
Chris Flanagan
Ray, Caroline, Emma & Kate
        Fletcher
Alison Foote (née King)
Sharon Ford
Ian & Lynn Gibson & son Grant
Christina Glass
Mrs Pat Goldstraw
Pat & Jim Gorin
Jonathan Granger 1974-1980
Mrs J Gray
G R & C J Haines
Carol Hall
John & Julie Hall & family
Mrs Peggy Hancock
Ann E Harris
Mr & Mrs D Hartwell
Jack Hartwell
Norman Hartwell

Tony & Rosemary Hartwell
Richard & Pat Harvey
Stanley Hayes
Eileen Heeks
John G Hemming
G M Heritage
Tony Heritage
Ms Nanci Herring
Sophie Rhian Hible
Elaine Hill
Sarah, Rhodri, David & Alice
        Horton
Lorna Howarth
Mr G Hughes
Councillor Kelvin R Hughes
Hutchings & Son
Jean James
Barbara & Tony Jerram
Cecil Jones
G R Keen
Vera Keen (Girlie)
Celia Keyte
M Anne King
David King
Martin King
Jocelyn King
Mr & Mrs H L Knight
Dennis & Mary Knight
Laraine & Russell Knight
Paul Knight
Jane Knight
Reg Kyte
Gordon J Lashford
J E Lavell
Mrs R Lazarus (née Syril)
Jean Leng
Mr & Mrs W T H Lewis
Jean Lewis (née Collett)
Richard Locke
Mrs Mary Lowe (née Hartwell)
Enid Major
Ian Major
Christine Malin
Carol Marshall
Ivor Martin
Roger Martin
Fred Mason

Harry Mason
John & Joan Mason
Marion McGowan
Rosalie Merrett (née Addis)
Margaret Merriman
David Miller
L & H Mitchell
Emily & Chloe Moore
Mr & Mrs W Moore
Lucy Moran
Peter Moran
Muriel Morcombe
P Morcombe
B E Moss
George Mountney
Ruth Mutch (née Jelfs), Canada
Audrey New
John Newbury
Samantha Newman
Mrs E Nicholls
Beth Norman
Lizzie Noyes
David Osborne
Mrs Jayne Osborne
Mr M Overd
Roy & Mary Page
Sarah, Julian & William Pask
Peter & Louise Phillips
Richard Phillips
E N Porter
The Pratt Family
Wendy Pritchard
In memory of Bernard
      Redgewell
Brian Redgewell
Christine Redgewell
Gillian Redgewell
Norman Redgewell
Evelyn Ritterswuerden
Fiona Roden
Zena Rogers (née Bennett)
Sheila & Cliff Sage
Dorothy & Rene Sandford
Robin Sandford
Roger Savory
Joanna Sellick (née Ealey)
Mr & Mrs R Simms
Anne Smith
Brian & Hazel Smith

Charles Smith
Liz & Pete Smith
Mr T N A Smith
Miss Susan M M Smith MBE
Mr V C E Smith
Jake & Emily Smitten
Mr & Mrs Arthur Sparrow
Mr & Mrs P Sparrow
Terry & Sandra Sparrow
Elizabeth Spencer
Peter Spencer
Guy Spencer
Tony & Jonathan Spinks
Millie Squires
H Stanton
In memory of Mary Stead
Peter Stewart
Wendy Such
Louisa Such
Catherine Such
Nicholas Such
John L Summers
Des Syril

N Syril
Jackie & Mick Thomas
Daniel Rees Thomas II
Jane Thompson (née Ellison)
Mrs Susan Thompson
Mr & Mrs Neil Thould
Mr & Mrs R A Thould
Mrs E Tomes
Stephen, Connor, Alexander &
      Claudia Trotman
A S Tucker
Jennifer Tweney
Peggy Tyler
Diana Wallis
Helen Walter
Jean Ward (née Poole)
Bert Weaver
Pat & Graham Westmacott &
      family
Harry Wheatley
S Wilce (née Evans)
Andrew Wilkes & Peter Wilkes
Andy Wilson & Carolyn Worth

'Those Carefree Summer Days'
Children from Bower's Hill walking to school across the grounds during the summer months. Cowslips, Buttercups and Cornflowers were picked from Mr Johnson's meadow for their nature class. The main road was walked during the winter months.

INDEX OF SURNAMES AND PLACES